"This book tells the truth. The authors kn̶ .... and they offer hope rooted in God's Word to transform conflict into grace in lives, families, churches, and communities."

Charles Colson, founder, Prison Fellowship

"The rifts in the Christian community are legion and legendary. The breakdown between two people or in our own walk with God saps more energy for the gospel than any one factor. Whatever the cause, the tragedy is most Christians don't have hope for repentance, reconciliation, and restoration. This bold and compelling book by two wise Christian mediators and peacemakers is a tour de force in offering a pathway for rebuilding broken relationships. Judy and Tara live and breathe what they write and know personally and professionally the glory of fighting for peace. Their labor of love will draw you back to the one who gave his life for our peace. Take it and read with hope and courage."

Dan B. Allender, president, Mars Hill Graduate School

"*Peacemaking Women* is not just for women and is not just about peacemaking. This powerfully honest book is about the peace the gospel brings every heart that applies the truths of the gospel to past wounds and present brokenness. And this book is about how personally embracing this gospel of peace makes each of us a loving instrument of God's grace to others."

Bryan Chapell, president, Covenant Theological Seminary

"If I could put one book in the hands of every Christian woman, in addition to the Bible, it would be this one. The book is marked by courage, vulnerability, integrity, respect, variety, and scholarship. It is a delight to read and a joy to ponder. Reading it has been beneficial to me as I am sure it will be to many."

Laura Mae Gardner, International Personnel Consultant for Wycliffe Bible Translators and Summer Institute of Linguistics

"*Peacemaking Women* is worth a dozen counseling sessions. The chapter on romantic love is worth the price of the book."

Charles Mylander, coauthor of *Blessed Are the Peacemakers*

"Judy Dabler and Tara Barthel weave into *Peacemaking Women* their wealth of wisdom and experience in counseling and conciliation. They show that conflict resolution demands more than communication techniques and negotiation strategies. Real peace (with God, others, ourselves) flourishes only when the deep drives of our hearts are captivated by the God of peace. In other words, the gospel of the crucified and risen Christ alone contains the life-changing mercy and power to heal our relationships with our Maker, each other, and our own conflicted hearts.

"Real people populate these pages, not only the authors but also the women (and some men) whom they have helped find peace in the love of Jesus (and some whom they've tried to help—their realism also admits that not everyone wants peace on God's terms). Their stories, told with refreshing humility and honesty, show how concretely practical the Bible's theology of peace is and speak hope that God's shalom can and does invade our broken lives and relationships in sovereign grace. I learned much about women, myself, and my God and his grace from *Peacemaking Women*. I highly recommend it."

Dennis E. Johnson, academic dean and professor of practical theology,
Westminster Seminary California

"Women know how conflict can threaten to tear apart relationships and homes. And worse yet, this conflict frequently begins within our own hearts, working its way out in demands and desires that can seem over-whelming. *Peacemaking Women* isn't just another book on communication or conflict resolution. It will open your eyes to the role our idolatrous hearts play in our conflicts and then point you back to the Peacemaker who took peacemaking so seriously he was willing to die for it. I strongly recommend it!"

Elyse Fitzpatrick, author, *Overcoming Fear, Worry, and Anxiety: Becoming A Woman of Faith and Confidence*

"Living in a world of conflict, we desperately need to discover the art of peacemaking. Tara Barthel and Judy Dabler use the wisdom of their own experience to apply God's truth to the deep wounds of our lives, showing the path to intimacy with God, reconciliation with others, and shalom in our hearts. This biblical, insightful, sensitive, and practical book will open the door of hope for many women."

Colin S. Smith, pastor, Arlington Heights Evangelical Free Church

PEACEMAKING
Women

Biblical Hope for Resolving Conflict

Tara Klena Barthel
and Judy Dabler

BakerBooks
Grand Rapids, Michigan

Published by Baker Books
a division of Baker Publishing Group
P.O. Box 6287, Grand Rapids, MI 49516-6287
www.bakerbooks.com

Printed in the United States of America

Library of Congress Cataloging-in-Publication Data
Barthel, Tara Klena.
    Peacemaking women : biblical hope for resolving conflict / Tara Klena Barthel
and Judy Dabler.
        p.   cm.
    Includes bibliographical references.
    ISBN 10: 0-8010-6495-3 (pbk.)
    ISBN 978-0-8010-6495-1 (pbk.)
    1. Christian women—Religious life. 2. Female friendship—Religious aspects—
Christianity. 3. Interpersonal relations—Religious aspects—Christianity. 4. Peace—
Religious aspects—Christianity. 5. Conflict management. I. Dabler, Judy. II. Title.
BV4527.B367 2005
248.8′ 43—dc22   2005000971

11   12   13   14   15   16   17   12   11   10   9   8   7   6

CONTENTS

FOREWORD

Peacemaking Women is a life-changing book. It contains a wealth of wisdom and encouragement for women who want to learn how to turn any conflict into an opportunity to build deeper and closer relationships.

My friends Tara and Judy write out of rich personal experience. God has refined them in the furnace of their own personal, family, and professional conflicts. As a result, they write with a winsome authenticity and vulnerability, and their teaching is laced with captivating personal examples to which every woman can relate.

Tara and Judy have been further refined by successfully guiding hundreds of other people through many kinds of conflict. Thus readers can readily apply Tara and Judy's insights and counsel to the conflicts of daily life, whether at home, in church, in the workplace, or at that "dreaded" family gathering.

The greatest strength of this book is that it is consistently Christ-centered. Instead of calling women to work harder in their own strength, the authors urge women to rest more fully and confidently in the redeeming work of Christ. The gospel—the good news that Jesus has saved us from all our sins—is woven into every aspect of this peacemaking model. The more that Christians embrace this model, the more we will understand what Jesus meant when he told us, "My yoke is easy and my burden is light."

Peacemaking Women is also utterly practical. The authors address a wide array of conflict scenarios that women face in today's com-

plex world and provide detailed and realistic steps for resolving
all kinds of personal issues. Readers who recognize the depth and
practicality of this book will return to it again and again to mine
its pages more deeply and discover the many jewels of wisdom that
God has planted here.

Prepare to be challenged and encouraged, convicted and inspired.
You may find yourself torn between wanting to devour this book
and needing to pause and let the truths soak in. When you have
read to the end and have begun to practice what you've learned,
your life and your relationships will never again be the same.

Ken Sande, president
Peacemaker Ministries

ACKNOWLEDGMENTS

I (Judy) would like to give my deepest thanks to the staff of the Center for Biblical Counseling & Education. You received far too little help and attention from me last year as I worked on this manuscript. Your commitment, loyalty, patience, and prayers have shaped me in ways you may never know. In particular, Dave Holden's love and support and the sacrificial friendship of Joani Nester leave me humbled and in tears. I am truly grateful to the Session and pastoral staff of The Kirk of the Hills Presbyterian Church for their willingness to allow me to pursue this project. While this book took me away from focusing on some important responsibilities, your unwavering belief in me leaves me fiercely determined to serve my Master well. Many thanks to my dear friends who encouraged me along the way. I could never have persevered without you. To my precious family, may the Lord bless you for your many sacrifices on my behalf. I love you so much.

I (Tara) would like to thank my husband, Fred, for his steadfast love for God and the church, and also for believing so strongly in women's ministries that he happily sacrifices his own comfort to enable me to write and travel to teach women across the country. I am also indebted to my pastors, Jason Barrie and Alfred Poirier, and each of the elders and deacons at Rocky Mountain Community Church (PCA)—thank you for teaching and ministering the whole counsel of Scripture and for loving your sheep well. Thanks, too, to the women in my church whose spiritual maturity, relational grace, and great wisdom help me each day to grow in faith and godliness. Special thanks to Samara Lynde, Melissa Skiles, and Kitty Routson for joyfully and generously giving of your love and time to care for Sophie so that I could work on the manuscript, and to my sister Kali Klena for lavishing your love and encouragement on me. *Thank you, friends!*

We would both like to thank Ken Sande for encouraging and facilitating the publication of this book and Bill Gleason for spending countless hours reviewing and editing the initial drafts. We are also grateful for the people who prayed for us, read our draft manuscripts, and shared their counsel with us: Pastor Jason Barrie, Fred Barthel, Rebecca Bowman, David and Pat Edling, Dom and Sandy Feralio, Edna Gleason, Len and Anne Greski, Allison Haltom, Susan Hunt, Dr. Paul Jensen, Carla Johns, Prof. Dennis Johnson, Kelly Kennison, Kali Klena, Jane Patete, Pastor Alfred Poirier, Kitty Routson, Molly Routson, Judy TenHarmsel, Cindy Zimmer, and Rich, Susan, and Melodee Mattson.

INTRODUCTION

Now may the Lord of peace himself give you peace at all times and in every way. The Lord be with all of you.

2 Thessalonians 3:16

Only one thing is strong enough to overpower a stormy life: what God promises to do in and through Jesus Christ.

David Powlison[1]

Clarissa was notorious for being a gossip and always seemed to be in conflict with others, but now she is known as a trustworthy and loving woman who helps others address their conflicts biblically.[2] Instead of turning to sugary desserts and buttery popcorn to escape her worries and anxieties, Lynne now feasts on the Bread of Life and walks through life in quiet confidence. Once extremely depressed, Teresa lived a lonely and isolated life, but now she enjoys true friendship and genuine relationships. Katie had been terrified to leave her home, afraid she would say the wrong thing or look stupid, but now she leads a Bible study to help other women to learn how to rest in security and contentment. Regardless of their circumstances, God's grace has given these women *peace*.

How is such peace possible? Knowing all we know about the trials and troubles of our lives, what hope do we *really* have for peace? Plenty! Why? Because of the grace and glory of God:

I lift up my eyes to the hills—
    where does my help come from?
My help comes from the LORD,
    the Maker of heaven and earth.

He will not let your foot slip—
    he who watches over you will not slumber;
indeed, he who watches over Israel
    will neither slumber nor sleep.

The LORD watches over you—
    the LORD is your shade at your right hand;
the sun will not harm you by day,
    nor the moon by night.

The LORD will keep you from all harm—
    he will watch over your life;
the LORD will watch over your coming and going
    both now and forevermore.

Psalm 121

Our help comes from the Lord. He is our righteousness (1 Cor. 1:30) and "the fruit of righteousness will be peace; the effect of righteousness will be quietness and confidence forever" (Isa. 32:17). If you are seeking help to grow as a woman of peace, Jesus is the biblical hope we offer you.

Why We Wrote This Book

Many Christian women today are not at peace. We claim to know the gospel—that we are saved by grace—and yet we live as though God's love for us is based on our performance. When we do the "right" things, we sense God's approval and pleasure, but when we struggle with sin, we feel distant and estranged from him. We know intellectually that Jesus is all we need, and yet we clamor for more. We lust after the desires of our hearts—money, a godly husband, the perfect career, beautiful children, and successful ministries. Though we may have great wisdom in many areas of life, we sometimes relate to others like unbelievers. Instead of faithfully blessing and never cursing (Rom. 12:14) or doing good even when treated unjustly (1 Peter 2), we subtly attack through gossip couched as "prayer requests" or through emotion-laden letters written to confront and rebuke. Failing to draw grace and strength from the biblical admonition that "If anyone says, 'I love God,' yet hates his brother, he is a liar" (1 John 4:20), we struggle with bitterness and hatred toward the people who have rejected, abandoned, or attacked us. Many of us suffer from shame—we have a vague sense that no matter how hard we try, we will never be good enough. We are prone to fear, worry, and anxiety. Our hearts are often heavy and depressed.

The result is that the body of Christ, the church, is struggling because of sin, fallenness, and spiritual attack. The number of Christians in psychotherapy is staggering. "In 1988 Americans spent an estimated $273.3 billion on mental health services. [In response], churches, Bible colleges and seminaries, Christian speakers, and Christian publishers across the country are promoting mental health programs."[3] Christian marriages crumble at an alarming rate, and homes are too often war zones of divided, angry people.[4] The Christian counseling ministry I (Judy) oversee in St. Louis has received over five thousand contacts from Christians seeking help in the last five years alone. I have personally helped hundreds of pastors, church leaders, and lay people in their struggles against sexual sin, addiction, and myriad other struggles. During my time as director of the Institute for Christian Conciliation, a division of Peacemaker Ministries, I (Tara) managed hundreds of requests for help every year from people on the verge of lawsuits, divorces, church splits, or simply the end of life-long friendships.

The impact of our personal conflicts on our churches and communities is profound. To paraphrase the great preacher D. Martyn Lloyd-Jones, conflicted Christians are, to say the least, a poor recommendation for the Christian faith.[5] For Jesus himself taught us that the world would know him when Christian relationships are marked by unity: "May they be brought to complete unity to let the world know that you sent me and have loved them even as you have loved me" (John 17:23). Only as we overlook, forebear, forgive—*love one another*—will Christian women reflect Christ to the world (John 13:34–35).

From Conflict to *Shalom*

The Hebrew word for peace, *shalom*, is a rich word encompassing far more than the absence of conflict. Where there is *shalom*, life is good and sound. *Shalom* is often described according to the threefold model of:

peace with God
peace with others
peace within

In the words of Eugene Peterson, "Shalom, peace, is one of the richest words in the Bible. You can no more define it by looking up its meaning in the dictionary than you can define a person by his social security number. It gathers all aspects of wholeness that result from God's will being completed in us. It is the work of God that, when complete, releases streams of living water in us and pulsates with eternal life."[6]

Almost every person in the world longs for peace within. But there can be no peace within unless there is first peace with God and peace with others "as far as it depends on you" (Rom. 12:18). Our restored relationship with God through Christ is the foundation for our peace with others and with ourselves. But the answer to our conflicts is not just a saving relationship with Christ—if that were true, there would be no broken relationships among Christians. Instead, as we grow in faith and are conformed to Christ, we learn how to do the hard work of biblical peacemaking.

Why Should We Be Peacemaking Women?

Peacemaking is a difficult, complicated, and often painful ministry. So why should we invest the time and effort? We are busy women with lots of things to do. Can't we just entrust this whole "peacemaking" thing to someone else? Simply said, no, for at least three reasons.

Christ compels us. As Christians, not all of us are called to youth ministry, music ministry, or work with the homeless, but we are *all* called to be peacemakers: "Blessed are the peacemakers, for they will be called sons of God" (Matt. 5:9). In our lives, the defining mark of Christ is *peace*. Do you want to be known to be a Christian? Jesus himself taught us that our peaceful *relationships* show whether we are truly his disciples (John 17:23). As his followers, we are to make every effort to live at peace with one another (Eph. 4:3).

If you are a Christian woman, you are called to be a peacemaking woman. This is not our idea. It is Christ who compels us. The admonition to "go and be reconciled" (Matt. 5:24) is the call to reflect the very heart of God in our lives. The gospel itself is the greatest message of peacemaking—we are reconciled to God through Christ. That same gospel is our foundation for reconciliation with other people. We earnestly strive to experience reconciliation and unity with the people around us because, in so doing, we are forgiving as the Lord forgives us (Col. 3:13). We reflect the nature of God when we are slow to anger, quick to forgive, and filled with love and faithfulness (Exod. 34:6). We demonstrate our reverence toward God and love for God when we obey his commands (John 14:15).

God is the first and ultimate peacemaker. I (Judy) first encountered the gospel at age six when I heard the story of how King Solomon wisely determined the true mother of the baby claimed by two women (1 Kings 3:16–28). As I heard the nun teaching catechism, time stood still. For the first time I realized that true love was *being willing to give up what you love to save what you love.* I never forgot the story I heard that day. I spent the next twenty years trying to fill a huge emptiness inside of me as I looked for real love. When I was twenty-seven, my husband and I were invited to a Bible study where we heard about a God who loved me so much that he gave up his Son to save me. A bell rang in the back of my mind, reminding me of that message I had heard many long years before. And by faith I embraced that saving love.

The gospel is the good message of sacrificial love. The gospel tells of the work of Christ that bridges the gap between God and man. Because Christ is fully God, God incarnate (Col. 1:19), he is able to serve as Redeemer and Reconciler through his death on the cross (Col. 1:20). Through the work of Christ, God built the bridge that enables mankind to cross that gap into a real relationship with him. Because of Christ, God is not against us; he is for us. In Christ, God's fundamental posture toward his children is one of love and acceptance. The whole world is destined to be completely at peace one day because God himself is the ultimate peacemaker.

God enables us to be peacemaking women. Our peacemaking efforts will succeed only to the extent that they reflect God's merciful act of redemption. In response to God's astounding gift of peace with him, we, the blessed recipients of this redemption, are called to spread this glorious message of salvation to others. As we personally rest in the promises and love of God, his grace enables us to grow as peacemakers.

We become true peacemakers through repentance, faith, and rightful worship of God alone. We are ambassadors of peace when we trust in God's grace, count others as better than ourselves, bear one another's burdens, and forgive our offenders. In short, we are peacemaking women when we drink so deeply of the peace of God that it becomes a lasting part of us and the motivating factor in all we do and say. Our only true hope for reconciliation with others is our reconciliation with God—for what else in all of life would ever motivate us to love our enemies or do good to those who hate us?

When we were God's enemies, we hated him in our hearts. We spit in his face. We were an offensive stench in his nostrils. But God, who is rich in mercy, forgave us all our sins and adopted us as his precious children. While we were yet enemies, he made us his friends (Rom. 5:10). In response to his grace, our hearts are fixed on Christ, and *his love* enables us to bear with the people in our lives and forgive—just as the Lord forgave us. *We* don't make peace. *God* makes peace to rule in our hearts because of his Son, Jesus. Our only hope for reconciliation is found in the gospel of Jesus Christ. In the words of Phillip Yancey, "A cease-fire between human beings depends upon a cease-fire with God."[7]

Your Authors Struggle to Be Peacemaking Women

Our realization of the costliness of conflict and our conviction that the Bible gives practical wisdom and guidance for building and maintaining strong relationships have led us to write this book. Yet even though we are writing a book on peacemaking, we both have failed in the past to live lives of Christlike unity and love—and we continue to struggle to this day. We even experienced heartbreaking conflict with one another while working on this manuscript! (We'll tell you more about that in the Conclusion of this book.)

Consider just two examples from our professional lives. I (Tara) once asked an employee for feedback on how I was doing as her supervisor. Her candid words rightfully embarrassed me: "Tara, you think you can do everything better than me, and maybe you can . . . but it makes me wonder why I am here at all. You expect everyone to be like you. But I just can't respond as fast as you do. You make me feel like a baby. I am overwhelmed because I can't even imagine what the game plan for a project might be—and you expect me to come out of the starting gate with the finished version."

As you might imagine, I was mortified! In fact, I was para-lyzed—what could I do? How could I change? I was an (ostensibly) mature, Christian woman who had served in the church for years and even taught peacemaking. Yet here I was, unaware of the con-flict I was causing and oblivious to my unloving relational skills. I didn't *want* to be this way, but I had no idea how to become the patient woman I desperately longed to be. I needed help.

And I (Judy) can relate similar examples of causing conflict and not relating well with others. During my twenties, I was a domi-neering and harsh woman. After one of my particularly pointed verbal arguments (the kind where winning really means losing), my mother softly spoke some life-changing words to me: "Judy, when you leave a room, you leave behind bleeding and wounded people." Her words burned into my heart, and I knew they were true. My mother's sad reflection about me greatly helped me to resolve to change and become a person whose words brought heal-ing, not harm.

In light of relational struggles we all face, how do we become peacemaking women?

Biblical Hope

As we prayerfully worked to provide biblical and practical hope in this book, one of our greatest concerns was that we would somehow imply that "If you follow steps A, B, and C, then all of your struggles will go away, your heart will be in perfect peace, and all of your relationships will be fully reconciled." As nice as that may sound, there is simply no way that such a paradigm could be true. Until heaven, we may experience moments of joy, even seasons of peace, but there is no guarantee that we can make any of our problems disappear. In fact, Jesus teaches us just the opposite: "In this world you will have trouble" (John 16:33). However, he also promises us in the same verse that he has "overcome the world." Therefore, as we turn to him in faith, God's grace enables us to rest in him and to have hope—regardless of our circumstances. Where is hope found? Biblical hope is found in God's grace that transforms our hearts and minds as we trust in Christ alone.

Our hearts. What does it mean to turn to God in faith? First of all, we must understand that our relational conflicts and lack of internal peace reveal with great clarity the condition of our hearts. The biggest enemy we face in our efforts to make peace with God, others, and ourselves is our *own hearts.* According to the teaching of Christ in Luke 6, our problems go much deeper than poor management, organization, or communication skills. Our lives and conflicts reflect a heart condition: "No good tree bears bad fruit, nor does a bad tree bear good fruit. . . . The good man brings good things out of the good stored up in his heart, and the evil man brings evil things out of the evil stored up in his heart. For out of the overflow of his heart his mouth speaks" (vv. 43, 45).

Jesus taught us that we act and speak the way we do because of the motivations and attitudes that rule our hearts (Luke 12:13–15). Because every human being has a heart problem, any effort to address outward behavior alone, rather than the heart itself, produces superficial, temporary change at best. Mere behavioral change does not provide lasting hope or peace. Scripture reminds us to "guard your heart, for it is the wellspring of life" (Prov. 4:23). It is our hope that this book will help you better see and understand your heart so that you can address the deeper causes of the conflicts that rob you of peace.

Our minds. Our way of thinking and of viewing God, others, and ourselves is founded on values and convictions that interpret and control how we live our lives. How we live our lives directly impacts our experience of *shalom*. The beliefs that reside deep in our minds impact the way we see and understand the world. Few things are more powerful than conflict for revealing what we truly believe.

Over the years, I (Judy) have come to understand better how my view of God, the world, and myself controlled me. As my beliefs have changed in accordance with the truth of God's Word, my life has seen dramatic differences. At a family reunion over twenty years ago, my siblings and I played a board game. The point of the game was to help the players know one another better by posing thought-provoking questions for discussion. One particular question, as I recall it, was "Who is God?" The multiple-choice answers were a white-bearded kindly father, an invisible spirit, or a distant, uncaring force in the universe. My family had a heated argument over the answer to this question, and I remember being profoundly shocked by the realization that *I didn't know who God was*. The absence of this truth from my life had serious consequences. My pre-Christian years were filled with despair, ongoing conflicts, and aimless wandering from job to job. I often said, "I hate people." Only after I became convinced of who God really is, who I am, and why I was created did my daily life begin to see transformation. As I grew in faith, God's grace enabled me to discard my old beliefs in favor of scriptural teaching. When I came to the point of believing that each human being has purpose, and life has value because God loves his creation, I moved away from a decade of toying with self-destructive thoughts and actions. I discovered a growing passion for life with the purpose of serving God and others. Above all, I finally became willing to risk loving others. Knowing that I was loved—and loving in response—transformed me from a miserable, lonely people-hater to someone who truly enjoys people and finds joy in life's many blessings.

As we learn to walk through life firmly rooted in God's grace, living for his glory, we constantly *identify and evaluate* our thoughts and convictions in light of the truth of Scripture. Instead of only addressing our behavior, we ask, "What are the deeply held beliefs that influence my emotions, thoughts, and actions?" and "How do my beliefs line up with Scripture?" We then reject any beliefs that are false, affirm those that are true, and take practical steps to live out our faith in a loving Christian community.

In short, we learn how to live out Romans 12:2: "Do not conform any longer to the pattern of this world, but be transformed by the renewing of your mind. Then you will be able to test and approve what God's will is—his good, pleasing and perfect will." By God's grace, we hope to help you better identify and evaluate your thoughts so that as they become more biblical, you can enjoy the freedom and peace that come from living by the truth (John 8:31–32).

Christ alone. Throughout this book, we hope to provide you with biblical truth and practical examples to help you identify, evaluate, and reconstruct how you respond to conflicts with God, others, and within—all in the context of authentic Christian relationships. As you meditate on the Scriptures in each chapter, we encourage you to pray and carefully consider how you can implement what you are learning. "You were taught, with regard to your former way of life, to put off your old self, which is being corrupted by its deceitful desires; to be made new in the attitude of your minds; and to put on the new self, created to be like God in true righteousness and holiness" (Eph. 4:22–24).

Our concern, however, is that you will be prone to focus on the law—the "you shoulds" and the "you musts" of Scripture—just as we are often tempted to do. We find it extremely easy to fall into this temptation when talking about biblical peacemaking: "You should forgive her." "You must confess your sins." "You ought to stop being angry." Our tendency as human beings is to interpret these verses to mean, "Pull yourself up by your own bootstraps, get your act together, and *do better.*"

But the truth, extraordinarily evident in peacemaking, is that only God's love and grace working in us can enable us to live lives of obedience that bear good fruit. Only as we remember the gospel—that we have been forgiven all our sins—will we be motivated to forgive those who wrong us (2 Peter 1:9). It is *God* who grants us peace as he enables us to rest more and more in the truth that in Christ we are already "holy and dearly loved" (Col. 3:12).

As you read this book, we hope and pray that you will put your faith fully in Christ—not in any theory, philosophy, or "practical steps" (Col. 2:8). Truly, Christ alone is our Savior. Christ alone is our hope.

As We Begin

Writing one book on so many diverse topics has not been easy. We fully realize that hundreds of books have been written on the subjects of each chapter, and so we do not attempt to fully address any one topic. However, we do pray that this book will be a resource to encourage you on to further hope in Christ, providing biblical and practical counsel for growing as a woman of peace. We particularly hope that the questions for reflection, scriptural prayers, and recommended resources at the end of each chapter will help you in your further study and reflection.

Living as a woman of peace does not come naturally or easily, but it is possible. In the context of loving relationships within the body of Christ, we learn to turn to God for mercy so that our hearts and minds can be brought more in line with Scripture. God's grace empowers us to walk as daughters of the King. Within the church we receive support, teaching, and the ministration of the sacraments. We learn to develop nurturing and caring relationships where our faith is developed and matured. Our brothers and sisters in Christ, though imperfect themselves and growing in sanctification, help us to remember the height from which we have fallen (Rev. 2:5), the home to which we are headed (John 14:2), and the great and glorious love of God (1 John 3:1).

Of course, we will continue to struggle! Until we are perfected in glory, we have much to learn. But we "press on to take hold of that for which Christ Jesus took hold of me" (Phil. 3:12). And along life's journey, no matter the sorrows that come, the people who betray us, the terrors that assail us, *we have peace.* Jesus promises us: "Peace I leave with you; my peace I give you. I do not give to you as the world gives. Do not let your hearts be troubled and do not be afraid" (John 14:27).

With our hearts fixed on Christ, strengthened by his gospel of grace, and committed to his holy Word, let's grow together as women of *shalom*.

PART ONE

CONFLICTS WITH GOD

For we do not have a high priest who is unable to
sympathize with our weaknesses, but we have one who
has been tempted in every way, just as we are—yet was
without sin. Let us then approach the throne of grace
with confidence, so that we may receive mercy and
find grace to help us in our time of need.

Hebrews 4:15–16

We are cruel to ourselves if we try to live in this world
without knowing about the God whose world it is
and who runs it. The world becomes a strange, mad,
painful place, and life in it a disappointing and unpleasant business, for those who do not know about
God.

J. I. Packer[1]

As I (Tara) worked to prepare this manuscript, I read
through nearly twenty years of old journals—hundreds
of handwritten pages of conflicts and angst captured throughout
my Christian life. Although I knew the "right" answers about God,
my relationship with him was often filled with anguish:

"What do you think of me, God? Am I detestable to you?"

"Why did this happen? Have you forgotten me altogether?"

Even as I served on mission trips, led Bible studies, and sang on worship teams, my heart continued to cry out with despairing questions. Sadly, all too often I did not respond to my own questions with scriptural truth. When my emotions ran amok, I indulged in "stinkin' thinkin'."

As my journals demonstrate, a mere "head knowledge" of theology often fails to accomplish real change in our lives. When our relationship with God becomes cold and distant, or when we face conflict and internal strife, we rarely think to ourselves, "I may have a theology problem." Instead, we usually look for quick fixes in self-help "how-to's." If we stop to realize the importance of biblical thinking, we come to understand that our conflicts with God and others are often rooted in bad theology.

The term *theology* may be a bit intimidating. Some might immediately envision a thick book filled with doctrinal minutiae. In reality, however, every Christian is already a theologian on some level. We all preach "sermons" to ourselves every day whether we realize it or not. We give sermons to our children and friends on a regular basis on a multitude of day-to-day topics. Theology matters—it affects all of life. What is your theology?

Theology can be narrowly defined as "the study of God." For our purposes, we prefer to paraphrase John Frame by defining theology as *the application of the whole of Scripture by the whole person to the whole of life*.[2] First Timothy 4:16 teaches us that we are called to "watch [our] life and doctrine closely." If our theology is shaky, aspects of our lives will decay and collapse. If it is strong and deep, we will have "everything we need for life and godliness" (2 Peter 1:3). Theology is good theology when it changes us—when our hearts are controlled by the theology we confess (Mark 12:30). As Christians, we are to be *doers* of the Word: "But the man who looks intently into the perfect law that gives freedom, and continues to do this, not forgetting what he has heard, but doing it—he will be blessed in what he does" (James 1:25). As David Powlison reminds us, "People change when biblical truth becomes more loud and vivid than previous life experience."[3]

The first chapter of our book is meant to establish a foundation of biblical thinking about God so that we can experience peace in our hearts and lay a solid foundation for peacemaking with others. In chapter 2 we turn our attention to the truth that God alone is worthy of our devotion and worship. Unless we grasp this foundational truth, we will never understand and turn away from the cravings that bring frequent conflicts into our relationships. Chapter 3 addresses how we can experience peace in the midst of intense suffering because we are anchored to the one eternal God whose ways, though sometimes puzzling and painful in the short run, are always purposeful and directed to our good (Rom. 8:28–29).

Since you are investing time in reading a book on peacemaking, you may be tempted to skip over these apparently "theoretical and theological" chapters about God to "get to the practical stuff" of how to resolve conflicts with others. We urge you, however, to meditate carefully on the truths presented in the first three chapters because knowing what it means to have an authentic relationship with God *is* practical and is the *only* way that we can be women of peace. Peacemaking is not a set of rules or how-to steps; it is heart-change and gospel ministry. Only God's grace enables us to be free: "If you hold to my teaching, . . . you will know the truth, and the truth will set you free" (John 8:31–32).

The ultimate relationship in our lives, our relationship with God, establishes our foundation for godly relationships with others and for peace within ourselves. It is not enough to know all the right "Sunday school" answers about God. Conflicts often arise when we experience a disconnect between our *confessional* theology (what we profess to believe about God) and our *practical* theology (how we actually think and live). Because relationships clearly demonstrate our practical theology, biblical truth must deeply penetrate our hearts if we are to experience relationships of *shalom*.

Let's now journey into "the trenches, where theology and life collide and real theologians are made."[4] We do so not as wandering orphans who have no home but as beloved children of the one true God (1 John 3:1).

1

THINKING ABOUT GOD

The LORD, the LORD, the compassionate and gracious
God, slow to anger, abounding in love and faithfulness, maintaining love to thousands, and forgiving
wickedness, rebellion and sin.

Exodus 34:6–7

What comes into our minds when we think about God
is the most important thing about us.

A. W. Tozer[1]

A young Christian woman named Elizabeth struggled in
her relationship with God. At times she feared God and
exhausted herself with Christian activities meant to please him.
During these frenetic seasons, she felt "like a good Christian" and
envisioned that God ranked her performance as "acceptable." At
other times she gave in to habitual lust or pride, and her behavior
and thought life looked like that of a nonbeliever. When she failed
in her performance, she thought God stopped loving her. She had
a vague notion that when she was ready "to be good," God might
"take her back." Elizabeth's relationship with God was a seesaw of
legalistic performance and licentious indulgence. She "felt" God's

love and approval when she lived up to her self-imposed standard of "goodness," and she "felt" God's rejection when she failed to measure up.

All too often Christian women relate to God as Elizabeth did. What are we to do? How can we have peace with God, lay a foundation for peace-filled relationships with others, and enjoy genuine peace within? To have peace with God, we first must have a personal relationship with him. In order to have a relationship with him, we must understand who he is, not who we mistakenly think he is or want him to be. Inasmuch as our finite minds can wrap themselves around infinite mysteries, we seek to grow in our knowledge of God.[2] In the words of D. Martyn Lloyd-Jones, "The Christian faith begins and ends with a knowledge of the Lord."[3] We will focus on four biblical truths to help counter our unbiblical thinking about God. These truths are essential to developing the comprehensive *shalom* we all long for.[4]

God Is Holy *and* Merciful

We will lack deep peace if we fail to understand that God is both completely holy and wonderfully merciful.

God is holy. He is completely free from all impurity and imperfection (Lev. 11:44). God is great and glorious. He is above all things and yet intimately associated with all things (Isa. 40:12–26; Ps. 145:3). Because God is holy, we ought to experience a sense of awe when we think of God. If our attitude toward God is that he is only our "buddy," then we probably have little motivation to obey him when the going gets tough. If we have no fear of God or sense of his majesty, why would we ever follow the difficult and seemingly foolish command to love our enemies (Luke 6:27)? But if we truly know God, we will describe him just as Mr. Beaver in *The Lion, the Witch and the Wardrobe* describes the Christ-figure, Aslan: "Safe? 'Course he isn't safe. But he's good. He's the King, I tell you."[5] As the holy King, God is to be honored and obeyed.

We are glorious ruins. We simply cannot revere God as we ought. Compared to his holiness, even our best is filth (Isa. 64:6). We are "glorious ruins" created in God's image and likeness but damaged by the Fall (Genesis 1–3).[6] Apart from the Spirit of Christ dwelling within us, we are totally without the ability to do good or to choose what is right. All of us share in Adam's sinful state of rebellion against God (Ps. 51:4). We are deceived and enslaved by sin (Ps. 19:12–13). Our thoughts, emotions, and actions flow out of our sinful hearts. Our sin traps us in a miry pit so deep that we cannot dig ourselves out. We are hopelessly lost in sin, unable to save ourselves (Rom. 1:18–3:20). The result of our sin is death (Rom. 6:23).

God is merciful. When the radiance of God reveals our sin, one temptation is to condemn ourselves and pull away from God. Like Elizabeth from the beginning of this chapter, we can easily enter into seasons of intense activity trying to "do all the right things" to earn God's love and approval. But since we can never be good enough to compel God to accept or love us, we are in desperate need of his mercy (Ps. 40:2). God demonstrates mercy by not giving us what we deserve. Our sin requires punishment, but the mercy of God withholds it and even lavishes life upon us!

Praise God! His mercy to us is vast and new every day (Lam. 3:22–24). *God* saves us from our sin and gives us new life. He does this not because we deserve or earn his mercy but because it brings him pleasure and demonstrates his great love for us (Eph. 1:3–5; John 3:16).

Jesus satisfies both the holiness and the mercy of God. The holiness and mercy of God meet in the crucifixion of Christ. Jesus's life and substitutionary death on the cross fulfill the righteous requirements of a holy God and provide a way for God, through Jesus Christ, to save those who are his. Jesus voluntarily gave his life to ransom us from our captivity to sin—and eventual eternal death (Matt. 20:28). He put himself in our place, became our substitute, and took on himself the penalty of our sins. *Through the cross of Christ, both the justice and mercy of God are fully satisfied.* In the words of John Piper, "The death of Christ is the wisdom of God by which the love of God saves sinners from the wrath of God, and all the while upholds and demonstrates the righteousness of God."[7]

Even children can embrace this truth with confidence. When my (Judy's) daughter, Robyn, was only ten years old, she gave her testimony at our church. As she proclaimed her faith publicly, I was moved to tears. Tears soon became laughter as Robyn surprised the congregation by saying, "I am grateful for Christ's double imputation." She explained how the righteousness of Jesus Christ had been imputed (credited) to her and how her sin was imputed (credited) to Jesus, which is why he died on the cross. I was amused to hear Robyn use this twenty-dollar phrase. Yet we are all called to remind ourselves of this truth whenever we are tempted to doubt God's love for us. Jesus took our place of punishment that we might stand in his place of perfection. When God looks at us, he sees Christ's own righteousness because he has made a judicial declaration that the righteousness of Christ is imputed to all who trust in him. We have done nothing to deserve God's gracious gift, but we are the grateful recipients of the blessings of a holy and merciful God. In this we delight like a bride on her wedding day: "I delight greatly in the LORD; my soul rejoices in my God. For he has clothed me with garments of salvation and arrayed me in a robe of righteousness, as a bridegroom adorns his head like a priest, and as a bride adorns herself with her jewels" (Isa. 61:10).

We must remember both ***God's holiness and God's mercy.*** We face a dual danger when considering both the holiness and mercy of God: when tempted to sin, we may want to focus on "grace"; when tempted to self-condemnation, we may want to focus on "law." When we give in to these dangers, we lose our peace. God's holiness *and* mercy together provide the way for us to be women of *shalom*. When our tendency is to focus on grace, we must never presume on God's mercy and use it as an excuse to sin. Instead we must remember his holy love. When our tendency is to focus on law, we must not condemn ourselves with our failures. Instead, when we are convicted of sin and repent, we must remember the merciful gospel. God calls us to believe on the promises of the gospel of Jesus Christ.

Marie's life beautifully demonstrates the blessings of God's holiness and mercy. Marie was a woman struggling with adultery. God's holiness convicted her that she needed to end the affair. But she had given her heart and soul to the man in an intimacy that went far beyond a mere sexual relationship. Marie did not want to end the relationship. Her rebellion rightfully deserved God's wrath, but in his kindness, God ministered mercy to her even as she struggled.

He did not withhold his love from her. He did not cast her away as rejected and abandoned. Instead, he lovingly called Marie to himself as his precious daughter. God's grace gave her the strength to trust him to care for her, and she ended the affair. Years later, she looks back on that difficult time with peace. She knows that her sin offended the holiness of God, but she also rests in the comfort of knowing that the mercy of God both paid the penalty for her sin and led her to repentance.

At a recent prayer group, my (Tara's) dear friend was burdened by a heavy sense of her unworthiness and her failures. She saw her sin and was disgusted by it. For days she had been reading God's Word and hearing only the law—all of the things she *ought* to do. She was discouraged and despondent because she saw only the ways she failed. I lovingly told her, "Susan, you need to remember God's lavish love *for you!* He delights in you, cherishes you, and forgives you because of Christ. Remember the gospel!" Susan's hope and joy were renewed as together we thanked God for his mercies in Christ.

But at that same prayer group, I was struggling with bitterness toward a family member. In my sin, I was trying to justify my attitude by claiming that the other person acted like an "enemy" and was "not to be trusted." My friends gently helped me to remember God's standard for how enemies are to be treated (Luke 6 and Romans 12) because I needed to be reminded of God's law. As I reflected on how I was called to be as a Christian, I saw my failures and knew that my only hope was to run to Christ. I was desperately in need of his mercy! Even God's good law brings us to the gospel, for only God's grace can enable us to obey his commands.

God Forgives His Adopted Children

We will lack deep peace if we fail to understand that God adopts forgiven sinners as his children forever.

God forgives us. Theresa was a ministry leader who struggled with experiencing God's forgiveness. She led Bible studies on God's forgiveness and communicated his grace to others with great clarity. But Theresa had a secret: as a teenager, she had an abortion and briefly married an abusive man. When he left her, she came to know

Christ and began a new life far away from her former home. While she loved God and encouraged others to trust in his forgiveness, deep down, she was miserable. How could God forgive *her*? What hope was there for *her*? Plenty! As Theresa prayed for the grace to believe the gospel, she cried out to God, "Please help me to say good-bye forever to my past and trust that it is covered by the blood of Jesus. Please, Lord, help me experience your forgiveness." Theresa learned to speak God's truth to herself, "I am righteous by faith in Jesus Christ. Through God's gracious gift of Jesus, I have been purchased by the blood of Christ, and I belong to him (Rom. 3:22, 24). Nothing can ever snatch me out of God's hand (Rom. 8:35). I am blessed! My sins are forgiven and will never be counted against me (Rom. 4:7–8)." This is the gospel that brings peace to God's adopted children.

God adopts us. According to many theologians, God's adopting grace is the utmost expression of the benefits of salvation and the highest privilege that the gospel offers.[8] "How great is the love the Father has lavished on us, that we should be called children of God! And that is what we are!" (1 John 3:1). As adopted children, we are fully accepted, brought out of bondage and destitution into the "safety, certainty and enjoyment" of the family of God.[9] If your family of origin reflected the steadfastness and delight of heavenly adoption, rejoice! Your ability to rest in the doctrine of adoption may come easily. But if your earthly home was not a safe refuge, you might struggle with the idea of God as your faithful, loving Father. The truth in Scripture, however, is that our position as children of God is even now permanently assured (Gal. 4:7). One day, your heavenly Father will "quiet you with his love, he will rejoice over you with singing" (Zeph. 3:17).

God delights in us. When you have placed your faith in the work of Jesus Christ for your salvation, you are the beloved child of the King of Kings! Because of his steadfast, passionate love, you will never be deserted or rejected. As a believer in Jesus, you are a member of the sought-after Bride of Christ, and your Groom gives you a new name. Just as adoptive parents seek out and delight in their children, your God seeks you out and delights in you: "No longer will they call you Deserted, or name your land Desolate. But you will be called Hephzibah [which means *the Lord's delight*

is in her] . . . for the L ORD will take delight in you" (Isa. 62:4, explanation added).

Through Christ, God looks on you with the gaze of a bridegroom who loves his bride fervently—even to the point of death.
It reminds me (Tara) of a wedding that I attended years ago. On a
normal day, the bride was absolutely gorgeous—not just physically
but spiritually and emotionally too. She radiated Christ. But on her
wedding day? She was the most stunning bride I had ever seen. As
she entered the church, the eyes of the entire congregation were
fixed on her—not just because it was tradition but because we were
entranced by the purity of her gown, the radiance of her face, and
the love cascading from her entire being for her groom. When she
reached the front of the chapel, the pastor had a twinkle in his eye
as he asked the congregation, "Isn't Melanie beautiful?" We all said
a loud, "Yes!" And then this pastor ministered the gospel to us all
when he said, "That is how God looks at *you* through Christ." Just
as a bridegroom delights in his bride, God delights in *you*.

We are God's beloved daughters. Do you see yourself as beautiful and precious in God's eyes? Or do you (like us) sometimes
think, "Yes, I'm saved, but I sneaked in the back door. If I stay
pressed against the back wall, maybe God won't notice what a terrible mistake he has made." One of the most common counseling
issues we address with women is that because they believe that they
cannot be good enough to merit God's love, when they sin and
repent they need a few days to feel they can approach God with
boldness and confidence. They wrongly feel as though they have to
earn their way back "up" to God before he will love them again.

Reject those lies. They come from your fallenness and sin. Believe the truth as revealed in God's Word: God passionately desires
that fallen, imperfect people be reconciled to him through belief
in Jesus Christ. He is the "hound of heaven" who pursues lost and
condemned people to adopt and save them.[10] You are the beloved
daughter of the King. God throws a party with you as the guest of
honor when you return home. It makes God happy to adopt you
into his family forever. He doesn't forgive you because you earn his
forgiveness by being good. He forgives you because he is a forgiving
God! He doesn't save you because he *has* to. He saves you because
he *wants* to save you. You are his precious child, forever.

God's Love for Us Does Not Depend on Our Performance

We will lack deep peace if we believe that God's love for us is based on our performance. God saved us not because of what we do but because it was his delight to do so. God loves us because he is a loving God, not because we earn his love or merit his kindness. In fact, before the foundation of the world was even laid, God chose us to be his beloved children. "In love he predestined us to be adopted as his sons through Jesus Christ, in accordance with his pleasure and will" (Eph. 1:5). Before we ever had a kind or selfish thought, blessed or hurt another, or even praised or blasphemed the God of glory, *God chose us.* God's love is not about us—what we think, feel, do, or say—it is about *him.*

God loves us particularly. Even though God's love for us is not based on our performance, his love for us in Christ *is* a particular love. He does not have some vague, generic love for mankind. God loves specific individuals. God loves me. God loves you. If God has breathed new life into your dry bones; if he has given you a heart of flesh for a heart of stone; if he has granted you the gift of repentance and you have transferred your trust for eternal life from your own performance to the finished work of Christ, then *your name* is forever engraved on his hands (Isa. 49:16). You could never merit such grace! Right now, in the throne room of heaven, God's hands are scarred with your name. Nothing can separate you from him or him from you.

God loves us because we are his. In response to this great truth, we rest secure knowing that we are wanted. There is a place for us in this world. We are safe in the arms of our loving Savior not because of what we do but because of what he has done for us. By God's grace we have been released from the covenant of our works (that leads to death) and brought into a covenant of grace (that leads to life and peace). This gospel of grace shows us the extent to which God loves us.

I (Tara) love to play a game with my husband, Fred, where one of us asks, "How much do you love me?" and the other responds with an extremely large number based on whatever we're doing at the time. When hiking in the Beartooth Mountains near our home in Montana, I might respond, "I love you more than the number of pine needles on all of the trees on all of the mountains in all of Montana." Or at a baseball game Fred might respond, "I love you more than the number of stitches on all of the baseballs that have ever been thrown in this ballpark." "Do you really love me that much?" "I do! I do!" It's a fun game and we enjoy it. But it's not my favorite.

My favorite game is when I ask Fred, "*Why* do you love me?" He always responds, "Because you're mine."This is God's response to you too: *"I love you because you are mine."* Not because of what you do or don't do. Not because of what you say or know, but simply *because you are mine.* Rest in this truth. Delight in it. Find yourself wholly defined by it.This is Christianity 101, the gospel in a nutshell.We are the blessed recipients of eternal love. God loves us more than the number of stars in the sky and grains of sand on the beach (or stitches on a million baseballs!).

In Christ We Are Perfect and Growing in Perfection

We will lack deep peace if we fail to understand that we live in tension between what theologians have called the "already" and the "not yet." We are already perfect by virtue of our union with Jesus Christ, and yet we look forward to the day in glory when our lives and thoughts will match this present reality. We are already perfect, yet we are growing in perfection. As Martin Luther reminded us, "This life, therefore, is not righteousness but growth in righteousness, not health but healing, not being but becoming, not rest but exercise. We are not yet what we shall be, but we are growing toward it; the process is not yet finished but it is going on. This is not the end but it is the road; all does not yet gleam in glory but all is being purified."[11]

We struggle and fail. For many Christian women, doubts and fears enter into our relationship with God when we continue to struggle with habitual sins and see areas of our lives that are not God-honoring.We may look at our struggles with the same sins and wonder if we are even saved at all. At times we can feel as though we are complete frauds. Am I "Tara the good Christian woman who loves God, loves her family, and serves faithfully in Christian ministry?" or am I "Tara the lazy glutton who would rather watch old movies on TV, eat cookie dough, and avoid any and all work"?

And yet we are perfect in Christ. While it is true that we must take sin seriously because it affects our fellowship with God and our testimony of his grace in our lives, we must also remember that we are *not* "either/or" (either a "saint" or a "sinner") but "both/and" (both "totally righteous in Christ" and "yet growing in righteousness"). We are both sinner and saint. We are sinners as a result of the fall and indwelling sin yet saints as a result of Christ's saving grace.

We are fully justified and we are being sanctified. We live in a state of tension, suspended between these two truths: we are already perfect and holy, yet we are growing in perfection and holiness. Theologians refer to these truths as *justification* and *sanctification*. When we are born again by the Holy Spirit (regeneration), we are fully justified—declared righteous—by our holy God. The doctrine of justification means that Christ's record has been imputed[12] to us once and for all. We are already perfect because Christ's perfect record is now ours. In other words, "God made him who had no sin to be sin for us, so that in him we might become the righteousness of God" (2 Cor. 5:21). If you have put your faith in the finished work of Christ on the cross, when God looks on you he always sees perfection because he sees Christ. You are already perfect.

On the other hand, the doctrine of sanctification means that we *are being* conformed more and more to the likeness of Jesus. Throughout our Christian life, we are growing in sanctification. We are not made perfect by our own strength or effort. God himself does this work in us. "He who began a good work in you will carry it on to completion until the day of Christ Jesus" (Phil. 1:6). We *are* growing in perfection (Rom. 8:29). We "are being transformed into his likeness with ever-increasing glory, which comes from the Lord" (2 Cor. 3:18). As we live each day, we see evidence of indwelling sin and fallenness. This is because we are *not yet perfect.* But we have great hope because *God* is growing us to be more like Jesus.

I (Judy) have often thought that the more any of us grow in spiritual maturity, the more of our own sin we are able to see. I am far more aware of my pride today than when I became a believer in 1989. I have often joked that I used to be blissfully ignorant of how rotten I really am, but now I see it much more clearly. This increasing awareness of my own sin can be very discouraging until I remember that it is the *evidence* of God's sanctifying work in my life. We are *being made perfect* by him, and nothing can thwart his accomplishing our sanctification.

We learn to give grace to others and ourselves. As we begin to understand the doctrines of justification and sanctification and to trust in God's grace toward us, we experience *shalom* as we extend that same grace to others and ourselves. Consider a lovely example of giving grace to ourselves in C. S. Lewis's little book *Letters to Children*. In this compilation of letters to his fans, Lewis gives grace to himself when he responds to nine-year-old Laurence, a little boy who worried that he loved Aslan more than Jesus. Mr. Lewis comforted the child by explaining, "the things Laurence loves Aslan for doing or saying are simply the things Jesus really did and said." He then goes on to demonstrate his confidence in God's justification and sanctification when he writes to Laurence's mother:

> If I were Laurence I'd just say in my prayers something like this: "Dear God, if the things I've been thinking and feeling about those books are things You don't like and are bad for me, please take away those feelings and thoughts. But if they are not bad, then please stop me from worrying about them" . . . That is the sort of thing I think Laurence should say for himself; but it would be kind and Christian-like if he then added, "And if Mr. Lewis has worried any other children by his books or done them any harm, then please forgive him and help him never to do it again."[13]

In day-to-day living, a genuine grasp of justification and sanctification results in grace—to others and to oneself. How remarkable that Lewis could be this gracious to himself! Wouldn't many of us condemn ourselves if our writings had frightened a little boy? But not C. S. Lewis. He knew his theology and doctrine too well. He knew that all we can do is our best in this life. Then we simply pray that the Lord will cover our feeble efforts with his grace. Lewis's words to Laurence reflect the truth that "nothing matters in the kingdom but the grace of God."[14]

From Unbiblical Thinking to Biblical Thinking

We have been talking about theology all throughout this chapter. To now demonstrate how biblical theology applies to real life, consider one of my (Tara's) journal entries from many years ago:

> Everywhere I go, I fail. When you see my selfishness, coldness, hardness of heart, and pride—what are your thoughts toward me, God? Is there any part of me that doesn't disgust you?

I'm sure I got up from that quiet time with very little peace, because *that* was the end of the journal entry. Not very hopeful, was it? Compare that with a more recent journal entry, one that reflects the changes in me as I have grown in my understanding of the doctrines of God, man, sin, redemption, and the glorious gospel of grace.

> Why is there no place for me in the world? I am such a failure! God, is there even anything in me that doesn't repulse you? Yes. You love Christ in me. "Not that we are competent in ourselves to claim anything for ourselves, but our competence comes from God" (2 Cor. 3:5). Father, please do not allow me to resist your hand in my life. Please forgive my anger at this great loss. Shall I accept good from you and not trouble? (Job 1 and 2). It was not the other person that caused this but you, Lord (Joseph in Genesis 45). My circumstance is difficult and humiliating, but I humble myself under your mighty hand because I know you are conforming my character to yours because you love me (Heb. 12:10).

I remember ending that quiet time with hope and joy even though my circumstances had not changed. What is the difference in the two journal entries? A deepening understanding of God in accordance with scriptural truth leads to more biblical thinking. The more we know who God is, the better we are able to understand the gospel. The better we are able to understand the gospel, the deeper is the relationship we have with God. The deeper our relationship with him, the deeper our sense of peace. Peace in the deepest level of our hearts is impossible without intimate knowledge of the Prince of Peace.

As we grow in a biblical theology, we put our hope in God (Ps. 119:147) and are enabled to experience deep peace with God, others, and ourselves. Through faith in God, *shalom* can abound in our lives as we rest in his love: "I pray that out of his glorious riches he may strengthen you with power through his Spirit in your inner being, so that Christ may dwell in your hearts through faith. And I pray that you, being rooted and established in love, may have power, together with all the saints, to grasp how wide and long and high and deep is the love of Christ, and to know this love that surpasses knowledge—that you may be filled to the measure of all the fullness of God" (Eph. 3:16–19).

Personal Reflection

Questions for Reflection

1. How did you first become acquainted with the gospel? What are some of your favorite passages in Scripture that remind you of the riches of your salvation? Why are they precious to you?

2. Identify one problem that you have faced in the last year. Summarize in a paragraph what you think God intended for you in this situation. What was he doing? How was he at work? How does God fit into your story? Can you identify any of your beliefs about God and his purposes that are un-biblical?

3. Read Matthew 7:24–27. Biblical hope comes from knowing Scripture. We learn Scripture through attending church, reading the Bible, listening to audio teachings, watching videos, reading books, and attending Bible studies. What steps can you take this week to better know and understand the Bible? Pray through Psalm 119:33–40.

4. Read Romans 8:15 and Galatians 4:4–6. Based on these passages, what is the nature of your relationship with God? How does God view you? What impact does this have on your life? Would you say that you live more like a hungry and cold orphan or a wealthy child of the King? Why do you think this is so?

5. Do you feel closer to God when you are doing good things? Do you feel that God loves you more when you do righteous acts? If so, why do you think you try to earn God's love and approval instead of relying solely on Christ? Write out a paragraph on what it means to trust in Christ alone rather than on your own performance.

6. On a typical day, how do you deal with your sin? Do you try harder, give up and run away, or turn in faith to Christ? Read Psalm 51. What does this psalm teach us about repentance? How does Psalm 51 speak to the way you typically deal with your sin?

7. How would you define *sanctification* in your own words? In what ways have your heart and life changed since you were "redeemed from the empty way of life handed down to you from your forefathers" (1 Peter 1:18)? Write out five examples of sanctification in your life.

8. As you consider the theological truths we talked about in this chapter, how do you think about God? Read Isaiah 6:1–7. As you consider God's holiness, what feelings come to mind? Do you have confidence to approach him with your needs and desires? Why or why not?

9. In what areas of your life are you convicted of the need to repent? Are you afraid that God may be punishing you for your sins? Which sins? Read Psalm 103:12, Isaiah 1:18, and Micah 7:19. In the form of a letter to God, summarize what these passages teach about how God treats your sin. How do the truths in your letter to God affect your inner peace?

10. Have you ever said, "I just can't forgive myself"? Meditate on the forgiveness God offers in Psalm 103:2–4; 1 Corinthians 6:9–11; Ephesians 1:4–8; 1 Timothy 1:15–16; and 1 John 1:9–10. What does it mean if you refuse to believe God's Word that you are forgiven for your sins? Are you sitting in judgment on God? If so, write out a prayer of repentance for your unbelief based on Mark 2:5. Substitute your own name for "Son."

Praying Scripture to God

Dear God, I thank you that you have given me everything I need for life and godliness through my relationship with you because of all you have done for me in Christ. I thank you that you have removed my old heart of stone and given me a new heart of flesh. I thank you, God, that my past is covered by the blood of Jesus and I belong to you. You are my firm and steady rock, and nothing can snatch me out of your hand. I thank you that your Word is eternal. Your Word stands forever. Father God, please bring me word of your unfailing love, for I put my trust in you. By faith I turn away from my sinful, unbelieving heart, and I turn toward you. Father God, my hope is in you alone. Thank you for delighting in me because of Christ. Please help me to love in deeds and in truth. Please encourage me from your Word, for I put my trust in you.

(Prayer based on 2 Peter 1:3; Ezek. 36:26–27; Rom. 3:22, 24; Ps. 40:2; Rom. 8:35; Ps. 119:89; Matt. 24:35; Ps. 143:8; Heb. 3:12–13; Ps. 62:5; 1 John 3:18; Isa. 62:4; Ps. 119:65; Ps. 40:3.)

Recommended Resources for Further Study and Consideration

Carolyn Custis James, *When Life and Beliefs Collide: How Knowing God Makes a Difference* (Grand Rapids: Zondervan, 2001).

Robert D. Jones, *Forgiveness: I Just Can't Forgive Myself* (Phillipsburg, NJ: P&R Publishing, 2000).

W. Phillip Keller, *What Is the Father Like?* (Minneapolis: Bethany, 1996).

C. J. Mahaney, *The Cross Centered Life: Keeping the Gospel the Main Thing* (Sisters, OR: Multnomah, 2002).

J. I. Packer, *Knowing God* (Downers Grove, IL: InterVarsity, 1973).

Eugene Peterson, *A Long Obedience in the Same Direction: Discipleship in an Instant Society* (Downers Grove, IL: InterVarsity, 1980).

John Piper, *Desiring God: Meditations of a Christian Hedonist* (Sisters, OR: Multnomah, 1986).

John Piper, *Future Grace* (Sisters, OR: Multnomah, 1995).

R. C. Sproul, *The Holiness of God* (Wheaton: Tyndale, 1988).

R. C. Sproul, *Knowing Scripture* (Downers Grove, IL: InterVarsity, 1977).

R. C. Sproul and Robert Wolgemuth, *What's in the Bible* (Nashville: Word, 2000).

John R. W. Stott, *Basic Christianity* (Downers Grove, IL: InterVarsity, 1958).

Joni Eareckson Tada, *Holiness in Hidden Places* (Nashville: J. Countryman, 1999).

2

IDOLATRY

You turned to God from idols to serve the living and
true God, and to wait for his Son from heaven, whom
he has raised from the dead—Jesus, who rescues us
from the coming wrath.

1 Thessalonians 1:9–10

It is a blessed mark of growth out of spiritual infancy
when we can forego the joys which once appeared to
be essential, and can find our solace in him who de-
nies them to us.

Charles Spurgeon[1]

Humans were made to be worshipers. To worship is to
"ascribe worth" to something. Because God created us
with a need for *him*, it is not a matter of whether or not people *will*
worship. The question has always been, *what or whom* will people
worship? Our hearts are continually in movement either toward or
away from God. The objects of our worship are the things we value
supremely and the things in which we find our greatest pleasure,
joy, and security. We make minute-by-minute choices to worship
either the one true God or false gods. Peace is not our natural

condition because in our fallenness we often try to find peace by going after all sorts of things (financial security, professional success, educational achievements) and people (the "perfect" husband, friend, parent, child).

The biblical term for worship of anything or anyone other than God is *idolatry*. The Bible addresses many human problems but none so extensively as idolatry. Many Christians are not familiar with the term *idolatry* even though it is a frequent and dominant image in Scripture. In fact, sin can be summarized by the word *idolatry*, as Ephesians 5 demonstrates: "For of this you can be sure: No immoral, impure or greedy person—such a man is an idolater—has any inheritance in the kingdom of Christ and of God" (v. 5). All of Scripture teaches us that our hearts are prone to idolatry. In the words of John Calvin, the human heart "is a perpetual factory of idols."[2]

God is a jealous God, and he will not allow us to find ultimate fulfillment, satisfaction, or joy in worshiping idols. The issue of idolatry is so important that God himself addresses it in the first and second commandments:

> You shall have no other gods before me. You shall not make for yourself an idol in the form of anything in heaven above or on the earth beneath or in the waters below. You shall not bow down to them or worship them; for I, the LORD your God, am a jealous God, punishing the children for the sin of the fathers to the third and fourth generation of those who hate me, but showing love to a thousand generations of those who love me and keep my commandments.
>
> Exodus 20:3–6

Does idolatry in the twenty-first century look like someone worshiping a golden calf or a little statue on a table? Not usually. Most of us do not have shrines with statues in our homes. Yet we do have idols. Recently I (Tara) journaled about some of the conflicts in my life and the heart motivations that they revealed. This is what I wrote:

> I want to be comfortable. I want to be entertained. Like a big, fat, lazy cat—I want my tummy full, my curiosities satisfied with idle

frivolity, a pillow to nap on when I am tired. I want people to serve me, wait on me, and make me happy. I always want more. More sweets. More rest. More work. I want what I want when I want it. I am restless. My heart is never satisfied.

As I reflect on my journal entry, I see that my idols are, to name a few, comfort, sloth, greed, rebellion, and pride. These idols rear their ugly heads in my day-to-day living. For example, I struggle with the idol of my personal comfort and convenience. I am fairly patient in a number of uncomfortable situations, but what if someone says she is going to do something, I am counting on her, and she doesn't do it? Or what if I am delayed by a store clerk who is (in my eyes) incompetent at his job? A rolling boil of anger can seep to my head, and I become visibly upset. I hate this in me! I know that it is my idolatrous heart ruling me (Ps. 119:133). I demand personal comfort to such an extent that I think constantly about it and strive to attain it, and when I don't get it, I am unable to pray, rest, or even enjoy anything else in life.

When we indulge our idolatrous worship, we act like addicts. Our idols become our focus and goal of life; they rule our feelings, thoughts, and actions. Like a drug addict putting her children in harm's way for a fix or an alcoholic jeopardizing her career and livelihood to go after a hidden bottle, we will do anything to satisfy our idolatrous cravings.

Idols Cause Conflicts

Idolatry is, of course, first and foremost an offense to God, but some form of idolatry exists at the root of every human conflict (James 4:1). Consider Laura, a ministry leader and homemaker who struggles with making idols out of three specific desires:

- to get her work done in a timely manner with professional excellence
- to have a beautiful, hospitable home with well-behaved, obedient children
- to find fulfillment and joy in an intimate, romantic marriage

These longings to do good work, have a beautiful home, and enjoy peaceful and loving relationships are good desires. But when she elevates these desires to demands, Laura ends up frustrated and bent on destroying whatever is in her way—usually people. The idols in her heart ("You must do an excellent job"; "You must have a beautiful home and perfect marriage") take hold of her. Her sharp tongue and her frantic pace are evidence of her bondage to the idols. As the psalmist described, Laura is ensnared: "They worshiped their idols, which became a snare to them" (Ps. 106:36).

Laura coerces the people around her to meet her sinful demands, and when they fail her, she punishes them with a disapproving tone of voice and actions meant to communicate emotional withdrawal and broken relationships. In short, she sacrifices others on the altar of her idols. Even though nothing is inherently wrong with the things she wants, the problem is that she wants them too much.

When idols rule us, we stumble in our Christian walk and we attack or avoid other people. We do whatever it takes to defend and cherish what is precious to us. As we fixate and obsess on our false gods, our lives become reminiscent of the pathetic and pitiable creature Gollum and his hunt for his "Precious" in the Tolkien trilogy *The Lord of the Rings*. "We wants it, we wants it, we wants it!" our hearts cry, and if someone gets in our way, "We hates them," we "throttle them all" if we get the chance. When we are acting as functional idolaters, we are just like Gollum: "filled with hideous lust and rage."[3]

The Development of an Idol

Paul David Tripp, in his workbook *Instruments of Change*, explains that the slippery slope of idolatry begins with a desire.[4] Often, these desires are for good things.[5] James 4:1–3 states: "What causes fights and quarrels among you? Don't they come from your desires that battle within you? You want something but don't get it. You kill and covet, but you cannot have what you want. You quarrel and fight. You do not have, because you do not ask God. When you ask, you do not receive, because you ask with wrong motives, that you may spend what you get on your pleasures." In this passage, the term "desire" does not indicate a bad or sinful desire. It is a neutral term that could indicate either good or bad desires. It is not the *object* that is the problem—it is *how much* we desire it that is the problem. Idolatry is rooted in our own hearts, not in the thing we are worshiping.

I (Judy) have struggled with idolatry in the arena of relationships. For much of my early life, I had shut down my desire for friendship and relationship, restricting my involvement with others to a small, intimate group of family members. After attending a conference by Larry Crabb on the topic of connecting with others in the body of Christ, I began to realize that I had sinfully refused to participate in a God-ordained element of true Christian community. I began to pursue relationships, opening my heart to desire and affection. I began to proactively take steps for others to know, understand, and love me, and I sought to love others in return. I was vulnerable with some people, and, as is true of most people, my new friends occasionally let me down. I got hurt. But instead of responding with forgiveness and mercy, I punished them by withdrawing from them. I was polite and nice on the outside, but deep inside I seethed with cold anger as I resolved never to give my heart to another person.

In the ensuing months, God was gracious to reveal my idolatrous heart to me through the rebuke of a friend who became hurt by my withdrawal. I had made my good desire for fellowship into a demand to be loved "my way." When my demands were frustrated and I felt disappointed, I grew cold and indifferent. It wasn't until I was confronted with my lack of love that I was able to recognize my sin. I had looked to *people* to satisfy me, and when left wanting, I quit investing in the relationship. Idols often lead to more idols. I still struggle between courting the idols of self-protection and being loved my way. Yet peace prevails each and every time my idols are revealed and I seek to be reconciled to God and to the people in my life.

Idols Lead to Death

Scripture teaches that idols are nothing more than worthless frauds: "Every goldsmith is shamed by his idols. His images are a fraud; they have no breath in them. They are worthless, the objects of mockery; when their judgment comes, they will perish. He who is the Portion of Jacob is not like these, for he is the Maker of all things, including the tribe of his inheritance—the LORD Almighty is his name" (Jer. 51:17–19). As John Piper reminds us, "God is most glorified in us when we are most satisfied in him."[6] This is true because God's glory and our joy intersect. Any motivation for living other than finding satisfaction in God will eventually bring emptiness, despair, conflict, and ultimately death.

Idols give no lasting help or security. Beth craved financial security. She believed that money would bring her a sense of accomplishment and worth. The more money she had, the better she felt as a person. Her expensive car, large diamond ring, and fashionable hair and clothes all testified to her wealth. She believed that they secured for her the respect and affirmation of others. When Beth's financial security was in question because her husband left her for another woman, her rage and depression resulted in a suicide attempt. However, through counseling, Beth came to realize that she had been living a life in which she attempted to use money to fulfill her longings for security and significance. Beth had turned away from God as the source of her security and placed her trust in bank accounts and mutual funds. These man-made idols easily vanished through court battles and legal fees, leaving Beth frightened, alone, and unsatisfied.

Beth's experience was reminiscent of Israel's experience as recorded in Habakkuk 2: "Of what value is an idol, since a man has carved it? Or an image that teaches lies? For he who makes it trusts in his own creation; he makes idols that cannot speak. Woe to him who says to wood, 'Come to life!' Or to lifeless stone, 'Wake up!' Can it give guidance? It is covered with gold and silver; there is no breath in it. But the LORD is in his holy temple; let all the earth be silent before him" (vv. 18–20). Just like the worthless idols of ancient Israel, at the end of the day, Beth's idols had no value and could offer no help to her.

How much security do you find in your own finances, relationships, or professional stature? Imagine how you would feel if they all disappeared tomorrow. We all like to imagine that such a tragedy will never happen to us, but we learn from Job and the rest of history that we never know what tomorrow will bring. Eventually all our idols will pass away, and we who cling to those worthless idols forfeit sweet grace that could otherwise have been ours (Jonah 2:8).

Idols blind us. Idols cloud our vision and keep us from seeing what we ought to see. In the words of the Old Testament prophet Ezekiel, "These men have set up idols in their hearts and put wicked stumbling blocks before their faces" (Ezek. 14:3). When our idols blind us, we walk through the day with only partial vision. We cannot see clearly—it is as if a net is over our head and face. We can see some things, but they are obscured because our idolatrous desires have blurred our vision. When we turn to money, shopping, food, television, or other "escapes" to find our comfort, we are no different from the Israelites who worshiped the golden calf (Exod. 32:4). We choose false gods, idols, over God himself. In so doing, we both avoid God and set ourselves up in opposition to him. Instead of loving as we ought, we live to please ourselves and feed our idols. And our lives bear the fruit of our false worship: dissatisfaction, lack of peace, and distorted vision.

Idols enslave us. Carol was devastated when the pastor's wife, Patricia, pulled back from their friendship. Carol wanted to be best friends with Patricia and came for counseling because she was overwhelmed with sadness at Patricia's rejection of her. At her counseling session, she was asked, "Carol, what does your friendship with Patricia mean to you?" Listen to her candid reply: "If I am a friend of the pastor's wife, then I must be something special. The pastor's wife wouldn't want to spend time with someone who wasn't interesting, spiritually mature, and gifted. When Patricia chose to be my friend, people viewed me as trustworthy and valuable. I just can't lose her friendship! If she doesn't stay close to me, she'll be sorry."

Carol's answer revealed that the problem involved the level of significance that she had attached to a relationship with Patricia. Instead of finding her identity and fulfillment in her relationship with Christ, she was looking to a temporal friendship to define her personal value. She was *enslaved* by her friendship to Patricia. But it was Carol's response to her disappointment that was most revealing: *"She'll be sorry."* When a desire is frustrated, are we quick to punish? A demand for vengeance or a lasting bitterness always reveals the presence of an idol and shows how we are enslaved by our idols.

Idols cannot give us meaning or fulfillment. When we commit ourselves to a false god, we expect it to give us something in return for our devotion. Idols do tend to give us a degree of meaning, purpose, and value. Unfortunately, they are counterfeit answers—they look like the real thing, but they have no value and lead us away from the true source of fulfillment (2 Peter 2:19).

God himself is the only one who can inform his creation of the meaning, purpose, and value of anything. And yet we often look to things and people to define us instead of to the Lord. For example, nothing is wrong with wanting to look presentable when we leave the house. But what does it mean if we must have makeup on before we are willing to leave the house?

Trina had not left her home without makeup in over twenty years. In fact, she would wake up two hours before she needed to leave the house for work in order to get ready. On the weekend, her reason for not committing to social events was that she wanted a break from putting on her makeup and doing her hair. When I (Judy) asked her about this, Trina told me that she could not feel good about herself without her makeup. She also felt that others would not like or approve of her unless she always looked her best. Her desire to look good and be accepted by others ruled her life. In fact, she was enslaved by her belief that looking her best would give her value and acceptance. Trina tried to find her meaning and fulfillment in looking good—but like all idols, this idol left her empty and unsatisfied.

Idols lead to death. The terrifying thing about giving in to false worship is that over time, we become spiritually deadened or insensitive. We become useless like the idols we are worshiping: "But their idols are silver and gold, made by the hands of men. They have mouths, but cannot speak, eyes, but they cannot see; they have ears, but cannot hear, noses, but they cannot smell; they have hands, but cannot feel, feet, but they cannot walk; nor can they utter a sound with their throats. *Those who make them will be like them, and so will all who trust in them*" (Ps. 115:4–8, emphasis added; see also 2 Kings 17:15). We stop listening to the Holy Spirit's guidance when we turn away from the Word.

Idolatry is not a minor issue but a serious, lethal sin that results in death. Only God's grace enables us to see how serious this is. Idolatry is sin and Satan himself, the father of lies, is behind our idol worship. When our life motivations are idolatrous, we neither worship nor fear God. Our accomplishments are in vain. Our spiritual disciplines are empty. We cannot grow in our sanctification when we intentionally look for fulfillment and blessing from idols. We cannot feast on the Bread of Life when we are gorging ourselves at the trough of idols. Idolatrous worship is incompatible with growth in Christ.

Margaret's relationship with her husband and children was conflicted. She had no peace within, and she did not want to pray to God. As I (Tara) asked her questions, the problem readily became clear. Margaret explained that over the years, she had become increasingly dissatisfied with her looks. She wanted to have cosmetic surgery to look better, and she asked me if she should do so. Of course, I had no idea whether she should or shouldn't have the surgery, but one thing was clear: Margaret had made an idol out of her desire for plastic surgery. Her own comments demonstrated her false worship:

I don't care what my husband says; I will have the surgery and nothing and no one can stop me. I don't want to pray because I don't want God to tell me that I can't have the surgery. I am depressed and angry. I just know that everything in my life will be better if I have this surgery—the only thing that will make me happy is to look pretty again. My eleven-year-old daughter says she is fat and talks about the plastic surgery she needs—I feel bad about that, but I still want to be beautiful again!

Do you see the problem? She wasn't just struggling with a decision that required wisdom (to have the surgery or not); she was guilty of wrong worship. Her daughter, her husband, and even her God all became secondary to her goal of achieving the "one thing" that she was sure would make her life better. Her idolatrous heart was saying, "My will be done!" but as a Christian, she was called to say, "If the Lord wills . . ." I led her in praying through Zephaniah 3:17: "The LORD your God is with you, he is mighty to save. He will take great delight in you, he will quiet you with his love, he will rejoice over you with singing."

Through this verse, I helped Margaret to see that she was caring more for plastic surgery than for her relationship with her Savior and King who "rejoiced over her with singing." The turning point came when I asked her to describe for me the conversation she would need to have with her daughter in which she would explain that she cared about her physical appearance more than her marriage relationship and even her relationship with God. She began to see how her false worship of this one "god" could soon transform into another idol as she followed her commitment to indulge her sinful desires. Today it was plastic surgery—would tomorrow bring a demand for a new wardrobe or a young and attentive lover to prove her beauty? Things that were once repulsive to us (adultery, sexual molestation, murder) may become less vile in our hearts every time we indulge in "lesser" sins and live for "lesser" idols—flirtation, sexually explicit movies, and bitter hatred of others. Idolatry leads to death.

In this circumstance, God was gracious to grant Margaret a humble and repentant heart as we prayed together. As she meditated on specific Scripture passages reminding her of all that Christ has done for her and as she shared with me specific examples of God's grace in her life, Margaret turned away from her false god and did not continue to demand her own way. She did not have the surgeries but instead found her joy in Jesus—her Savior who captivated her heart and satisfied her with his eternally abundant love.

Turning Away from Idols

Idolatry is heart worship—devotion to anything in all of creation other than God (1 Cor. 10:18–22). Any true hope and help to turn away from idols results from applying the truth of God's Word to the deepest part of our hearts. How do we do this?

Identify your idols. The first step in repenting of our idols is to identify them. Sometimes idolatry is hard to detect because it occurs in our invisible hearts and because idols blind us. In order to better identify the idols ruling your heart, complete the following statements as honestly as you can:

- I would be completely happy if only . . .
- I don't care how my husband feels about it, I *will* . . .
- All I want is . . .
- I feel hopeless whenever . . .
- Sometimes I dream that . . .
- If only I could avoid . . .
- Don't ask me to give up my . . .
- If I could force someone to do something, it would be . . .

If you complete any of these statements with something other than a Christ-oriented response, you are engaging in idolatry. For example, the statement "All I want is Christ" reflects rightful worship, but "All I want is a loving and godly husband" reflects idolatrous worship.

We urge you to take time in the next few days and weeks to identify the idols that are ruling your life. We firmly believe that all Christians should be able to list the top four or five idols that they struggle with on an ongoing basis. Seek the counsel of a mature Christian friend who loves you enough to tell you the truth and help you to see deep into your heart. What really pleases you? What really angers you? What do you sacrifice on the altar of your idols? What is in the place of God in your life? To what do you look in order to feel that you are loved and valuable—your career, approval and acceptance from others, success, pleasure? Nothing but the knowledge that Jesus loves you and has rescued you from eternal death should rule your heart. Desires are normal and often harmless unless they become the focus of living. Jesus Christ himself belongs as the focus of our lives.

Prayerfully wield the sword of the Spirit. As you engage in faith's fight against sin, you would be wise to prayerfully identify some specific Scriptures with which to battle your temptation to indulge specific idols. Applicable passages from God's Word embedded deeply in our hearts can guide us in our struggle against the pull of idolatry. We have everything we need to live a life of godliness so that no sin rules over us (2 Peter 1; Ps. 119:133).

As you develop a list of biblical passages to direct you, we encourage you to be specific. You may even want to prepare cue cards with specific Scriptures for your specific areas of temptation. In my battle against gluttony, I (Tara) am helped by a biblical paraphrase of Philippians 3:19: "I am an enemy of the cross of Christ if my god is my belly." When I (Judy) struggle with temptation, I sing the hymn "Be Thou My Vision," focusing on the scriptural truths found within. Whatever Scriptures help you the most, be diligent to pray through them on a regular basis. Look at them each day during your devotions. Post them around your home and put them prominently in your day planner.

This battle is a fight of faith (1 Timothy 6). When we battle our idolatry, we are battling our own unbelief. We do so by resting in the promises and present power of God. "The grace of God . . . teaches us to say 'No' to ungodliness" (Titus 2:11–12). Instead of trying to satisfy our hunger elsewhere, we remember that Jesus is the Bread of Life. Our battle must include fighting to hold on to and believe in God's promises in his Word.

Get help. As members of one body, we are interdependent (Rom. 12:4–5; 1 Cor. 12:12–26). We are not meant to battle against sin on our own. As you are convicted of your idols, reach out to trusted, wise, and mature Christians for help. Ask your church leaders to pray for you, counsel you, and help you stay accountable. Warn your friends about your idolatrous temptations and ask for their loving help to avoid tempting areas. I (Tara) have specifically asked my friends to help me in my battle against the idol of food. So, not always (wouldn't that be unpleasant?) but quite often, when I invite a friend out to lunch, she will lovingly check in with me by asking something along the lines of, "Tara, I know that you have a big deadline coming up and that sometimes you are tempted to turn to food to avoid difficult work. Are you inviting me to lunch so that we can enjoy a fun time of redemptive fellowship? Or would such an outing lead you into sin?"

Idols thrive in darkness. By God's grace, take proactive steps to shine the light of God's Word into the deepest crevices of your heart. Your husband, church leaders, and closest friends can be key in your battle against idolatry.

Remember that God is faithful. If you know your propensity to make idols out of certain things, you can wisely arm yourself with the Word of God to battle your temptations in those areas. If you are mindful of your frequent idols, you can learn to say: "I'm not getting my way, but this isn't worth sacrificing someone on the altar of my idol. In fact, this is an opportunity for me to lay down my own life, my own desires, and take up my cross and seek the good of others." Remember, "no temptation has seized you except what is common to man. And God is faithful; he will not let you be tempted beyond what you can bear. But when you are tempted, he will also provide a way out so that you can stand up under it. Therefore, my dear friends, flee from idolatry" (1 Cor. 10:13–14).

Turning toward the Lord

Once we have identified the idols that tempt us, we are called to reject and replace them with rightful worship of God. This is what it means to *repent*. As John Piper teaches, "Repentance is not just regret. It means following through on that conviction and turning around—changing your mind and your heart so that you are no longer at odds with God but in sync with God. That is repentance: turning from darkness to light and from Satan to God. It is a reversal of the direction of your life—toward God."[7]

Don't just turn to another idol. It is not enough to just "turn away" from ungodly motivations and idols of the heart lest we turn to another idol. For example, I (Tara) remember a time when I was eating lunch with a friend, Karla. Karla used to be a "large woman" like I often am. (My weight fluctuates a lot.) But now she is a tiny, lean, petite woman. As we were eating, Karla remarked on my large meal, "I used to love food too."

Well! At first I was offended. But then I realized that what she said was true. At that moment, I was loving food more than practically anything else. I wasn't interested in obedience to God, self-discipline, health, or godly modeling for my daughter. I just wanted to eat my sandwich, chips, and cookies and drink my extra-large real-sugar cola. God convicted me. Later in the conversation, however, God also granted me a precious insight when Karla told me that she would get up two and three times in the night to weigh herself because she was so afraid that she would gain her weight back. I realized that she had turned away from the idol of food only to turn to another idol—thinness. How prone we all are to do this!

To truly repent of our idols, we are called not only to turn away from our idols but also to turn toward the Lord Jesus Christ (1 Thess. 1:9–10). As we gaze on his beauty, holiness, majesty, and power and meditate on what he said, we will learn to hate our worldly motivations and be motivated by his glory and pleasure alone.

Christ delivers us. Sin is our core problem. The moment we believe that sin is no longer our primary problem, the gospel of Jesus Christ is no longer the most important thing in our lives. Sin is much more than open rebellion against God. It is also a "blinding power that wants to control and enslave us."[8] As Martin Luther emphasized in *The Bondage of the Will*, "our will is powerless apart from the power and grace of God poured out on us."[9] Only Christ can deliver us from our idolatry.

God's grace changes what we love. We cannot simply choose to change our desires. God's grace changes our hearts—as we draw close to the Lord, he changes what we love. Ezekiel reminds us of this great and precious promise:

> They will return to it and remove all its vile images and detestable idols. I will give them an undivided heart and put a new spirit in them; I will remove from them their heart of stone and give them a heart of flesh. Then they will follow my decrees and be careful to keep my laws. They will be my people, and I will be their God. But as for those whose hearts are devoted to their vile images and detestable idols, I will bring down on their own heads what they have done, declares the Sovereign LORD.
>
> Ezekiel 11:18–21

I (Judy) have struggled throughout my life with the idol of self-sufficiency. I have simply hated to depend on anyone. As a child, in the years following my family's bankruptcy, I developed the firm belief that I could, should, and would be my own source of care and help. I learned to cook, clean, and pay bills long before I became a teenager. I left home at seventeen, paid my own way through college, and essentially provided for myself financially, emotionally, and physically. Throughout the years I developed a kind of arrogance, believing I really could do everything for myself. Several years ago, however, my attitude changed when I worked for two years to try to purchase a building for my ministry but all my efforts met with failure. When one of my board members discovered that I was grieved and defeated because I thought the contract for the property had fallen through, he called me. When he asked, "Judy, will you let me help you?" I came to a crossroads: do I continue to trust in my own efforts or do I allow others to help me? In one hour my board member handled the real estate problems that I had shouldered and carried for days. As the tears poured down my face, sitting in his office and allowing him to intervene for me, I knew that I could no longer love my self-sufficiency. Instead I was called to accept the help and care of others. God's grace enabled me to turn away from my idol of self-sufficiency and instead trust that God ministers to me through the body of Christ. Not only is my life richer but I can actually help others to "fulfill the law of Christ" when I allow them to bear my burdens (Gal. 6:2).

God hears us when we call to him. I (Tara) remember a time when I was struggling from motivations that were clearly idolatrous. Judy counseled me to engage in battle by calling on the Lord for help in breaking the hold of idolatry in my heart. *Knowing* that God can help is one thing. Actually *turning* to him for help is yet another. How do we turn to God for help? We call out. We talk to him. We plead. We write letters, songs, and poems to him. Many of us fail to realize the power of prayer because we fail to pray. The result? We fail to enjoy the blessing of answered prayer. As Judy counseled with me, I wrote in my journal:

> Please Lord, don't just take away these ungodly motivations . . . but Lord Jesus Christ, captivate me. Change me so that I want your desires above all else. Please change me so that I know you in such a way that life apart from you cannot compare to life with you. Please have mercy on me! My idols will rule me if I continue to indulge them. They will only increase, never decrease. Things that are wicked and distasteful to me now (adultery for example) could become attractive and enticing to me if I do not turn from sin and throw myself on your grace. Please purify me Lord Jesus! I trust only in you.

What comfort we find in knowing beyond a shadow of a doubt that God hears our prayers! As Isaiah reminds us, God is the one who delivers us: "Yet the LORD longs to be gracious to you; he rises

to show you compassion. . . . O people of Zion, who live in Jerusalem, you will weep no more. How gracious he will be when you
cry for help! As soon as he hears, he will answer you. . . . Whether
you turn to the right or to the left, your ears will hear a voice behind you, saying, 'This is the way; walk in it.' Then you will defile
your idols overlaid with silver and your images covered with gold;
you will throw them away like a menstrual cloth and say to them,
'Away with you!'" (Isa. 30:18–19, 21–22). Why? Because idols are
deaf (Ps. 115:6) but God hears us when we call to him.

From Idolatry to *Shalom*

A heart that hungers after idols is a heart without peace. Although
we are children of God by grace through faith in Christ, we are too
often *functional idolaters* as we seek satisfaction in things outside of
the Lord and are guilty of wrong worship. Idolatrous living robs us of
shalom—that sweet relationship with God, others, and ourselves.

I (Tara) remember hearing a speaker once tell a story about a
journalist in India who was swimming in a river when he saw a
woman bathing across the way. He felt lust for the woman and decided to act on his impulses. As he swam toward her, he fantasized
about her beauty and how she would satisfy his licentious desires.
But when he was only a few feet away, he realized that she was a
toothless old leper woman.

Idols are like that. From a distance, idols appear to be alluring
and beautiful. We think to ourselves, "If only I could have that,
then everything would be great." But when we get closer to the
idol and give in to its lure, we are left unsatisfied, enslaved, and
blind. Our idolatrous hearts entrap us in the filth and muck of the
grave (Prov. 9:18).

To be peacemaking women, our hope is to rest in God's grace
as we turn from these false gods. This is a lifelong battle. It is our
ongoing calling to turn away from idols and turn toward the Lord.
This is one of the foundational aspects of our sanctification and
conformity to Christ. We must never think, "If I only can have victory over this idol, then my life will be great." No! As Christians
we fully realize that even as God's grace enables us to knock one
idol over and banish it from the altar of our hearts, another idol is

waiting to take its place. That is why we must pray by faith each day to be *continually* turning away from idols and to the Lord. We pray that he will change our very desires so that we desire, crave, long for—worship—God alone.

As you consider carefully the idols that are fueling your conflicts and learn to repent of them, remember this: *God* battles for you. He carries your burdens. He sustains you by his amazing grace and love. *He* empowers you to turn away from false worship and pursue right worship—worship of him, your true God. Women of *shalom*, we lean on him and he promises us, "Even to your old age and gray hairs I am he, I am he who will sustain you. I have made you and I will carry you; I will sustain you and I will rescue you" (Isa. 46:4).

Personal Reflection

Questions for Reflection

1. Read Jeremiah 17:9; Proverbs 20:5; Luke 24:25; Romans 10:10; Hebrews 4:12; and 1 John 2:16. What does Scripture say about the nature of our hearts?
2. List three things that you have longed for in life that you thought would satisfy you but left you feeling empty after receiving them. Why did these things not satisfy? How did you respond when your longings were fulfilled but you experienced further dissatisfaction?
3. We do things for many reasons: to avoid pain or to achieve pleasure, comfort, joy, meaning, or happiness. To help discover what you value and what rules your heart, complete the following statements:
   - I would be completely content or happy in my life if only . . .
   - All I want is . . .
   - I get most sad and depressed when . . .
   - I feel hopeless when . . .
   - Sometimes I dream that . . .
   - I just want to avoid . . .
   - Don't ask me to give up my . . .

4. From the above answers, what desires can you identify that motivate you to do the things you do or feel the way you feel? Read Deuteronomy 6:5; Jeremiah 17:5–8; Luke 6:43–45; and 1 John 2:15–16. Write a paragraph about what your desires reveal about who or what you worship, trust, and love.

5. Are you convicted that you may be struggling with an idol? Name this idol and make a list of the consequences you have experienced or might experience in the future because of it. How would your life be different if you were to turn away from this false god? Read 2 Chronicles 14:2–6. What did King Asa do to gain peace and rest?

6. Read 1 Samuel 7:3, 12:20–25; Matthew 6:24; and 1 John 3:10. What is God calling *you* to do?

7. The following are practical steps to help you turn away from the idols of your heart.[10] By identifying our idols, evaluating them in light of Scripture, and taking steps to live in obedience to God's Word, we begin to experience freedom from idolatry. How would you complete these statements?

    • I am struggling with . . .
    • The root (idol of my heart) is . . .
    • God promises me that he has already done for me . . .
    • God promises me that he *will* do for me . . .
    • God warns me in his Word that the consequences of my sin are . . .
    • God commands me in his Word to put off . . .
    • God commands me in his Word to put on . . .
    • I will ask _____ (brother or sister in Christ) for help and accountability with this sin by _____ (date and time).

8. Write out your own prayer to the Lord Jesus Christ expressing your gratitude for his love and acceptance despite your temptation to indulge in idolatry. Ask for his gracious help to live in a manner worthy of your calling as a Christian.

Praying Scripture to God

Dear God, by faith in Christ I commit myself to not having any false gods before you, for you are a jealous God. Please deliver me from my worthless idols and help me to worship you alone. I thank you, Lord, that you are close to me. Please come quickly to help me. When I hide my sins and worship other gods, my life is burdened and heavy. Please lead me in the way of godly sorrow and true repentance. Cover me with your hand, Lord God. I thank you that you hear when I call to you, and I worship you, God. You alone are worthy of my adoration and praise. You are great and glorious, and all my idols are revealed as worthless in light of your radiance. I cling to you, God, and I thank you for loving me, delivering me from my idols, and teaching me to worship you alone.

(Prayer based on Exod. 20:2–5; Matt. 4:10; Ps. 22:11, 19; Ps. 38:4; Prov. 28:13; 2 Cor. 7:10; Ps. 80:17; Ps. 4:3.; Ps. 61:1; Isa. 42:8; Ps. 111:3; Isa. 12:5; Ps. 31:6.)

Recommended Resources for Further Study and Consideration

Elyse Fitzpatrick, *Idols of the Heart* (Phillipsburg, NJ: P&R Publishing, 2001).

Kris Lundgaard, *The Enemy Within: Straight Talk about the Power and Defeat of Sin* (Phillipsburg, NJ: P&R Publishing, 1998).

John Piper, *A Hunger for God* (Wheaton: Crossway, 1997).

David Powlison, *Seeing with New Eyes* (Phillipsburg, NJ: P&R Publishing, 2003).

Edward T. Welch, *Addictions—A Banquet in the Grave: Finding Hope in the Power of the Gospel* (Phillipsburg, NJ: P&R Publishing, 2001).

Edward T. Welch, *When People Are Big and God Is Small: Overcoming Peer Pressure, Codependency, and the Fear of Man* (Phillipsburg, NJ: P&R Publishing, 1997).

3

SUFFERING

For when we came into Macedonia, this body of ours had no rest, but we were harassed at every turn—conflicts on the outside, fears within. But God, who comforts the downcast, comforted us.

2 Corinthians 7:5–6

Nothing can reach us, from any source in earth or hell, no matter how evil, which God cannot turn to his own redemptive purpose. Let us be glad that the way is not a game of chance, a mere roll of dice which determines our fortune or calamity—it is a way appointed, and it is appointed for God's eternal glory and our final good.

Elisabeth Elliot[1]

When the darkness and pain of life overwhelm us, we may be tempted to close our hearts to God. Ongoing conflict, injustice, betrayal, and other forms of trauma can all combine to lead us into deep conflict with God. Suffering tempts us to doubt the goodness of God and is often used by Satan to attack our faith (1 Thess. 3:4–5). In our darkest hours, twisted theology can overtake us when we feel as though God is singling us out to punish and hurt us.

I (Tara) remember experiencing intense burning and pain when I was using the bathroom as a child. As an adult I look back on that memory and think, "I must have had a urinary tract infection or a bladder infection." But in the ignorance of my youth, I cried out to God, "Please stop hurting me like this, God! I promise I'll be a better little girl." My view of God was that he was easily angered at me, I had failed to be a good enough child, and thus he was punishing me with the pain. Instead of turning to him for love and help, I was afraid of him. Bad theology coupled with intense suffering can easily lead us away from faith and reliance on God.

While we cannot thoroughly address the problems of evil and suffering here, we must at least speak to the issue of suffering. The longer we live and the more we serve God, the clearer we see that the way of the Christian life is the way of suffering. In the words of a common baptismal prayer from the sixteenth century, this life is "nothing but a constant death."[2] Of course, there are moments of justice, seasons of joy, and even extended periods of relative peace. But over time, we suffer. We suffer as a result of our own sin and fallenness. We suffer at the hands of others. The fallen world we live in, spiritual attack, our fallen bodies, and our troubled times all bring agony and affliction.

The apostle Paul understood both the despair that comes from intense suffering and our need to rely on God in our suffering. He wrote: "We do not want you to be uninformed, brothers, about the hardships we suffered in the province of Asia. We were under great pressure, far beyond our ability to endure, so that we despaired even of life. Indeed, in our hearts we felt the sentence of death. But this happened that we might not rely on ourselves but on God, who raises the dead" (2 Cor. 1:8–9). How can we, like Paul, learn to rely on God during times of suffering? First, we must understand why we suffer.

Why We Suffer

While the Bible is in no way silent on the topic of suffering, still no simple response can be given to the question of why we suffer.

Volumes and volumes have been written on the problem of pain and the causes of suffering. Some posit that we suffer because God ordains it for a greater good. When asked to explain the reason for one man's blindness, Jesus answered that it "happened so that the work of God might be displayed in his life" (John 9:3). Others argue that God is in the business of "soul-making," and our response to suffering sanctifies our souls for good and prepares us for heaven. Romans 8 links our suffering to God's glory (his presence, beauty, and light) being revealed in us: "Now if we are children, then we are heirs—heirs of God and co-heirs with Christ, if indeed we share in his sufferings in order that we may also share in his glory. I consider that our present sufferings are not worth comparing with the glory that will be revealed in us" (vv. 17–18).

We will not attempt to make an exhaustive treatment of why God allows suffering. However, we do hope to provide an overview of this important topic and an introduction to resources that can be of further help to you as you face your own suffering or seek to help others. So what do we know from Scripture about why we suffer?

We are fallen people living in a fallen world. Broadly speaking, the Bible teaches us that suffering is a result of the sinful and fallen state of the world (Genesis 3). All suffering ultimately relates back to the fact that we live in a world that is in bondage to corruption (Rom. 8:20). When my (Judy's) son, Ryan, was born, he arrived seven weeks early and was immediately taken to intensive care for respiratory distress. The first time I got to hold him, he stopped breathing. As the doctors grabbed my tiny baby out of my arms, resuscitated him, and placed him on a respirator, all I could think was, *What have I done to bring about this suffering?* For days I held Ryan's hand through a plastic incubator, searching my heart for sins I had committed that were the reasons for Ryan's premature birth. After he came home and for the next six months, I experienced severe agoraphobia. I was unable to leave my home because of excessive anxiety that my sins (of which there were many) would bring further punishment and suffering on my family and myself. Years later, in seminary, I learned about the concept of a fallen world—that much of our suffering is simply a result of being fallen creatures in a fallen world. Our world is cursed, and illness, calamities, and struggles—even the struggle of a preemie baby to breathe—can often be attributed directly to this fallenness.

God uses suffering to lovingly discipline us. Scripture instructs us to endure hardship because God himself uses it as a form of loving discipline. God disciplines us as beloved children so that our lives will produce "a harvest of righteousness and peace" (Heb. 12:7–11). This is always to our benefit and the benefit of others. Most discipline is unpleasant by nature. Our distress may be so great that we might barely be able to whisper a prayer (Isa. 26:16). This is especially true when our discipline comes in the form of apparent injustice. And yet God draws straight lines with crooked sticks—he works all things for good for those who love him (Rom. 8:28).

As we reflect on God's discipline, we are called to remember that Christians are *not punished by God*, even as God is dealing with their sin. That is, even though a Christian may be disciplined by God due to sin, she is not eternally separated from God. The punishment for all believers has been dealt with *fully* on the cross of Christ. The Lord laid upon him the iniquity of us all so that we would not have to bear that penalty. Therefore, God's dealings with us are never penal in nature. Even though our suffering may be terribly painful, we are called to resist the temptation to think that God is punishing us out of hatred and to instead remember that he only disciplines us out of love: "Those whom I love I rebuke and discipline" (Rev. 3:19).

Suffering conforms us to Christ. Suffering helps conform us to the image of Christ by providing us with greater insight into life and a better understanding of the ways of God. One example of this comes from my (Tara's) college years. I had greatly hurt a young man, Christopher, when I dated him knowing that he desired to marry me but I did not love him. Ultimately I ended the relationship, and he was rightfully hurt and angry. While I apologized for hurting him, it wasn't until years later, after a different man had broken *my* heart, that I began to truly understand just how much sorrow I had caused my dear friend by my sin. I went back to Christopher and expressed again my sadness over the pain I had caused. He could see that my own suffering had helped me to understand better my sinful contribution to his suffering. My deeper understanding and more complete confession helped him to find even greater freedom from his lingering resentment. One reason God allows suffering is so that we might reflect him more profoundly in our lives by being more conformed to Christ. As the psalmist writes, we learn God's decrees when we suffer: "Before I was afflicted I went astray, but now I obey your word. You are good, and what you do is good; teach me your decrees. . . . It was good for me to be afflicted so that I might learn your decrees" (Ps. 119:67–68, 71).

Suffering grows our faith. All of Scripture indicates that God sovereignly rules over our suffering for the strengthening of our faith (see Heb. 12:3–11 and 2 Cor. 12:7–10). One young mother, Trisha, was facing the death of her husband after a seven-year battle with cancer. Her friends and family prayed earnestly with each blood draw and MRI, anxiously wondering how long he might survive. But Trisha's response was different. She said, "God is writing the letter of my husband's life. The doctors are just opening the envelope and reading me the message. When I remember that, it guards me from anxiety and being scared of what the doctors are going to say." Even in this, her worst suffering, Trisha trusted in the sovereignty and goodness of God. She believed that her husband's illness was not a surprise to God, nor was her heart-wrenching pain. Rather, she knew that it was "granted to her for Christ's sake to suffer" (Phil. 1:29).

Suffering deepens our relationship with God. Intimacy with the Lord often comes at the price of our suffering (Phil. 3:7–14). Do you want to know Christ? Then you must be prepared to suffer. Alison was a young woman who expressed to me (Judy) that although she knew a lot *about* God, she did not think that she truly knew *him*. We began to pray together that she would grow to know God intimately. Little did either of us know that in the coming months, Alison would experience more sorrow and pain than in all of her previous years combined. This season of life was excruciating for her—she never cried so much or hurt so deeply. And yet years later we both look back on that season with amazement at just how much she grew in her relationship with the Lord.

Was that the reason for her suffering? Maybe in part. The full reason for her suffering remains a mystery to this day. However, the *outcome* of her suffering was, in fact, a deeper intimacy with the Lord—though at the real price of pain. Years later, Alison told me how 2 Timothy 3:12 became much more real to her after her season of suffering: "In fact, everyone who wants to live a godly life in Christ Jesus will be persecuted."

Different Kinds of Suffering

Our suffering can come in many different forms. Some of our worst suffering may tempt us to go to extreme lengths to try to avoid or deny it because we wrongly convince ourselves that *shalom* is found by avoiding and denying pain. We may grow weary of pain in any form and try to numb ourselves with food, sleep, shopping, books, and even drugs. In our agony we may be tempted to shake our fists at God and even hate the person associated with our pain. What is it about suffering that affects us so deeply? Why is it that our pain sometimes drives us to such despair? Although suffering comes in many forms, the following types of suffering are some that we observe most frequently in the lives of Christian women and in our own lives.

Fallenness. At its most basic level, all of our suffering comes from the fact that we are fallen people living in a fallen world. Our bodies are constantly in the process of aging; we live in a world that experiences natural disasters. The sin of others invades our lives in stark horror. From the tragedies of terrorist attacks to the traumas caused by hurricanes and earthquakes, the fallenness of our world often leaves us reeling in shock, hurt, and despair.

By the time I (Judy) was eight years old, I had lived through a major flood that threatened to wash away my hometown, a fire where one of the residents became badly injured as he jumped from a second floor window and landed at my feet, and a devastating earthquake that rocked Southern California. At the time of the earthquake, my family lived in a one-bedroom apartment not far from the epicenter. For months I would try to block out the memory of my mother's screams and the radio reports about elderly people being pulled from the rubble of a hospital. I grieved a long time for people I never even knew, even as I lived in constant fear of another catastrophe. For decades entering stores and buildings felt life threatening to me. Hiking in the mountains, swimming in the ocean, or enjoying amusement park rides seemed unnecessarily risky. Allowing my son to get his driver's license triggered oppressive fear of not being able to guarantee his safety. As a result of the disasters I experienced, suffering for me came in the loss of joy and peace as even sweet moments of happiness were shaded by sorrow and fear.

The fallen world is a source of much suffering for its inhabitants. We experience disease, fatigue, pollution, and political instability. When our suffering comes as a result of things beyond our control, we hurt deeply even as we grapple with the truth that we have no other option but to grieve and mourn.

Loss. We suffer when we lose a loved one to debilitating disease or death. We suffer when we lose a job, a friend, or a beloved pastor. Loss in any form brings heartache. When we lose sight of the truth that we do not yet live in heaven but live in the "Promised Land," our losses are even more devastating. Promised Land living brings struggles, challenges, and frequent battles. Experiencing our losses causes us to long for heaven—that perfect place where all is well. We hunger for a time when "he will swallow up death forever. The Sovereign LORD will wipe away the tears from all faces" (Isa. 25:8). For people who have lost loved ones to death, the promises of God bring a hope and a comfort to an ache that will one day fully end in glory. "He will wipe every tear from their eyes. There will be no more death or mourning or crying or pain, for the old order of things has passed away" (Rev. 21:4).

Betrayal. One reason the pain of betrayal is so great is because our greatest suffering often comes at the hands of those we trust the most. This makes sense because strangers cannot betray us. If we neither respect nor care for someone, we will not be devastated by her rejection or maltreatment of us. We suffer because that is the price of risking our love. When we open our hearts to another person, we risk betrayal. Even Jesus was betrayed by a friend (Matt. 26:47–50).

I (Judy) experienced a profound betrayal by a friend whom I considered my best friend for more than ten years. We spoke by telephone on most days, our families got together weekly to watch our favorite television show, and we cared for each other's children.

During her darkest days I was there for her. When my dark days came, she terminated our friendship. Her reason? In an email she said, "I know this sounds selfish, but I don't want needy friends. I just want friends who will be there for me." Scripture testifies that the deepest wounds many Christians have experienced are at the hands of other Christians: "If an enemy were insulting me, I could endure it; if a foe were raising himself against me, I could hide from him. But it is you, a man like myself, my companion, my close friend, with whom I once enjoyed sweet fellowship as we walked with the throng at the house of God" (Ps. 55:12–14). That was true of me.

Attacked by one of my dearest friends, my heart broke. I was tempted to remain behind an emotional wall for the rest of my life. I did not want to reach out again because I wanted to guard myself from more suffering. But I realized that suffering would just come again in a different form. And in the interim I would have missed out on the joy that comes from faithful, loving relationships with others. God created us for intimacy with each other. We dehumanize ourselves if we cut ourselves off from others even though it is risky to love. I learned that instead of running away, suffering as a result of betrayal provides us all with the opportunity to share in Christ's suffering as we entrust our sorrow to him (Phil. 3:10).

Complex pain. Another reason our suffering can devastate us is that we often experience suffering on two different levels. The pain from the current situation may "tap into" our past experiences. Lilly had been let down by her Christian employer. Even with all of my years of counseling, I (Judy) was surprised by the depth of her angst and the level of devastation this conflict caused in her life. As we continued to work together, however, I learned that her boss's promise to care for, protect, guide, and accept her coupled with his ultimate rejection of her for not "being good enough" were eerily reminiscent of Lilly's childhood. Lilly had been tossed back and forth from house to house as a young child because neither of her parents wanted her. Her boss's actions in the present hurt her, but they also tapped into feelings of rejection, abandonment, and shame from her childhood. Lilly had been badly damaged in her life by people who should have been faithful, wise, and mature. And she was now experiencing suffering on two levels, past and present, and both were in desperate need of the gospel.

When our experience of pain seems disproportionate to the actual situation we are in, we need to look deep into our own hearts to see if a life-altering trauma might be surfacing in the current conflict. Sometimes we may even need help to do so because our pain may cloud our vision and make it difficult to see clearly. Grief and despair, while rooted in past hurts, can be reflected powerfully in current circumstances and present suffering. Of course, even as we seek to gain wisdom and insight into our complex pain, our suffering never gives us an excuse to sin. God calls us to honor him regardless of our past or present circumstances. As David Powlison reminds us, "Knowledge of a person's history may be important for many reasons (compassion, understanding, knowledge of characteristic temptations), but it never determines the heart's inclinations."[3]

Those we love suffer. We experience severe pain when someone we love is badly hurt—physically or emotionally. Extraordinary suffering comes when we watch a beloved family member or friend agonize through a deadly illness. I (Tara) will never forget the horrible sorrow and helplessness I felt when my friend was dying of cancer. She was so covered with open sores that she could not find one position that would afford her any relief. Even the morphine and other medicines were powerless to release her from her distress. In addition to the difficulty of witnessing such horrible physical agony, parents frequently agonize when their children are dealt emotional blows; wives grieve when their husbands are wounded at work; we are hurt when others criticize a dear friend.

One child, Bobby, joined a children's Wednesday night Bible club at his neighborhood church. New to the neighborhood, he joined shortly after his move to the area in January and worked hard to memorize all of his Bible verses. Every week Bobby earned the praise of his leaders, and his verse chart never failed to be initialed to show that he had successfully recited his verse. When the "graduation" service came in May, the students who had learned all of their Bible verses arrived at the special ceremony to earn their trophies. Bobby and his parents were among the crowd. When all the children had been called up to receive their trophies, Bobby alone remained uncalled. In tears, Bobby begged his parents to take him home. When Bobby's mother went to the youth leader to ask if a mistake had been made, she was told that Bobby had not learned the verses from September through December, the four months before Bobby had begun attending the Bible club, and would not be earning a trophy. Bobby's hurt was great, but it was nothing compared to that of his parents. A month later, when Bobby's trophy arrived in the mail with a brief note of apology, they still felt grief. Over time Bobby and his parents were able to have peace about this sad situation as their suffering helped them to remember the goodness and wisdom of the Lord.

Hopelessness. Sometimes we don't see a way out of a painful situation. Our hopeless questions lead to despairing answers, and before we realize it, our suffering feels overwhelming and unbearable. For instance, we may lose hope if we answer no to the question "Will this ever end?" or yes to the question "Has she ruined my life?" Sometimes our emotions take over our thinking and we give the people "causing" our suffering more power in our lives than they should rightfully have.

I (Tara) remember a dark time in my life when I really felt as though a sister in Christ had destroyed any chance I had for peace or happiness. In the midst of this pain, I told my husband, Fred, that I did not even want to celebrate our wedding anniversary. "Tara," he responded, "you are giving this woman too much power in your life. You are letting her control your emotions. We're going to be okay. God's grace gives us faith. Our love and marriage are strong. Our future is bright. We've got each other. She is a tiny part of our life. I know it feels like she stepped in and ruined our lives, but she can't. And besides, every word she says and every action she does is accountable before God." Because the hurt was deep, God used Fred's love to comfort me and his counsel to help me regain a godly perspective on the situation. Even though I felt otherwise, the situation was not hopeless.

How Others Help Us

We cannot give ourselves certain things in life. Encouragement and comfort are two of these things. As Christians we are exhorted to encourage and to comfort one another: "Praise be to the God and Father of our Lord Jesus Christ, the Father of compassion and the God of all comfort, who comforts us in all our troubles, so that we can comfort those in any trouble with the comfort we ourselves have received from God" (2 Cor. 1:3–4; see also 1 Thess. 5:11; Heb. 3:13). When we are suffering, others comfort and encourage us in many different ways.

Shared grief. When we suffer, others help us by being present with us as we grieve. Sometimes suffering leads to weeping. Crying and wailing are often part of facing fully the sorrows of life. Rarely will a person feel safe enough to sob in the presence of others. But if we do not have one or two friends to whom we can turn during heart-wrenching times, we are missing out on one of God's greatest blessings. Our dear friend Ruth Brewer, who was a young missionary when she lost her beloved husband due to a doctor's misdiagnosis, explained, "If you don't cry, you are not going to heal. God has made us that way." As John Piper has said, "There are things to see in the Word of God that our eyes can only see through the lens of tears."[4]

Like Christ himself, we can cry out with the words of the psalmist: "My God, my God, why have you forsaken me? Why are you so far from saving me, so far from the words of my groaning? O my God, I cry out by day, but you do not answer, by night, and am not silent. Yet you are enthroned as the Holy One; you are the praise of Israel" (Ps. 22:1–3). When others grieve, it is often wisest to withhold judgment and even counsel. When our ability to think is shut down in grief, we cannot process information or advice. In sharing the suffering of another person, there is a time for loving silence—to simply give empathy and care (see Job 2:13).

Biblical hope. Katrina was a young woman who had been forced to watch as her mother was beaten, raped, and sodomized. She was told to put on a brave face and explain as a part of her Christian testimony how "God brought good out of it" and how "God knew she was a strong little girl and could take it." As I (Tara) listened to her story, my heart broke at the truth that a terrible, evil thing had happened to a defenseless child. No reason was good enough to explain her suffering. My first response was to weep for her and with her. As I held her, I reminded her that through every moment of that awful time, God was with her, loving her, and one day she would suffer no longer. I held out biblical hope for her.

When I (Judy) am seeking to share biblical hope with someone who is suffering, I will often bring her to Psalm 34:

> I will extol the LORD at all times;
>> his praise will always be on my lips.
> My soul will boast in the LORD;
>> let the afflicted hear and rejoice.
> Glorify the LORD with me;
>> let us exalt his name together.
>
> I sought the LORD, and he answered me;
>> he delivered me from all my fears.
> Those who look to him are radiant;
>> their faces are never covered with shame.
> This poor man called, and the LORD heard him;
>> he saved him out of all his troubles.
> The angel of the LORD encamps around those who fear
>> him, and he delivers them.
>
> Taste and see that the LORD is good;
>> blessed is the man who takes refuge in him.
> Fear the LORD, you his saints,
>> for those who fear him lack nothing.
> The lions may grow weak and hungry,
>> but those who seek the LORD lack no good thing.
>
> Come, my children, listen to me;
>> I will teach you the fear of the LORD.
> Whoever of you loves life
>> and desires to see many good days,
> keep your tongue from evil
>> and your lips from speaking lies.
> Turn from evil and do good;
>> seek peace and pursue it.
>
> verses 1–14

Even the righteous will have many troubles (v. 19). And yet it makes perfect sense to trust God in the midst of our suffering. God is the only one who ultimately has the power to answer prayer and to deliver us from all our fears (v. 4). Psalm 34 provides the biblical hope we all need when we are suffering: our deliverance follows on the heels of pursuing the Lord. Even if our circumstances do not change, freedom comes when our *experience* of them changes. As we are delivered from our fears, even in the midst of our suffering, we express our new freedom by boasting in the Lord (v. 2); glorifying the Lord and exalting his name (v. 3); seeking the Lord (v. 4); calling on the Lord (v. 6); fearing the Lord (v. 7); tasting the goodness of the Lord (v. 8); and taking refuge in him (v. 22).

Biblical hope reminds us that real peace is not a by-product of suffering-free living but a by-product of trusting God even in the midst of intense suffering. God's grace enables us to remember that no one and nothing can act more powerfully in our suffering than the God who saves us out of all our troubles (v. 6), gives good things (v. 10), stays close to the brokenhearted (v. 18), and protects our bones (v. 20). This deliverance is called redemption, and it means being purchased out of bondage into freedom forever. "The Lord redeems his servants; no one will be condemned who takes refuge in him" (v. 22). On the basis of knowing that our eternal redemption is real, we are content to rest in the goodness and sovereignty of God despite the intensity of our pain and suffering.

Wise counsel. Suffering sometimes clouds the eyes of our heart and mind. Suffering can overwhelm us and blind us. Therefore, one of the most important things we can do when we are suffering is to seek godly counsel. Mature and wise friends will love us enough to comfort us, grieve with us, and also remind us of biblical truth. Wise counsel helps us to glorify God. The way we can glorify God in the midst of suffering is to know him, trust him, and obey him. In essence, we must remember all of the doctrinal truths outlined in chapter 1. This is difficult to do, and even more difficult to do alone. That is why we benefit from the help and counsel of others.

In our suffering we are easily tempted to take our eyes off of the Lord and to put them on the other person or our circumstances. Whenever we take our eyes off of the Lord, we will despair. Even in our suffering, praying and loving friends persevere with us and give us good counsel. Instead of surrounding ourselves with people who tell us what we want to hear—"Wow, she really treated you terribly. You have every right to be angry. She deserves it anyway.

God understands."—godly counsel helps us to remember that God knows just what we need in order to grow. "We also rejoice in our sufferings, because we know that suffering produces perseverance; perseverance, character; and character, hope" (Rom. 5:3–4). By God's grace, we can endure disappointment and sorrow as we rejoice in the hope of the glory of God. He will never give us more than we can bear—even if we *feel* otherwise.

Some Gentle Warnings

Sometimes people let us down. Sometimes people will respond to our suffering in unloving and inappropriate ways. I (Judy) remember a breakfast Bible study during which I shared with some women about suffering in my life. One woman actually held her hand up in my face and said, "Stop! I don't want to hear this. It's too depressing." Instead of receiving love and comfort, I was silenced and rejected. I look back on that sad exchange with sympathy for the woman who stopped me.

Don't give up! When people let us down, we are called to not give up. Instead, in love, we can continue to seek out trustworthy, abiding friends to walk with us during our dark times. I (Tara) am reminded of a time when I was at my friend Kim's home. Her three sons were playing in the living room when one of them let out a scream and began to cry. The other two scattered to their rooms. Kim quickly assessed that a flying fire truck had caused no serious injury, and she comforted the sobbing child. Then she did something I will never forget. She called the other two boys to her, got down on her knees in front of them, looked them right in the eyes and said, "Sons, when your brother is hurting, you don't run away from him. You run *toward him* and you *help him.*" When others run to us in our time of suffering, we are blessed and comforted. However, quite often others will not arrive when and where we need them. How will we respond? Depending fully on the grace of God, we must continue to reach out to others for help, not holding their failure against them. "At my first defense, no one came to my support, but everyone deserted me. May it not be held against them. But the Lord stood at my side and gave me strength, . . . and I was delivered from the lion's mouth. The Lord will rescue me from every evil attack and will bring me safely to his heavenly kingdom" (2 Tim. 4:16–18).

Be merciful, just as your heavenly Father is merciful. When someone responds inappropriately to our suffering, we can consider gently challenging her with well thought-out advice on how she might be able to minister more effectively to those who are hurting. We can pray for the grace to retain a merciful attitude toward people who do not enter into our pain, especially because we are mindful of how easy it is for us to let people down too.

To enter into another's suffering is a precious gift. I (Judy) remember a time when I was the one who was unable to enter into the pain of a friend. Years ago, I deeply envied a friend of mine. I'll call her Kari. My mother lived 800 miles away, and I felt overwhelmed by children, school, and work; Kari's mother lived ten minutes away and frequently helped my stay-at-home friend with babysitting and household errands. Our finances were in distress; Kari's family was just about to move into a large, beautiful home in a wonderful neighborhood. I was feeling depressed and unhappy as I struggled to lose 35 extra pounds; Kari was thin, filled with energy, and extremely beautiful.

As I envied Kari in my heart, I used to think that she could never understand my suffering. Although I never shared my struggles or even gave her the chance to minister to me, in my heart I felt bitterness toward her and rejected her for not ministering to my pain. Within a few years, however, our circumstances had radically changed. My mother had moved in with our family and was providing amazing help to us. Our finances had improved dramatically, and I physically felt good and strong. My friend Kari, however, was experiencing terrible suffering. Her mother had died unexpectedly from a heart attack. Her husband had just lost his job. Their newborn baby was extremely fussy from terrible colic. And Kari was struggling with postpartum depression and the physical challenges of 30 pounds of extra weight from the pregnancy.

As I stood at Kari's mother's coffin, I was filled with inexpressible sorrow over how I had felt toward my friend during the years when I was suffering and she was not. I knew without a doubt that I had failed to allow her to suffer with me. A willingness to share our own suffering with others sets them free to share their suffering with us. I had not allowed my friend to share in my suffering, and as a result, I stood helpless at her mother's coffin. I desperately wanted her to feel the freedom to allow me to shoulder some of her burden, but I had not earned the privilege. I could help her in some ways, but ultimately, I had let her down. That bitter lesson taught me anew how precious it is to enter into another person's suffering. And yet my own previous self-centered silence deprived me of this Christian privilege. I was reminded how quickly days of joy turn into days of suffering and how quickly suffering can be swallowed up by joy, even when we least expect it. As brothers and sisters in Christ, let us pray for the grace to minister to one another—especially when we are suffering.

Suffering Well

I (Tara) remember a time when I felt truly wronged by a woman in authority over me. I knew many theological truths applied to the situation: God works out his will through authority; I was to make respectful appeals and entrust the results to the Lord; regardless of how she treated me, I was to do only good to her, bless her, pray for her, and love her. But to be honest, when push came to shove, I *really* wanted *her* to change. I wanted our pastor to make her stop hurting and wronging me. I longed to be protected and defended. I craved justice, and I didn't get it. It was one of the worst experiences of suffering I have ever gone through. For years I was tempted to be bitter. But wise counsel and gentle rebukes from friends, my elders, and my husband all helped me to remember that if I want to grow in perseverance and maturity, then in Christ I am called to suffer well. How do we suffer well?

Remember that God is with you. I (Tara) remember my friend Trisha telling me of a recurring dream she had during the long years when her husband was dying of cancer. She dreamt that as she swam in a pool, she had the definite sense that if she could only reach one side of the pool, the side with the cabana, her husband would live and they would go on to raise their young children together in life. But if she swam to the other side of the pool, he would die. So she strained and strained, and kicked and pulled—trying with all of her might to get to the side where her husband would live. Over time, however, she became exhausted and gave up. She said to herself, "Fine, I'll just go to the side where he dies." But try as she might, she could not reach that side of the pool either. She grew more tired with each passing moment—how long could she stay afloat? In her last dream of this sort, Jesus appeared on the diving board and threw her a life preserver. She was thrilled! "Jesus! Pull me out! Rescue me!" But he didn't. He gave her all she needed to stay afloat and then promised to *stay with her.* But he did not take her out of the pool.

Trisha was comforted in her suffering by Jesus. She prayed with the psalmist, "When I am afraid, I will trust in you. In God, whose word I praise, in God I trust; I will not be afraid. What can mortal man do to me?" (Ps. 56:3–4). Like Trisha, let us all remember that it is enough that Christ is with us. He is *Immanuel*—God with us. This is our hope and our security. God not only ordains our suffering, he promises to be in it with us (Isa. 43:2).

Resist bitterness. Often our suffering can tempt us to yield to anger, resentment, bitterness, and hatred. We suffer well when, by faith, we decide each day not to be bitter toward those who have caused us suffering. By faith we choose to love them *especially* when they disappoint us, hurt us, and let us down. Jesus taught that even pagans and tax collectors love their friends. But Jesus said, "I tell you who hear me: Love your enemies, do good to those who hate you, bless those who curse you" (Luke 6:27–28). And Romans 12 says, "Do not be overcome by evil, but overcome evil with good" (v. 21). When we do so, we show ourselves to be Christians.

During a horrible season when I (Tara) was struggling with bitterness, I was convicted and helped by 1 John 4:19–21: "We love because he first loved us. If anyone says, 'I love God,' yet hates his brother, he is a liar. For anyone who does not love his brother, whom he has seen, cannot love God, whom he has not seen. And he has given us this command: Whoever loves God must also love his brother." And 1 John 3:15 says, "Anyone who hates his brother is a murderer, and you know that no murderer has eternal life in him." I wrote in my journal, "Please guard me from being a liar because I cannot love you, Lord God, and at the same time be continually hating her."

Trust in God's sovereignty. When we suffer well, we remember that we do not have to fret, scheme, manipulate, or try to force things. God is in control. We are called to trust in his sovereignty. If anyone wants to lift a hand against us, he or she will only do so with God's permission. Therefore, although we do not need to celebrate evil or pain, God's grace enables us to maintain a merciful attitude toward those who wrong us.

Ashley had survived a tragic childhood. Her mother had died when she was only six years old, and her father married a physically and emotionally abusive woman who held Ashley's hands over the burner of the stove until her flesh charred. She moved in with distant relatives but missed her father terribly. Instead of understanding the longings of a little girl to be with her father, her relatives told her she was ungrateful because she wanted to go home. They refused any further contact with this young child who desperately needed stable, loving relationships. When Ashley returned home to live with her father, her stepmother continued to abuse her. On her eighteenth birthday Ashley left home and lost contact with her family. Now married to a godly Christian man, this woman has a gentle, loving relationship with her children and enjoys the good fruit of a beautiful home. I (Judy) wept as I listened to her story and marveled that she could share it without bitterness or anger. Instead, her testimony is that God has used it for his glory and enabled her to persevere in life and faith. Ashley did not try to overspiritualize what had happened or ignore it. She simply lived by the conviction that God is sovereign and it was enough that he was with her, even in all of her pain.

Compare correctly. The truth is, we are more like the people who cause our suffering than unlike them. We are all sinners in need of God's grace. I (Tara) was reminded of this sobering truth as Fred and I were driving in the Beartooth Mountains, enjoying a tape of a lecture by Dr. R. C. Sproul. In his lecture, Dr. Sproul illustrated a teaching point by asking the listener to imagine a large stage with Christ at one end and Hitler at the other. He told us to pretend that they were on a continuum and to place some profoundly giving, loving, selfless woman somewhere on the stage. With Christ at one end and Hitler at the other, where would the saintly person go on the continuum? I cried out, "She would be in a bear hug with

Hitler." And a few moments later, Dr. Sproul explained that she would be hugging Hitler. You see, I knew my doctrine. Compared to the holiness of Christ, apart from the justification that comes from God in Christ, even a beautiful, lovely, godly person is more like Hitler than she is like Christ. "All our righteous acts are like filthy rags" (Isa. 64:6).

I knew the theology, but two days later I struggled to live it out in real life when my pastor confronted me on my judgmental heart toward the woman who had betrayed me and publicly embarrassed me. He lovingly reminded me that I was "just like her"—we were both in need of God's grace and salvation in Christ. But trapped in my bitterness and anger, my heart defiantly cried out within me, *"I am not like her. I would never do what she's done."* Of course I was only kidding myself. Apart from God's grace, I was and am capable of much worse than she did to me.

My pastor gently explained that in my anguish, I wanted to compare myself with her so that I could self-righteously demand justice. He counseled me to compare correctly instead—I was to compare myself with the holy God, because then I would cry out for mercy. "Tara," he told me, "if you want to place your hope in justice, then you will be a person of justice and you will be judged and die by justice. As a Christian, you are utterly dependent on the mercy and grace of God, just like the woman who wronged you. The very things that are in her heart are also in you. By faith, do not compare yourself with her but compare yourself with God." And so by faith, every Sunday when I saw this woman, I would say to myself over and over again, "I am more like her than unlike her. I am more like her than unlike her."

Persevere. Hebrews 12 is an important reminder that we are called to throw off everything that hinders and the sin that so easily entangles and run the race God has marked out for us. We are not to compare our race to other people's races because we don't all run the same race. Our responsibility is to run *our* race. And our race is custom-made for each of us—by God himself.

Of course, when the path marked out for us is uphill and rocky, it can be tempting to give up. Johanna, a woman in her fifties who lives alone and collects disability checks, has suffered greatly throughout her life. Years ago she was treated unjustly at work and lost her job, thus incurring a tremendous financial burden. Divorced by her husband, alienated from her only child, and misunderstood by fellow Christians, Johanna became bitter and wanted nothing to do with God. She turned away from her faith in Christ and withdrew from all of her relationships. In the face of her suffering, Johanna gave up. On the other hand, Jane lost her only son in utero due to a nurse's error. Yet she has forgiven the nurse and holds out the hope of meeting her "little quarterback" one day in heaven. One woman experienced physical agony and relational rejection and has shaken her fists at God in rage for years. The other endured the torturous task of carrying and delivering her dead baby, all the while faithfully witnessing to God's goodness even as she grieved.

What makes the difference? How can we persevere in suffering? It is a miracle of God's grace that he turns our hearts away from the things of this life to the things of eternal value. Instead of being constantly focused on our happiness, our hearts are fixed on eternity and our hope is in God: "We also rejoice in our sufferings, because we know that suffering produces perseverance; perseverance, character; and character, hope. And hope does not disappoint us, because God has poured out his love into our hearts by the Holy Spirit, whom he has given us" (Rom. 5:3–5).

The grace to persevere to the end depends on our absolute commitment to feed continually on Jesus as our Bread of Life (John 6:35). God doesn't take away our troubles. He does, however, reveal his own strength in the midst of our weakness (2 Cor. 12:9). He is strong in us as we display the faith that perseveres to the end (Hebrews 11). The journey is long, but faith outlasts our suffering. And our perseverance produces an abundant bounty of blessings. As Jesus said, "The seed on good soil stands for those with a noble and good heart, who hear the word, retain it, and by persevering produce a crop" (Luke 8:15). As we learn to persevere in suffering, we can say along with the apostle Paul, "I consider my life worth nothing to me, if only I may finish the race and complete the task the Lord Jesus has given me—the task of testifying to the gospel of God's grace" (Acts 20:24).

Stay fixed on eternity. Especially during times of intense suffering, we must commit ourselves to living for eternity and not for this life. Otherwise, suffering will always lead us to despair. In this

Suffering   85

life we will never see complete justice—not until the Lord returns and rights every wrong. In this life, even in the body of Christ, we have days of growth—but not perfect healing. But the day is coming when all injustices will be righted and all injuries cured. In the interim, we can let go of our resentment because we believe God when he says that he will repay every wrong that has been done (Rom. 12:19). What does it mean that God will repay every wrong? For believers, this means that all of their sins have been paid for at the bloody cross of Christ. Christ's substitutionary death satisfies God's just requirements. For nonbelievers, their wrongs will eventually lead to eternal damnation. Either way, all injustices will be fully addressed by our just God.

In light of these truths, we can choose daily not to grow bitter or give up hope as we live for our true home—heaven. "Therefore we do not lose heart. Though outwardly we are wasting away, yet inwardly we are being renewed day by day. For our light and momentary troubles are achieving for us an eternal glory that far outweighs them all. So we fix our eyes not on what is seen, but on what is unseen. For what is seen is temporary, but what is unseen is eternal" (2 Cor. 4:16–18). During a recent Bible study, my (Judy's) friend and pastor, Mike Kennison, stunned me when he mentioned that eternal life is like a vast ocean, filled with tiny droplets. Of all the uncountable droplets in the ocean, only one of those droplets represents our life on this earth. The entire, vast ocean is filled with pain-free, suffering-free living—save one tiny droplet. This life is our only opportunity to suffer and to grieve. Mike asked us, "Are you making the most out of your one brief opportunity to suffer?"

This world is not our home. It may feel like our home because we can see it, taste it, and touch it. It feels "real" to us. But our few years of life are short and eternity is very, very long. Humility and wisdom come when we properly understand that we are but a vapor (James 4:14) and that "a thousand years in [God's] sight are like a day that has just gone by" (Ps. 90:4). Our state is transitory, so we learn "to number our days aright, that we may gain a heart of wisdom" (Ps. 90:12) because this life will never satisfy our deepest desires and hopes. In the words of C. S. Lewis, "If I find in myself a desire which no experience in this world can satisfy, the most probable explanation is that I was made for another world."[5]

To persevere through intense suffering, we remember that heaven is our home, not this world. Our suffering in this life reflects how much we long for a family where they shout in joy, "She is ours!" and we gratefully acknowledge, "I belong. I'm safe, protected, understood, wanted, and loved." We long for heaven because, in Christ, we have been re-created to live in God's presence. We keep our hearts fixed on eternity, for there will be no more suffering in heaven. The depths of our sorrow have a bottom, but the bliss of joy in Christ is utterly limitless. He is enough. "The God of all grace, who called you to his eternal glory in Christ, after you have suffered a little while, will himself restore you and make you strong, firm, and steadfast" (1 Peter 5:10).

Peace Even amidst Suffering

As we learn to rely on God, we learn to endure and even embrace our suffering in a God-glorifying way. To develop into peacemaking women, we are called to carefully address our past and current suffering as we learn to persevere by trusting God's providence. The result is that we risk sharing our burden with someone—allowing her to come alongside and support us. We learn to honor suffering *both* as an enemy *and* as a friend—it is against God's original design, yet it is an instrument for our sanctification and ultimately a pathway to glory (Romans 8).

Our dear friend, Pastor Dennis Reiter, has experienced great sadness in his life. He has endured betrayal, attacks, and relational anguish. Once during a time of prayer, he sensed an image of the Lord opening a large book in front of him—the book of his life. He was given an eraser and told he could erase any parts of his life, any experiences that he chose. As he contemplated erasing the grief, sorrow, and agony, he realized that were he to do so, he would erase his entire ministry. His growth in Christ, his deepening faith in the Lord, and his ability to minister compassion and assistance were all tied to his suffering. His pain taught him how to comfort in the way he had been comforted (2 Cor. 1:3–4). Instead of cursing his suffering, Dennis learned over time to consecrate it to the Lord. He responded to his suffering much like Hannah responded to hers, trusting in God's promise and the fulfillment of that promise: "My heart rejoices in the LORD; in the LORD my horn is lifted high. . . . The LORD brings death and makes alive; he brings down to the grave and raises up. The LORD sends poverty and wealth; he humbles and he exalts. . . . For the foundations of the earth are the LORD'S; upon them he has set the world" (1 Sam. 2:1, 6–8).

The road to glory winds along the path of sanctification, and suffering is a part of this path. As God's grace enables us to trust him because we know who he is, we learn to suffer well and consecrate our pain to the Lord in humble reliance upon his goodness. Otherwise, we will curse our suffering and the God who allows it—missing out on a deeper relationship with God, greater ministry opportunities, and lasting peace within. In the words of Eugene Peterson, "A Christian is a person who decides to face and live through suffering. A man or woman of faith who fails to acknowledge and deal with suffering becomes, at last, either a cynic or a melancholic or a suicide."[6]

The bottom line is that at all times, in every circumstance, we are called to trust in God's goodness. "For our light and momentary troubles are achieving for us an eternal glory that far outweighs them all" (2 Cor. 4:17). Our sufferings may not *feel* light or momentary, but we can trust based on God's Word that good comes from enduring suffering. We can trust that God does not waste pain. In the words of that great preacher Charles Spurgeon, "There is nothing better than health. Except for suffering."[7] May God grant you peace, even amidst your suffering, as you trust fully in him.

Personal Reflection

Questions for Reflection

1. Read Genesis 37–50; 2 Corinthians 1; and Romans 8:28–29. Do you believe that God is truly sovereign and purposeful and that he has a good and holy reason for everything he does? Write a paragraph to reflect on what it means that God is sovereign. Look up a definition of *sovereign* to assist you.

2. How do you feel toward God because of the pain and suffering you have experienced in life? Do you doubt his goodness and care for you? Meditate on Psalm 23. How do these truths comfort you?

3. Read 2 Thessalonians 1:3–10. Make a list of three wrongs that you have suffered or that someone you love has suffered. What does it mean to you to know that one day God will right every wrong? What wrongs do you most look forward to seeing God make right?

4. Read 1 Peter 4:1–2. What does the attitude of Christ look like in real life? If you were to have the same attitude of Christ in your suffering, how would God's grace enable you to address the discouragement associated with your suffering?

5. Read 2 Corinthians 1:3–4. Can you recall a way that someone has ministered to you because he or she experienced suffering similar to your own? How might God use your suffering to comfort others?

6. Have you ever felt abandoned by God and others during seasons of suffering? Read Job 19:1–22. What one verse in that passage strikes you the most? Why? How have you responded when others have failed to minister to you in your suffering? If you could change one of your responses, what would it be and why?

7. Meditate on Psalms 37 and 73. Make a list of five to ten thoughts from these psalms that you identify with. On what are you focusing? Did earthly or heavenly concerns make the list? What does it mean for you to keep your eyes fixed on eternity? How will your suffering be dealt with in eternity (Ps. 73:23–28)?

8. Read Exodus 16. Can you recall a time when you sinned in the midst of your suffering? Have you grumbled against your circumstances, other people, or the Lord? Write a short letter to God as a response. When you are finished, read Romans 8:35–39. Did the truths found in this passage find their way into your letter to God?

9. Read Matthew 26:30–27:44. In what ways did Jesus experience suffering like yours?

Praying Scripture to God

I thank you, God, that you carry my sorrows. Dear
Lord, please help me to remember that although outwardly I

am wasting away, inwardly I am being renewed day by day.
Father, I thank you that your grace enables me to persevere
in my suffering, becoming "mature and complete, not lacking
anything." O God, please turn my mourning into gladness and
give me comfort and joy instead of sorrow. Please restore me
and make me steadfast even after I have suffered. Thank you,
God, for refining me like silver, even through the fire of suffering.
Thank you that one day you will right every wrong. Whatever
my circumstance, may I run with perseverance the race marked
out for me, for you are with me. May I rest in you, Lord, and
wait patiently for you. I trust you, God, even when it is granted
to me for Christ's sake to suffer.

(Prayer based on Isa. 53:3–4; 2 Cor. 4:16; James 1:4; Jer. 31:13; Ps. 66:10; 1 Peter 5:10; Ps. 11:6; Ezek. 38:22; Heb. 12:1; Isa. 43:2; Ps. 37:7; Phil. 1:29.)

Recommended Resources for Further Study and Consideration

Horatius Bonar, *Night of Weeping: When God's Children Suffer* (Geanies House, Scotland: Christian Focus Publications, 1999).

William Bridge, *A Lifting Up for the Downcast* (Carlisle, PA: Banner of Truth Trust, 1995).

Jerry Bridges, *Trusting God: Even When Life Hurts* (Colorado Springs: NavPress, 1988).

Jeremiah Burroughs, *The Rare Jewel of Christian Contentment* (Carlisle, PA: Banner of Truth Trust, 2000).

Lawrence J. Crabb, *Shattered Dreams: God's Unexpected Pathway to Joy* (Colorado Springs: WaterBrook Press, 2001).

Linda Dillow, *The Blessing Book* (Colorado Springs: NavPress, 2003).

Elisabeth Elliot, *A Path through Suffering: Discovering the Relationship Between God's Mercy and Our Pain* (Ann Arbor, MI: Servant Publications, 1990).

Elisabeth Elliot, *The Path of Loneliness* (Nashville: Thomas Nelson, 1988).

Steven Estes and Joni Eareckson Tada, *When God Weeps: Why Our Suffering Matters to the Almighty* (Grand Rapids: Zondervan, 1997).

John Flavel, *The Mystery of Providence* (Carlisle, PA: Banner of Truth Trust, 1995).

Elisabeth Kübler-Ross, *On Death and Dying* (New York: Macmillan, 1991).

John Murray, *Behind a Frowning Providence* (Carlisle, PA: Banner of Truth Trust, 1990).

Edith Schaeffer, *Affliction* (London: Hodder and Stoughton, 1984).

Phillip Yancey, *Disappointment with God: Three Questions No One Asks Aloud* (Grand Rapids: Zondervan, 1997).

PART TWO

CONFLICTS WITH OTHERS

How good and pleasant it is
    when brothers live together in unity!
It is like precious oil poured on the head,
    running down on the beard,
running down on Aaron's beard,
    down upon the collar of his robes.
It is as if the dew of Hermon
    were falling on Mount Zion.
For there the LORD bestows his blessing,
    even life forevermore.

Psalm 133

When believers are bitterly embroiled in disagreement
or coldly estranged from one another, few people will
pay attention when we try to talk with them about the
reconciling love of Jesus Christ.

Ken Sande[1]

As Christians, we are called by God to spend time and energy striving to be women who live at peace with others because God commands it: "Make every effort to keep the unity of the Spirit through the bond of peace" (Eph. 4:3). But in addition

91

to the joys that come from obeying God, we also experience blessings from reconciliation. Unity is not only morally good, it feels good too. "How good *and pleasant* it is when brothers live together in unity!" (Ps. 133:1, emphasis added). As with most areas of life, God's glory and our good intersect at the same point. To pursue the one is to experience the other.

Of course, the thing we are called to be—united in love—must be *given to us by God*. Left to our own devices, we will be kind to those we like and hold grudges against our enemies—just like the pagans do (Matt. 5:47). Only God can enable us to be kind and tenderhearted, forgiving one another, imitating God, and living a life of love (Eph. 4:32–5:2).

The first two chapters in this section will focus on general principles for developing relationships of *shalom*. In subsequent chapters, we will turn our attention to the conflicts we face in several specific relationships—romantic, parenting, in-laws, church, and leadership. In each context, our relational goals are summarized in 1 Peter 3:8–9: "Finally, all of you, live in harmony with one another; be sympathetic, love as brothers, be compassionate and humble. Do not repay evil with evil or insult with insult, but with blessing, because to this you were called so that you may inherit a blessing."

4

BIBLICAL PEACEMAKING

As a prisoner for the Lord, then, I urge you to live a
life worthy of the calling you have received. Be completely humble and gentle; be patient, bearing with
one another in love. Make every effort to keep the
unity of the Spirit through the bond of peace.

Ephesians 4:1–3

Jesus gives the world the right to judge whether the
Father has sent the Son on the basis of whether the
world sees observable love among all true Christians.

Francis Schaeffer[1]

No section on conflicts with others could be complete
without introducing you to the foundational biblical
peacemaking principles developed and taught by Peacemaker Ministries. The mission of Peacemaker Ministries is "to assist and equip
Christians and their churches to respond to conflict biblically." Both
of us have benefited greatly—personally and professionally—from
their teaching. Whenever we serve in the ministry of Christian conciliation, we do so according to Peacemaker Ministries' principles
because they are rigorously biblical and graciously practical.

As you begin to work through your conflicts with others, please consider reading *The Peacemaker* by Ken Sande and studying the other excellent resources available through Peacemaker Ministries.[2] This chapter will provide a concise overview of their basic principles, but we cannot do justice to the wealth of wisdom you will gain from immersing yourself in all that Peacemaker Ministries has to offer. Our goals are to supplement their concepts, particularly as they pertain to conflicts women face, and hopefully motivate you to further study.

A Biblical Theology for Conflict Resolution

The Bible provides powerful and practical instruction for resolving conflict, but most Christians have a "devotional theology" for resolving conflicts—their approach to peacemaking often depends on where they are in their daily devotions. One day, Proverbs 19:11 seems to coach them to overlook an offense: "A man's wisdom gives him patience; it is to his glory to overlook an offense." Another day, Luke 17:3 counsels them to rebuke the person who has offended them: "If your brother sins, rebuke him, and if he repents, forgive him." These passages may seem contradictory at first glance and may leave us confused about how to deal with conflict in biblical ways. But God does not contradict himself. Instead, the Bible gives us a coherent set of principles to help us understand that there is a time to overlook, but there is also a time to confront. To determine how to respond to conflict wisely, we need a systematic approach based on key passages about forgiveness, confession, and confrontation. Without such an organized approach to conflict, we will probably respond emotionally and impulsively. To be peacemaking women, we are called to approach conflict as biblically informed, Spirit-directed women.

Peacemaker Ministries summarizes a systematic framework for understanding and resolving conflict as "The Four G's":

- *Glorify God*—How can I please and honor God in this situation?
- *Get the log out of your eye*—How can I show Jesus's work in me by taking responsibility for my contribution to this conflict?

- *Gently restore*—How can I lovingly serve others by helping them take responsibility for their contribution to this conflict?
- *Go and be reconciled*—How can I demonstrate the forgiveness of God and encourage a reasonable solution to this conflict?

Glorify God. We are to glorify God in all areas of living: "So whether you eat or drink or whatever you do, do it all for the glory of God" (1 Cor. 10:31).

How does the gospel of Jesus Christ relate to our efforts to bring glory to God in the midst of conflict? The gospel reminds us of who we are and where we are going. We are called and expected to remember our identity and our destiny as his children and disciples. As Christians, our identity and eternal destination have been forever changed. Once we were children of the darkness, but now we are children of the holy God (Eph. 5:8). In light of this truth, our lives begin to reflect enduring gratitude at the life-changing realization that we have been completely and eternally rescued from the punishment we rightly deserve for our sins. The gospel says that God loves us and accepts us because of Jesus. In response, we live boldly as every aspect of our lives becomes a response to God's grace. Even conflict, a universally dreaded human experience, becomes an opportunity to respond to the glorious grace of God in our lives.

Our love stays fresh and powerful as we focus on the pleasure of glorifying God with our lives (Rev. 2:1–7). We remember the newness and excitement of our first love as we proclaim, "You are everything to me, my beloved!" To glorify God is not to give mere mental assent to his good attributes. It is to lift up, exalt, and delight in the Lord. We glorify God when our hearts cry out, "Nothing compares to you. I will live for your glory because of *who* you are—not because of The Four G's, not even because I'm a good Christian if I do, but because you are my first love." We glorify God when Jesus is our heart's delight.

We can easily forget the wonder of God's grace when others betray, misunderstand, or attack us. But during those times our opportunity to glorify God is greatest—for who else but a beloved child of the King of Kings could live to please God in the midst of such terrible circumstances? Living for God's glory makes the world look at us and ask, "What do you have that I don't? Who is this God that you trust even through your tears and distress?" Compelled by his grace, we respond, "He is the one true God, and he is trustworthy and good. Let me tell you about Jesus, my Lord."

My sister and I (Judy) were disowned by our father for a period of time. During those years, my sister remarked at how differently she and I handled our pain and frustration. When she asked me to explain my peace even amidst such a sad situation, I was able to tell her about my faith in God—how my relationship with Jesus Christ made all the difference in how I chose to respond to the conflict with our father. I bought my sister a Bible, even though she seemed indifferent. Several years later, my sister committed her life to the Lord. The conflict with our father was hugely instrumental in her coming to a saving faith and provided many opportunities for us to talk about the grace and glory of God. Rarely have I ever seen such dramatic change in another person. My sister is passionate in her desire to live for God's glory, and her love for God is evident when she speaks of his goodness.

Get the log out of your eye. This teaching of Jesus is difficult to obey: "You hypocrite, first take the plank out of your own eye, and then you will see clearly to remove the speck from your brother's eye" (Matt. 7:5). What does it mean to have a plank or a "log" in our eye? When Jesus refers to a log, he is referring to anything that blinds us and prevents us from seeing things as they really are. The logs in life are often personal sins or idols that prevent us from being able to accurately see our situation, God, and others. A log can greatly distort our ability to know the truth and be transformed into women of *shalom*. There are numerous types of logs, but anger, fear, and a refusal to take responsibility for our own words and deeds are logs with which many of us struggle when we are in conflict. We often need the help of others to see our sins.

What does obedience look like in this painful task of log removal? We may be tempted to minimize our sins and contributions to a conflict because we really want to get to the part about confronting our brother. We may feel frightened by our weaknesses and sins. Confessing what we view as a small contribution to the problem can be painfully difficult when we feel that the other person has sinned greatly. But the gospel makes us joyfully free to root out and admit our weaknesses and inadequacies because we know that we are safe and secure in the hand of God. As believers in the Lord Jesus Christ, we are comforted with the knowledge that we are already saved and headed for heaven. We can calmly look at what is unbecoming within us because we know that we are loved and fully accepted by God (Rom. 14:3). Nothing in us can make God love us less. Nothing we do can make God love us more. We are free to see and deal with our own sin because we are fully, eternally loved and our sins have been forgiven because of Christ's blood. The gospel of grace sets us free to be honest about our faults.[3]

To get the log out of our eye, we are called to rest so securely in God's love and ownership of us that, like Paul, we can delight in our weaknesses (2 Cor. 12:9). In light of God's love and acceptance, we can identify our weaknesses, confess them to God and others, resolve to forsake them in the power of Christ, and walk in a new way—all the while delighting in knowing that he is at work in us to make us perfect in Christ. This is the heart of repentance: we turn from sin and fully endeavor to walk in obedience. And this brief time on earth? It is but a vapor, so we can gladly work through these weaknesses as we boast in the hope of salvation. The gospel is profoundly present in our lives as we honestly and faithfully identify our logs and repent of them.

During an intense conflict in my (Tara's) life, I regularly sought the counsel of my friend Nancy. During one conversation, Nancy asked me to identify specifically how I had sinned in this conflict. I did not think I had sinned all *that* much. I really wanted to concentrate on the other person's sins, but Nancy wisely reminded me that, apart from Christ, my own sins were enough to damn me to hell for all eternity. Of course she was right. The grace of God helped me to see my many sins and confess them. Through a series of meetings with the man I had a conflict with, I apologized for my immaturities and weaknesses, the way I had communicated, and my bitterness and anger. To get the log out of my eye, I had to repent of various idols in my life that contributed to the ways I had hurt him.

These were not easy conversations—especially because he did not own up to his contributions to our conflict or demonstrate genuine remorse or regret. But remembering the riches of God's grace toward me enabled me to humble myself and own up to my contribution to the conflict anyway—to get the log out of my own eye—whether or not he ever repented, whether or not he ever asked my forgiveness, and whether or not we were ever fully reconciled. *I* was not the Holy Spirit. This man's repentance was not for *me* to determine or control. With a heart focused on glorifying God, my job was to confess *my own* sin and leave the results to the Lord. (We go into more detail on confession later in this chapter.) At an appropriate time, however, love for both God and this man compelled me to move on to the "third G"—Gently restore.[4]

Gently restore. As difficult as it is, sometimes we are called to go humbly to the people who have wronged us in order to help them to understand better how they have contributed to our conflicts. Of course, when appropriate, we should be quick to overlook (Prov. 19:11), and we must always first confess our own sins (Matt. 7:5). But if after we have confessed our own sins we cannot overlook the offense, we are called to help the person who has offended us by gently restoring her (Gal. 6:1) and helping her remove the speck from her eye (Matt. 7:5).

Apart from the gospel, such humble and loving confrontations would be unthinkable. Sinners simply do not have the right to point out someone else's sin, do they? Yes, they do. Genuine biblical love *requires* that sometimes we confront others. Jesus explicitly taught us: "If your brother sins against you, go and show him his fault, just between the two of you. If he listens to you, you have won your brother over" (Matt. 18:15). The fact that we too are sinners does not remove the responsibility to lovingly confront. Nowhere in Scripture does our own sinfulness remove from us the requirement to help others see their faults and deal with them. The grace of God is what enables us to minister truth, mercy, hope, and love to our brothers and sisters in Christ through biblical confrontation. We confront because we are compelled by love. As John Stott has often said, "Grace is love that cares and stoops and rescues."[5] One way we care for and rescue one another is to gently confront.

Galatians 6:1–2 says, "Brothers, if someone is caught in a sin, you who are spiritual should restore him gently. But watch yourself, or you also may be tempted. Carry each other's burdens, and in this way you will fulfill the law of Christ." The term "restore" in this passage means to mend in the same way we might mend holes in a net or set a broken bone. The term "caught," however, includes an element of surprise. In the same way that a fisherman might cast his net over the side of his boat only to realize, too late, that his leg is caught in the net, we can be caught off guard by our own sin. The weight of the net pulls the fisherman over the side and he begins to sink. He can barely hold on with one hand to the side of the boat, but if he lets go of the boat to try to free his leg, he will drown. He is not strong enough to pull himself back into the boat. He is *caught*.

Sadly, metaphorically speaking, if this fisherman was a Christian caught in sin, many of us would mock him: "Hey, Jerry! I thought you were a fisherman! No *fisherman* would ever let himself get stuck like that. Hey, you guys, come look at Jerry—he *claims* to be a fisherman. Can you believe what he did?" A woman is caught in the sin of gossip or gluttony and we cluck behind our church bulletins, "She claims to be a Christian." A man leaves his wife and children or is incarcerated for embezzling and we say, "No *Christian* would *ever* get caught in a mess like that." Instead of such a proud and condemning response, we ought to run to the side of the boat and *help our brother or sister*. "Jump in! Hold his neck up so he can breathe! Get a knife and cut the net! Go and get help! He's in trouble and he needs us!" This should be the response of the church.

Instead of such rescue, when someone offends us, our natural inclination is often to go angrily to confront her or embarrass her. But anytime we *want* to confront, we should see a red flag and know we would probably do best to wait. When we are *eager* to confront, we are often acting out of selfish motivations. If we are grieved to confront another person and we only do so prayerfully and lovingly, it is probably the right thing to do. Our purpose in going to the other person must never be to make ourselves "feel better." Godly confrontation seeks to restore by glorifying God, serving the other person, and helping to promote unity within the church.

One final point under "Gently restore": even if a proper and loving confrontation hurts, it will not ultimately cause harm. God would never command us to do something without also intending a morally good result. I (Judy) remember a time in my twenties when my supervisor assessed me for a promotion and rejected me. His candid words were deeply wounding, yet they provided me with opportunity for reflection and growth. As painful as his words were, they never ultimately harmed me. They were used by God to help me change. Paul writes of this godly sorrow in 2 Corinthians 7: "Even if I caused you sorrow by my letter, I do not regret it. Though I did regret it—I see that my letter hurt you, but only for a little while—yet now I am happy, not because you were made sorry, but because your sorrow led you to repentance. For you became sorrowful as God intended and so were not harmed in any way by us. Godly sorrow brings repentance that leads to salvation and leaves no regret" (vv. 8–10).

Go and be reconciled. As we embrace our holy calling to pursue unity with a heartfelt devotion, we have the hope of true reconciliation. The admonition to go and be reconciled is the call to reflect the heart of God in our lives. With the gospel as our foundation—God reconciling us to himself—we strive to follow the admonition in Colossians 3:13 to "bear with each other and forgive whatever grievances you may have against one another. Forgive as the Lord forgave you."

When we make our goal true reconciliation rather than revenge, then we are sharing in Christ's suffering and his glory. Our efforts to live like Christ please God and bring glory to him. The wonderful result is that we bear witness to Jesus and proclaim to a watching world that God loves you and sent his Son to die for you (John 17:23).

In our conflicts we often want to run away. But wise counselors remind us that the world sees and hears the Good News of the gospel when it sees conflicted believers faithfully work toward true reconciliation. No quarrel or conflict is just between the people involved. According to Scripture, our struggles are spiritual battles against evil (Eph. 6:12). We are called to remember that all of our conflicts are public—we do not have private lives. Even a fight in the privacy of home is public because it affects the message of the gospel going out to the world.

I (Tara) saw this truth perfectly illustrated during a recent hospital stay for the birth of my first child. When I mentioned the name of my church to the nurse, she asked if I knew a certain young woman, Rachel. I did, but mentioned that Rachel had left our church a few months previously. The nurse's reply grieved me: "Yes, I know Rachel left. She told me that some people hurt her. But didn't they even apologize publicly and really try to make it up to her? I don't understand why she left your church—aren't you Christians supposed to be all about forgiving and loving each other? I mean, what more could they have done for her?" By failing to persevere in reconciliation, Rachel missed an opportunity to show this nurse the gospel of Jesus Christ. Instead of hearing about how God's lavish forgiveness had motivated Rachel to forgive even her enemies, the nurse was left wondering how people who claim to be so loving could refuse to be reconciled.

Conflict is painful. Will we strive for unity and harmony? Or will we live in conflict or, worse yet, the apathy of denial? The gospel message of reconciliation is our mandate to show the world Christ. Our conflicts provide opportunities for us to impact the world by prayerfully, humbly striving to be reconciled inasmuch as it depends on us (Rom. 12:18). Forgiving is a lifelong event—we cannot just say, "I forgive you" once and move on. To walk in an attitude of mercy, to forgive over and over again each day when we are tempted to be bitter, these acts of faith and obedience keep us anchored in God's love because our conflicts constantly remind us of how much we need his grace. As we trust in the Lord and persevere in love, we carve out a vast space that holds God's grace in our hearts, for only he can enable us to obey the command, "A new command I give you: Love one another. As I have loved you, so you must love one another. By this all men will know that you are my disciples, if you love one another" (John 13:34–35).

Confession

A key aspect of biblical conflict resolution is confession. Most of us need instruction and assistance in how to make a helpful and good confession. We most likely have not been taught how to confess our sins and wrongs to others. In fact, we often teach and are taught to make ineffective confessions. How many of us "made peace" with a squabbling sibling when our parents dictated, "Say you're sorry right now or go to your room!" Our response? "Sorrrrreeeeeee" (while our hearts continued to seethe). From our earliest childhood days, we have been taught to be hypocrites when it comes to confessions. Sadly, poor confessions often cause more harm than good.

For instance, the likelihood of true reconciliation is small when I (Tara) raise my voice to my husband in anger, feel bad about it, and then make a confession like this: "Fred, I'm sorry that I yelled. But I've had such a stressful day! And I was really upset that you didn't call to say you'd be late—if you had just called, I'm sure I would have been more patient with you. So, anyway, I'm sorry I upset you. Will you forgive me?"

What does that confession actually say? "Fred, I'm feeling vaguely guilty about something, but I'm not really sure what (so you can count on me doing it again). But I can tell you're going to be quiet and withdrawn all night until I make some sort of token apology to get you off of my back. So I'll be the martyr and apologize. But of course, I wouldn't have anything to apologize for if you were a more caring husband. So really the problem is with you. Will you forgive me?"

What is the likelihood of us being at peace with each other following this confession? Quite low to be sure. Why? Because I have not *truly* confessed *anything* to him. In fact, I have simply used the false pretense of confession to level more attacks against him. I have not been convicted of my sin or failings. I am not thinking of the Lord and what would honor him. I am certainly not focused on loving, serving, encouraging, and blessing my husband. This "confession" shows my selfish heart and will not lead to true reconciliation.

A more thorough and effective confession can be summarized by what Peacemaker Ministries describes as "The Seven A's of Confession":

- Address everyone involved
- Avoid *if*, *but*, and *maybe*
- Admit specifically
- Acknowledge the hurt
- Accept the consequences
- Alter your behavior
- Ask for forgiveness

Not all confessions require all seven steps, but the next time you need to confess to someone, consider reviewing The Seven A's to see how you can make the most heartfelt, sincere, and helpful confession. A good confession is crucial to experiencing *shalom*. We will not attempt to restate all of the excellent instruction on a good confession found in *The Peacemaker*. Instead, we will highlight and expand on a few key points that we often encounter in our attempts to help people make peace with one another.

Address everyone involved. A confession should be as public as the offense. If no one at all is aware of the offense, God himself may be the only necessary recipient of our confession. If you envy your best friend in your heart and your friend is unaware of your sin, you may do best to withhold a confession from her in order to protect her feelings and the relationship. God, however, must hear your confession so that your fellowship with him can be restored. Other wrongs are public, however, and require a public confession. I (Judy) once coached an executive who had yelled at his secretary and called her a name in front of his sales support team. While not wanting to confess to his secretary in front of everyone, he understood the need to do so. That same day, addressing everyone involved, he gained not only the forgiveness of his secretary but also the deep trust and respect of his entire staff by making a public confession for his public offense.

Avoid the words **if, but,** *and* **maybe.** Three little words can destroy a confession. As effectively as an eraser obliterates a message on a chalkboard, these three words wipe out an entire confession. *If, but, maybe,* and all the variations of these three words (*perhaps, however,* etc.) shift the responsibility for the offense to something or someone else. These little words effectively disconnect the confession from the offense, allowing the offense to remain unresolved.

Admit specifically. A non-specific apology is generally heard as, "I'm sorry you are upset—maybe you could just get over it so that I don't have to be inconvenienced by your anger any more?" Such an "apology" is unlikely to facilitate true forgiveness and reconciliation. The confession of the offense must be specific and focused for forgiveness to wipe away an offense.

I (Tara) remember a time when I was working through a conflict with a friend. We were both eager to forgive one another, and we were doing our best to make full confessions and grant forgiveness. At one point in our conversation, I gently asked my friend about a few emails she had sent that had really hurt me. I did so because I wanted to truly forgive her for them so that every time I saw them on my laptop or thought of them, I would know they were covered by the grace of the Lord Jesus and were totally forgiven. She specifically confessed them to me and asked me to forgive her. Now whenever I see or think of them, I don't have a sense of hurt or dread but one of gratitude and worship because they remind me of how much God has forgiven me. Her willingness to confess specifically helped me to forgive fully.

Acknowledge the hurt. Christians should be the most sensitive people on the planet. Who can understand pain and sorrow better than those who share in the sufferings of Christ? To acknowledge the hurt that has been experienced by another is profoundly healing to the injured person. To tell someone, "I know what I did hurt you, and I'm so sorry for the hurt I caused" is to express genuine compassion and to own up to the full implication of the offense against the person. We all know what it feels like to be hurt, and we know the comfort and hope that comes when someone shares in our pain.

Six-year-old Anna was punished by her mother, who wrongly thought that Anna had broken a picture frame and refused to admit it. When Anna's father came home with a new picture frame to replace the one *he* had broken that morning, Anna's mother approached her daughter with deep sorrow. In making up, Anna heard her mother admit with tears: "I really hurt you when I didn't believe you, and I am so sorry." Grieved all evening, Anna's mother asked her at bedtime, "Are you still sad over what I did today?" Anna told her mother no. In surprise, her mother asked why. Anna said, "You took away my sad when you felt it yourself." Sharing another's pain occurs when we acknowledge it. Shared pain heals much faster than pain untouched.

Accept the consequences. Sometimes there are no consequences for an offense. Often, however, the consequences are complex and lingering. When trust has been destroyed, for instance, it may take years to rebuild it. Leslie committed adultery with a neighbor, carrying on her affair during the day while her husband was at work. When God's grace enabled Leslie and John to recommit to their marriage and do the hard work of rebuilding their relationship, John frequently called Leslie during the day to "just check and see how you are doing." Leslie became increasingly frustrated when John insisted on calling her four times a day. She had repented and confessed. "What more does he want?" she demanded. Leslie had to be reminded that one consequence of her breaking trust included the need for her to prove that she would be where she said she would be, doing what she said she would be doing. In other words, she had to work hard to earn back John's trust. His phone calls to her were one way for that to occur. Being reminded of the consequences of her actions, Leslie embraced them with grace. Today, Leslie and John have a vital marriage ministry to couples suffering from the after-effects of adultery.

Alter your behavior. Most of the time, the best we can do during a confession is to draw a verbal picture of how we hope to be different in the future: "I intend to do all I can to learn how to communicate more openly," "I am committing to try to speak respectfully and not in anger when I feel upset," or "I want you to know that I want to always speak the truth and never lie to you again." These types of words go a long way in making a confession complete. Of course, we must then follow through on our commitments and alter our behavior. The time to alter our behavior is before, during, and after a confession.

Ask for forgiveness. A statement does not require a response; a question does. Most people, in making a confession, make the statement "I hope you will forgive me." This statement of fact does little to complete the transaction of reconciliation. By asking the question, "Will you forgive me?" both parties in the conflict have the opportunity to fully resolve the open offense. The final step in a confession is the request to be released from the offense in the only way possible—forgiveness.

When hurts and offenses are grievous and complex, additional time may be needed before the injured person is fully able to extend forgiveness. One way we can help others to reconcile with us when we have hurt them deeply is to be willing to ask for forgiveness several times, over an extended period of time. When hurts are profound, forgiveness sometimes takes a little time, and a person's integrity may require them to not offer "full" forgiveness because they know that they need additional time to work through the pain.

We can help them to work through the hurt and come to complete forgiveness by genuinely expressing our sorrow and asking for forgiveness more than once.

Sinning versus Offending

As you consider your confession, understand the important fact that there are actually two types of confessions: a confession for sinning and a confession for offending. They sound similar; but they have a profound distinction. In a confession for sin, we are able to say, "What I did was wrong, and I am sorry." In a confession for offense, where sin is absent, we are able to say, "What I did really hurt you, and I am sorry." Sometimes we offend and hurt people without sinning.

One day several years ago, I (Judy) was counseling a man who confessed to criminal activity. Outwardly I appeared calm as I dealt with this revelation by calling all of the necessary parties and agencies. Inwardly, however, I was distraught. Two days later a co-worker stopped to ask me, "Judy, why are you angry at me?" I was dumbfounded. I told her I wasn't at all angry and asked her what made her think this. She responded, "When I passed you the other day and said hello, you didn't even answer me. I was extremely upset. I can't imagine what I did to make you so mad at me." I soon discovered that she had passed me in the hall the day of the criminal case. Focused on my task and engulfed in my own situation, I had passed her in the hallway without even seeing her. She was deeply hurt and offended by my lack of response. I could have become defensive when this co-worker confronted me because I had not sinned against her. But the truth was, I had injured her.[6] Knowing full well how such suffering can be a burden, I had an opportunity to help my friend release her pain and hurt. I did this by acknowledging the offense and asking for her forgiveness.

To help better grasp this distinction between sinning and offending someone apart from sin, picture two concentric circles representing sin and fallenness.

All sin is a result of the fall, but not all of the struggles we experience related to our fallenness is sin. Fallenness includes things like fatigue, cancer, air pollution, limited knowledge, and the inability

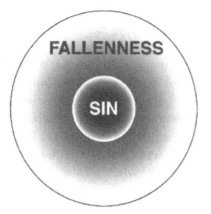

to understand others. Sometimes, in conflict, we need to confess our sins to one another. At other times, we need to acknowledge how we have offended them out of our fallenness. Often, offenses and hurts include a combination of both sin and fallenness.

Brian had no intent to harm or offend his wife and did not even realize that his words would hurt her so deeply. But Carol was crushed when Brian said, "Birthdays just aren't a big deal to me." Having invested many hours in preparing a surprise birthday party for him, complete with clues to find his hidden gifts, special treats for dinner, and homemade decorations, Carol felt frustrated by her failed attempts to communicate love to Brian. When she began to cry, he listened with embarrassment and sorrow. Brian came to realize that he invested little time and effort into understanding his wife and in helping her to understand him. While his words about birthdays were not intended to hurt and disappoint her (he was shocked to learn about the birthday celebration), his failure to reveal himself to her and pursue her to know her better was rooted in simple selfishness regarding his time and energy. Brian offended Carol both out of his sin (selfishness) and his fallenness (not knowing the whole story).

As fallen people living in a fallen world, we fail to understand, we mishear, we misspeak, or we are not available when others need us. The result is often genuine hurt—hurt that we must be prepared to acknowledge and from which we must seek to be released. An acknowledgment of hurt and a request for forgiveness (a release from the real or perceived injury incurred by our action or lack of action) is an act of love that profoundly assists others to obey God by getting rid of their rage, bitterness, and anger (Eph. 4:31).

Some people are reluctant to apologize when they don't believe they sinned. Let us not be those people. Only as we genuinely acknowledge another's hurt, even for unintentional offenses, do we experience the blessing of a reconciled relationship. Sometimes our best efforts hurt people because we are finite, fallen creatures living in a fallen world. As Christians acquainted with sorrow, let's be quick to confess our sins when we sin and quick to acknowledge hurt when we offend.

The Four Promises of Forgiveness

As we learn to confess our sins and offenses to one another, we have the hope of experiencing the joy of forgiveness. "Forgiveness is one of the chief acts by which God expresses the greatness of his glory (Exod. 34:7). . . . We cannot and must not reduce forgiveness to a therapeutic technique. . . . Forgiveness is something supernatural. It is a divine gift and power. It is a miraculous work."[7] But what does that mean for us when we are trying to forgive someone? How do these biblical truths apply in real life?

Peacemaker Ministries summarizes forgiveness with the following four promises:

- I will not dwell on this incident.
- I will not bring this incident up again and use it against you.
- I will not talk to others about this incident.
- I will not allow this incident to stand between us or hinder our personal relationship.

In our counseling with women, we often expound on these promises as follows:

- I will not dwell on or ruminate on this incident. Instead, when I become aware that thoughts about this incident pop into my mind, I will take them captive and commit them to Christ.

- I will not use this incident against you to cause you hurt, shame, or fear. Instead, I will only bring this incident up when it is necessary for our healing and growth.
- I will not gossip to others about this incident. Instead, I will only bring it up to others when it is necessary to ask for their assistance for God's glory and our good.
- I will not avoid you or neglect our relationship. Instead, I will pray, allow time, and faithfully labor toward our continued reconciliation and the true restoration of our relationship.

I will not dwell on this incident. This first promise is an opportunity for us to practice the spiritual discipline of "capturing and taming" our thoughts in a way that reflects the character of Christ. Memories of hurt will come into our minds from time to time. We need not feel ashamed or guilty when they do—as long as we handle them properly. Instead of chewing them over like a cow chews its cud, we remain committed to not dwelling on forgiven issues. Instead, by God's grace, we take our thoughts captive and make them obedient to Christ—which means, of course, exposing them to a scriptural critique (2 Cor. 10:5).

Many years ago I (Judy) struggled with anger toward my mother-in-law over an unresolved conflict. I remember many days of waking up, drinking my coffee, taking my kids to school, and returning home to shower and get dressed for the day. I would step into the shower relaxed and step out furious. My mother-in-law and I had a standing date to argue every morning in the shower. I would say one thing, she would say another, and before I knew it we were having a fight. Of course, she was never actually in the shower with me. It took me many months to realize that my thoughts had captured me and made me obedient to them. My thoughts pushed me to be angry. I had to learn to capture my thoughts and make them obedient to Christ.

When was the last time you thought about *what* you were thinking about? We are called to train our thinking to be biblical. What we do with our thoughts when a hurtful incident comes to our remembrance matters a great deal. In this example, by God's grace, I learned to preach truth to myself rather than dwell on an incident of pain. My morning sermon inside my head sounded something like this: "Well, here's another day. My first thought is of the critical comment my mother-in-law made to me. Father, please forgive me for failing to think first of your unfailing love. Please help me to worship you with my heart and 'sing for joy and be glad all [my] days' (Ps. 90:14). Please help me to remember your lavish forgiveness to me, an unworthy servant (Matt. 18:23–35). Help me grant forgiveness to her, forgiveness modeled on your lavish forgiveness of me. Lord, please empower me to 'bless and [never] curse' (Rom. 12:14) and 'do to others as [I] would have them do to [me]' (Luke 6:31)."

I will not bring this incident up again and use it against you. When we forgive as Christ forgives us (Eph. 4:32), we make a promise to the person who has wronged us that we will not mention the offense again in order to shame or attack her. When she asks for our forgiveness and we grant it, we are promising that she is free to interact with us in an open and safe relationship. Instead of guarding each word or protecting herself from our verbal attacks, the recipient of our forgiveness is free from our punishment.

I (Tara) have received forgiveness like this from my husband, Fred. During our courtship, I knew I had to confess my past impurities to him. I was terrified to do so. Fred was a godly, merciful man—but I did not believe he could truly forgive me and still want me for his wife. Thankfully, I was wrong. As I confessed my sins to Fred, he told me, "Of course I forgive you, Tara. I am such a sinner myself. How could I hold your sins against you? If I did, then God would hold my sins against me. And anyway, your past sins do not define who you are now. You are a new creature in Christ. The old is gone. The new is come." After true forgiveness like that, in all our years of marriage, I have never once been afraid that Fred would bring up my sins and use them against me. He forgave me and it was done. My sins were covered, removed, and gone forever. The fruit of this forgiveness is an intimate, loving, and safe friendship and marriage. Fred provides me with a taste of heaven because of his forgiveness toward me.

Contrast that godly and biblical forgiveness with the lie of false "forgiveness." I hurt a woman years ago. I have humbled myself and asked for her forgiveness on numerous occasions with the hope of having a reconciled relationship with her. Yet all too often when she is hurt or offended, she brings up the conflict from *years ago*. Ironically, she often begins these uncomfortable exchanges with, "Of course I've forgiven you, but I'll never forget the time you . . ." The fruit of this "forgiveness" is a lack of true friendship. I find it difficult to be open or vulnerable with her—to truly trust her—because I am always afraid that another attack will come and I will again have to face up to my sins from years ago. No relationship can be truly reconciled in the face of such false forgiveness.

I will not talk to others about this incident. When we forgive someone who has wronged us, we may be tempted to "share" about our reconciliation in such a way that we are actually gossiping. For example, we may genuinely want to give a praise report at our prayer group, but because we are not careful in our speech, we may actually end up sharing information that reflects poorly on the other person. "Marjie confessed that she had intentionally lied to me, I forgave her, and we were reconciled" would be an example of such unwholesome sharing. Although technically true, without Marjie's explicit permission to share her confession publicly, we should not talk to others about it.

At other times we may have even less noble motives in talking to others. We may actually *intentionally* share about the offense in order to tear others down and build ourselves up in the eyes of others. For example: "You know, Marjie intentionally lied to me. It hurt me terribly. I was devastated! But *of course*, I forgave her. *I* know enough to do good to her even though *she* doesn't deserve it and *she* has so many sin issues in her life. Well, let's pray for our sister Marjie." While we may be tempted to sin in this way, we are called to pray for the grace to not do so. It truly is God's grace that enables us to walk humbly, protecting the other person's reputation and not seeking our own advancement or glory.

Consider an example of when it would be appropriate to talk to others about something that we have forgiven: if I had a conflict with Marjie, even if she did lie to me—which is clearly a sin—you can be certain that I *also* sinned in the situation. I may have sinned with acts of commission (harboring bitterness, presuming the worst in her) or omission (failing to gently restore her, not praying for her, withholding my love, and not covering over a multitude of sins). If we meet together, mutually confess our sins to one another, and are reconciled, we *may* choose to share our reconciliation with others in order to bring glory to God. If we *mutually agree* to talk with others, we should be careful to rarely speak of the other person's sins and confessions. Instead, we ought to focus on how God worked to give us both gracious and repentant hearts and loving forgiveness toward one another. If we do share any specifics, we should only do so with the explicit permission of the other person, and we must be very careful to speak only in edifying ways about the other person.

Another reason we may mutually agree to talk to others would be for their assistance. For example, Marjie might explain that she would benefit from ongoing accountability because she has a habitual problem with lying. She may give me permission to "check in" with her husband or a close friend in the coming weeks and months in order to help her keep "on track" and in order to demonstrate that her repentance is genuine. Other than these two reasons (for God's glory and for future assistance), we ought not speak to others about offenses that we have forgiven.

I will not allow this incident to stand between us or hinder our personal relationship. What about our promise not to avoid the other person or neglect the relationship? Sometimes Christian women will say, "I forgive her. I just don't want to have anything to do with her ever again." Or, "I forgive him. I just know that God is calling me to a new church (or Bible study or job)." This is not forgiveness. If God forgave us in this manner, what hope would we have? What if God told us, "I forgive you; I just don't want to have anything to do with you anymore"? *We would be lost.* And yet that is the very "forgiveness" we so often offer one another.

Tamara's husband mistreated her and neglected her. During a counseling session on the Four Promises of Forgiveness, Tamara was convicted that she was offering false forgiveness to her husband. The breakthrough happened after she realized that she was willing to forgive him only when she was convinced that he *really* understood how badly he had hurt her. And she thought that would take some time. She reflected on the horrible thought of what it would be like if God treated her the same way. She realized that she would be lost if, after she confessed her sins to God, he responded by saying, "Tamara, you've really hurt me, and it's going to take some time, but after you earn your way back into my good graces, then I'll forgive you."

Isn't that the very "forgiveness" we so often offer others—even our own children? They do something wrong, they confess, and we claim to forgive them, but then we hold ourselves back from them emotionally and relationally. Maybe after a passage of time we are open, happy, and warm with them again. God have mercy on us and forgive us for modeling such unbiblical "forgiveness" to them! Instead, we ought to embrace them after disciplining them and say, "I love you, honey, just as though you had never sinned." *This* is forgiveness that reflects the Lord's forgiveness of us (Col. 3:13).

Relationships are damaged and our testimonies are diminished when we avoid or neglect someone after claiming to forgive her. For example, it was a red flag to me (Tara) when I realized that I had claimed to forgive a friend at church but I was actually changing pews on Sunday morning to avoid sitting next to her. Of course, I always couched my action in some way to try to hide my sinful heart ("Fred needs to be at the end of the pew in order to lead worship"; "Sophie needs more room"), but I knew the truth. I had claimed to forgive her, but I was not prayerfully working toward restoring our friendship. In fact, I was avoiding her.

True forgiveness sets us free to work toward restoration of the relationship. As is often the case, we may not feel like close friends at the end of the peacemaking process even though we have reached a point of reconciliation. This is because the need for *restoration* still exists. To better understand this concept, we find it helpful to make the distinction between reconciliation and restoration.

Think of the analogy of a broken bone. If a leg is broken, the doctor sets the bone and the gap is healed (reconciled). This is what happens when someone confesses to us and we forgive her. Yet in the same way that a freshly set bone is not ready to bear weight, a broken relationship, newly reconciled, often needs time and help to be fully restored. A broken bone might need a cast or physical therapy for complete restoration. The same thing happens to a relationship following reconciliation. It often takes prayer, time, and focused effort to build trust back into a formerly broken relationship. A good rule of thumb: the greater the fracture, the longer the recovery time. Just as a healed bone that never bears weight will never grow stronger, relationships that are avoided or neglected will never grow stronger. God's grace and mercy enable us to strengthen reconciled relationships. We may send cards or emails, take extra time to share a gift that truly communicates love, or perform other countless acts of kindness that communicate our commitment to the relationship. Reconciliation is an event, but restoration is a process that slowly restores the relationship.

Excusing Is Not Forgiving

The last point we want to mention about forgiveness is this: excusing somebody is not the same thing as forgiving her. Too often, even in the church, we are taught to excuse others rather than to forgive. Have you ever heard (or said) something like this: "Yes, she wronged me, but she was going through a really hard time and I really wasn't there for her—so I forgive her." This is not forgiving; it is excusing. Excusing says, "On the basis of some external criteria, I release you." True biblical forgiveness says, "On the basis of God's forgiving me for my sin, I forgive you."[8]

Excusing wrongs is like buying a cheap appliance—it is unreliable and breaks down quickly. Excusing does not last. Forgiveness lasts forever. Jessica told me (Judy) that her father had sexually abused her but she forgave him. She just didn't know why she was still hurt and angry. I asked her *why* she forgave him. She claimed that he had a hard life and was abused himself. Although she thought she had forgiven her father, she had in actuality only excused him. As we looked at scriptural passages on forgiveness, Jessica came to understand that there is no excuse for her father's sin against her but that she was called to forgive him. Jessica rejected her false forgiveness and by God's grace found real forgiveness for her father. She came to understand that answering *why* we forgive is the key to understanding that forgiveness is not excusing. As we ended one beautiful counseling session, Jessica shared: "Why do I forgive him? Because I am a sinner. I have sinned against the Lord, yet he has completely washed my sin away. On that basis, I can forgive my father even this horrible thing because it is a small debt in light of my great debt to God and because of the fact that my sins have been washed away by the blood of the Lamb."

Forgiveness requires that you acknowledge how bad the wrong actually was rather than minimize the wrong with an excuse. We say, "This was bad; this was wrong; it should not have happened." And God's grace empowers us to forgive—"I forgive you and release you of this because God has released me."

Before we move on from the "Four Promises of Forgiveness," a word of caution is in order. To grant forgiveness is to enter into a holy covenant with God himself as a witness. Whenever we say, "I forgive you," we have committed ourselves to these four promises in clear view of our merciful God who calls us to forgive in the same way he forgives (Col. 3:13). To break our promise of forgiveness is a serious matter because it is a breaking of an agreement with God as a central party. May we be women who are quick to forgive.

The Slippery Slope

The wide variety of possible responses to conflict are wonderfully represented by "the Slippery Slope."

Notice that the slope is divided into three segments: on the left are escape responses, in the middle are peacemaking responses, and on the right are attack responses. Some of us tend toward the escape responses—we don't really like conflict, so we seek to avoid it or pretend it doesn't exist. Others enjoy a lively debate—we tend toward the attack responses. But God wants us to do something much more productive with our conflicts. His desire for us is neither to attack nor escape but rather to reconcile *inasmuch as it depends on us* (Rom. 12:18). The peacemaking responses at the top of the Slippery Slope have a much greater likelihood of bringing about a just and mutually agreeable solution and a reconciled relationship.

What is your personal tendency in conflict? Are you someone who tries to *escape* conflict (a "peace-faker") or are you one who *attacks* in conflict (a "peace-breaker")? Often we ping-pong back and forth on the slope—one moment we shove our emotions down or deny that they exist; the next we explode in anger with a level of rage that is inappropriate to the situation. We may not even realize that our attempts at overlooking have shifted into denial and we are getting more and more angry with each passing moment. If we are not aware of our own hearts, we will probably just make the conflict worse. In your conflicts, are you modeling the Lord and demonstrating the fruit of the Holy Spirit as a peacemaker (Gal. 5:22)?

In Conclusion

As you consider the biblical peacemaking principles summarized in this chapter, you may be thinking, "I've struggled with conflicted relationships my entire life. I've read the books. I've gone to the 'how to be a better manager' seminars. I really don't think I can change. I can't become a peacemaker." In one respect, this is true. *You* do not have the strength or ability to change yourself. In another sense, you are wrong. God's eternal Word promises that you *will* be perfected in Christ. *He* is doing the work in you. Trust *him*, not yourself.

We must remember that "our tendency to self-sufficiency can only be overcome when our situation is beyond our sufficiency."[9] Even if the majority of your relationships are conflicted now, you can have great hope because God is passionate about peacemaking. As we live at peace with one another, we are God's ambassadors proclaiming the gospel of Jesus Christ so that men and women can be reconciled to God: "All this is from God, who reconciled us to himself through Christ and gave us the ministry of reconciliation: that God was reconciling the world to himself in Christ, not counting men's sins against them. And he has committed to us the message of reconciliation. We are therefore Christ's ambassadors, as though God were making his appeal through us" (2 Cor. 5:18–20).

Personal Reflection

Questions for Reflection

1. Have you ever known a truly peaceful woman? Describe her countenance. What were her words like? How did you feel in her presence? Do you think her life was free of all conflicts? Why do you think she was so at peace?

2. Read 2 Corinthians 4:7–10 and John 16:33. In this life we have troubles and conflict. Write out three promises from Scripture as to how you can be a woman at peace even amidst the storms of life.

3. Think of a person you feel has wronged you. List out the ways he or she has wronged you. On another sheet of paper, list out your wrongs against this same person. Which was easier to do? What might this reveal about your heart? Read Matthew 7:1–5 before you answer.

4. List the relationships in your life that are conflicted. Review the Four G's on p. 94–95 and read Proverbs 15:1 and Romans 12:21. Explain in your own words how Christians are called to respond to conflicted relationships, especially when people wrong us. Have you responded to your conflicted relationships in a biblically faithful way?

5. How do you usually respond to conflict as described on the Slippery Slope of conflict (see p. 115)? Peacemaking does not come naturally to us. Only God's grace can empower us to be peacemakers. What steps can you take this week to grow in your ability to work through conflict in a biblically faithful way?

6. Peacemaking is hard work. Even with the best of intentions, sometimes conflicts can worsen, and we may need to get help to work them through. Read James 5:19–20; Hebrews 3:12–13; Romans 15:14; and Proverbs 15:22. Whom can you turn to for help?

7. Can you identify an ongoing conflict in your life where you have not forgiven or where you have not been forgiven? Read Matthew 18:21–35. Do you relate more to the servant who owed many years' wages to his master or to the servant who owed a small amount of wages to another servant?

8. In what ways is it difficult for you to forgive others? How does the parable in Matthew 18:21–35 affect your desire to forgive those who have wronged you? If you become aware that you have not forgiven someone who has hurt you, whom can you talk with about this situation? What steps might you need to take?

Praying Scripture to God

Apart from you, Christ, I can do nothing good. Please cause me to abide in you, Lord Jesus. May I be wise with the wisdom that comes from heaven. May I be pure, peace-loving, considerate, submissive, full of mercy and good fruit, impartial, and sincere. My heart is at rest in your holy presence. May I do all things for your glory. Father God, please cause me to be completely humble, gentle, and patient. May I bear with my brothers and sisters in Christ in love, and may I make every effort to keep the unity of the Spirit through the bond of peace. When I am wronged, please help me to be quick to overlook and quick to confess my own sins. When necessary, may I humbly go to my brother or sister to help promote true reconciliation. May I show myself to be your disciple by my love for others and by the way I forgive others just as you have forgiven me. I thank you, God, that in Christ I am loved and fully accepted by you.

(Prayer based on John 15:5; James 3:17; 1 John 3:19; 1 Cor. 10:31; Eph. 4:1–3; Prov. 19:11; Matt. 7:5; Gal. 6:1–2; Matt. 18:15; John 13:34–35; Col. 3:13; Rom. 14:3.)

Recommended Resources for Further Study and Consideration

Jay E. Adams, *From Forgiven to Forgiving* (Wheaton: Victor Books, 1989).

Ted Kober, *Confession and Forgiveness: Professing Faith as Ambassadors of Reconciliation* (St. Louis: Concordia Publishing House, 2002).

Patrick H. Morison, *Forgive! As the Lord Forgave You* (Phillipsburg, NJ: P&R Publishing, 1987).

Corlette Sande, *The Young Peacemaker* (Wapwallopen, PA: Shepherd Press, 1997).

Ken Sande, *The Peacemaker: A Biblical Guide to Resolving Personal Conflict*, 3rd ed. (Grand Rapids: Baker, 2003).

Ken Sande and Ted Kober, *Guiding People through Conflict* (Billings, MT: Peacemaker Ministries, 1998).

5

SHALOM-FILLED
RELATIONSHIPS

By this all men will know that you are my disciples, if
you love one another.

John 13:35

On the last day, Jesus will not ask about our IQ, social
status, health, or wealth. He will ask how our relationships were. And the chief characteristic of a good relationship is love.

Alfred Poirier[1]

Before we examine how conflict impacts specific kinds of
relationships, we want to consider relationships in general.
Whether at work or church, in the community or at home, certain
key principles apply in building relationships and friendships hall-
marked by peace. The foundation for all peace-filled relationships
is the gospel of Jesus Christ. Reconciled relationships—relationships of *shalom*—entail much more than merely the absence of
conflict. They reflect the positive qualities of love, kindness, trust,
and compassion. Without intimate friendships and redemptive re-

lationships, our lives can feel like a wasteland. But in the presence of true friendship, our hearts dance and sing with blessed joy.

One of the most interesting passages in Scripture that reveals the importance and significance of relationships is Romans 16. In the final part of his letter to the Romans, the apostle Paul acknowledges nearly thirty individuals with whom he appears to share a special bond. Of this group, ten are women. Paul expresses his appreciation to them, affirming their contributions both to his own life and to the lives of others. Yet this written greeting from Paul to his friends does not express his affection and love enough. Paul asks them to "greet one another with a holy kiss" (Rom. 16:16). One imagines Paul smiling as he writes, reflecting on the joy of a loving Christian community expressing their affection for one another. Even as he sends his own greetings to the Romans from his entire ministry team, Paul acknowledges those who are with him. People were important to Paul. People are important to all of us.

So how do we learn to be a friend? We meditate on and experience God's friendship toward us. He calls us friends (John 15:15)! How do we learn to walk in love? We remember and drink in God's lavish love for us. God loves us (1 John 3:1)! As we consider how our gracious Father invites us into a relationship out of his own good and loving character, we have a glimpse of how relationships are *established*. As we reflect on how our faithful Father holds us in the palm of his hand, never leaving us or forsaking us, we understand how relationships are *sustained*. As we ponder the God of glory who makes all things new, we are filled with the anticipation of *perfected* relationships. As the Prince of Peace saturates us with grace, our relationships begin to overflow with *shalom*.

Obstacles to Relationships of *Shalom*

Relationships of *shalom* are blessings and joys. Our hearts are edified when a good friend greets us with a genuinely warm hug and a sweet kiss on the cheek. Knowing that we can call a friend any time of the day or night and she will be there for us brings us security and pleasure. When a friend forgives us, loves us, and bears with us, our lives are enriched. Friendships of *shalom* provide safe harbors for our hearts when the storms of life come. True friendship is a reflection and foretaste of heaven. But many of us put up obstacles to relationships. Some of the most common ones include:

A refusal to value relationships. God created us to be in relationships with one another. Even before sin entered the world, God looked at Adam in his perfect state and determined that it was better for Adam to have a companion. True companionship will only come if we value relationships and make them priorities in our lives. When we refuse to open our hearts and lives to one another, we cannot have genuine friendships. Jesus described the kingdom of God as being like many things (a mustard seed, new wine), but he *never* said, "The kingdom of God is like the Lone Ranger."

Relationships provide the opportunity for God to develop in us the fruit of the Holy Spirit. Such development, however, can be extremely painful. How do we grow in patience? Is it when we are sharing fellowship with a group of lovely ladies at a women's conference? No—they are all far too gracious and enjoyable. We grow in patience when we are called to relate to annoying and frustrating people. How do we grow in gentleness? When we are treated harshly by others but don't respond in kind. We grow in faithfulness when we are abandoned and rejected by others but continue to persevere in love. God uses *people* to help us grow to be more like *Christ*.

In 1 Corinthians 12, Paul reminds us that we are all members of one body (v. 12). He then goes on to explain how we all need one another: "The eye cannot say to the hand, 'I don't need you!' And the head cannot say to the feet, 'I don't need you!'" (v. 21). Rugged individualism is neither biblical nor viable. It's not right and it doesn't work. As Christians, we are called to share our lives so that we can all live out the second greatest commandment by loving one another. In the words of Edgar Metzler, "Created by God, we are born into relationships and destined to fulfill our potential in and through relationships."[2]

A refusal to set aside self to serve others. Apart from God's sanctifying work in us, we are easily trapped into interacting with people solely on the basis of what they can do for us. If they meet our needs and we enjoy them, we choose to have relationships with them. But if they are immature, annoying, or just plain different from us, we do not pursue them. We love like tax collectors by loving those who love us (Matt. 5:46). We do not naturally love as God does—reaching out to the unlovable, the rejected, and the despised.

To show Christ to the world through our relationships, we are sometimes called to go against the grain of our natural inclinations in order to serve and love others better. Instead of doing what is pleasant and easy for us, our focus is to be on God's glory and the good of others. "We who are strong ought to bear with the failings of the weak and not to please ourselves. Each of us should please his neighbor for his good, to build him up. For even Christ did not please himself" (Rom. 15:1–3).

One way we refuse to set aside self to serve others is refusing to understand and enjoy the fundamental differences in people.[3] We often have an easier time loving people who are like us. Fast talkers and workers enjoy people who talk and work fast. Careful and contemplative people feel safer in reaching out to careful and contemplative people. We often value the qualities in others that we ourselves have, and we have a hard time loving people who are different from us.

I (Tara) am an incredibly task-oriented person. I *love* to make lists. At one point I actually had over a thousand tasks on my Microsoft Office Task List. My husband, Fred, asked, "Is that really a list? Or is it just an electronic pile?" But it was a list—categorized, sorted by date, and prioritized. I love organization! I'd enjoy a date night to the container store. I love making order out of chaos. It truly is one of my pleasures in life, and I've been this way my entire life. Once Fred found a letter I wrote to Santa when I was only six years old. It read: "Dear Santa, I am trying to be good. Please send me office supplies. Love, Tara."

You can imagine how I have struggled over the years. I often sacrificed people for the tasks and goals in my life. For example, if my to-do list at work said that a 300-piece mailing would go out but somehow the day had gotten away and it looked as though we wouldn't make my self-imposed "deadline," I would often become harried and put unloving pressure on my staff. Instead of seeking their best, I made an idol out of my desire for organization and efficiency. I was so busy doing tasks that I often failed to set aside my own interests, serve others, and in so doing, love my neighbor as myself.

A refusal to understand. First Thessalonians 5:14 recognizes that to be at peace with others, we are called to understand their true hearts. Paul instructs his readers to respond to people as they *really* are at the heart level: "And we urge you, brothers, warn those who are idle, encourage the timid, help the weak, be patient with everyone." Paul describes how three types of individuals, all with different kinds of heart issues, are to be treated. The appropriate response to idle people is warning; to the timid, we provide encouragement; and to the weak, assistance. Patience is in order for everyone, and our love looks different as it is expressed to various people.

Women aren't always who they seem to be. What would happen if we seriously misunderstood someone? Suppose we helped an overwhelmed, stressed out woman who was actually an idle person? She would be encouraged to remain idle. What would happen if we encouraged a weak woman—even one who did not acknowledge that she wanted or needed help—instead of giving her practical help? She would remain weak, and probably grow discouraged, because she would continue to lack the resources she needed to solve her problems. What would happen if we warned a timid woman—even though she actually looked like she confidently "had it all together"? We would only increase her fear. Great harm occurs when we refuse to understand who a person is and respond appropriately.

A refusal to be vulnerable. Another obstacle to developing *shalom*-filled relationships is an inability or unwillingness to be vulnerable with one another. We crave intimacy and fear it all at the same time. To protect ourselves from others, or even to protect others from ourselves, we put up walls. These walls have the capacity to keep us from seeing others and ourselves as we really are. Without being able to see others clearly, we easily remain disengaged and lonely.

Many women who have experienced severe hurts, such as a divorce or the death of a child, have expressed deep disappointment over how friends and acquaintances withdrew from them at their time of greatest need. Our lives are messy, and we need a great deal of faith and humility to be vulnerable with another person. But friendship is not about superficial tea parties and meaningless conversation. It is about being there through struggles like cleaning up after a sick child and handling the terrifying trauma of a spouse's abandonment.

At this point perhaps you are thinking that it is unsafe to be vulnerable with people. God can know you, because he is good and loving. But people? They are fallen sinners who hurt, misunderstand, and judge. Why would any of us, especially if we have been hurt by others, allow anyone to know us? We are able to take this risk because Jesus himself modeled this kind of risk-taking in his relationships. Faced with the knowledge that his friends would desert him (Matt. 26:56), deny him (Matt. 26:75), and disappoint him by failing to provide him the emotional and spiritual support they should have (Matt. 26:40), Jesus nevertheless promised to remain in relationship with his people "to the very end of the age" (Matt. 28:20).

To be like Jesus, our faithfulness and love require a commitment to relationship—a commitment that requires us to know and be known. We are to entrust ourselves to the Lord and be vulnerable enough to love and be loved. Scripture teaches us, "There is no fear in love. But perfect love drives out fear" (1 John 4:18). True friendship requires us to vulnerably share our physical, spiritual, and emotional struggles with one another so that we can "rejoice with those who rejoice; mourn with those who mourn" (Rom. 12:15). Those are the marks of a true friend.

Of course, until the day that all divisions are broken down forever and sin is destroyed, our love for one another must be constrained by wisdom. Wisdom tells us that the heart is "deceitful above all things and beyond cure" (Jer. 17:9). Wisdom tells us that if we open ourselves up to any fallen person, it is only a matter of time before we will be hurt. Wisdom tells us that some people are not trustworthy and that to consider them worthy of trust would be an act of foolishness. As our friend Pastor Dennis Reiter taught us, love is like the gas pedal that pushes relationships forward toward greater intimacy, and wisdom is the brake that responds to the road signs and signals when reality calls for caution and care.

A refusal to accept one another (including ourselves). We are often tempted to compare ourselves to others and conclude that we simply do not fit in. I (Tara) felt this way for years. I looked at all Christian women as being sweet, petite, gentle women who were gifted at hospitality and mothering. As much as I valued these crucial areas of women's ministry, for years I was an attorney who didn't know how to cook, had no children, and couldn't figure out how to work a glue gun. I used to think to myself, *I will never have female friends.* In my immaturity, I truly believed there was one proper model for the "Christian woman" and I was not it. I was a round peg trying to fit in a square hole. Rejecting others before I could be rejected, I did not accept the women in my life "just as Christ accepted [me]" (Rom. 15:7).

Another obstacle to relationship is that we don't accept *ourselves* as we are. By taking the time to understand how God has created us and by learning to steward our gifts appropriately, we are better prepared to embrace others as we realize how we can learn from them and how their gifts complement our own. What is more, when we know our weaknesses—which we need not be ashamed of because Christ's grace perfects them—we grow in our ability to be vulnerable and less critical of others. It has taken me (Tara) *years* to begin to embrace who God made me to be as I learn how to share my gifts with grace. For instance, just because I need to focus on slowing down and relating in a gentle manner with people does not mean that my fast-thinking, driven personality is "bad." In fact, in appropriate settings, my gifts in acting decisively and force-fully can be quite loving and good. Once Fred and I were leaving a grocery store with a full basket of groceries. In the parking lot we saw that the engine of a pickup truck was on fire—flames were licking the side of the truck and jumping into the air. Fred froze. I quickly assessed that no one was inside and no one was in danger near the truck. I went back into the store, told them to call 911, asked for a fire extinguisher, and returned to the parking lot. Fred was still standing there. His many other gifts did not help in this situation. In a crisis setting my ability to assess a situation and act decisively was a good thing.

Realistically, most of life is not filled with crisis situations, so I need to learn when to put my gifts to use because they are helpful or loving and when to set them aside because they are annoying or damaging. But in any case, I am learning to accept myself as God's precious daughter, not because I'm "good enough" but because

Christ has bought me with his precious blood. Finding ourselves wholly defined by God is a critical step in being able to accept people and have genuine relationships with them.

A refusal to persevere. At other times, relationships do not develop into true friendships or friendships fade because we are unwilling to persevere when the going gets tough. People let us down, fail to meet our needs, or demonstrate some selfish or ugly traits, and we give up on them. Instead of seeking to emphasize their beauty or edify them, we see only their rough edges and faults and pull away. Instead of seeing the people in our lives as beloved children of God or unsaved sinners in need of redemption, we reject them.

I (Judy) was once profoundly hurt by my closest female friends. I had been going through an incredibly intense time in my life with professional and academic stresses that made me feel like I was not succeeding on any front. At our ladies' night out, I shared my burdens with my friends with the hope of receiving grace and encouragement. Instead, they confronted me over my choices that were contributing to my stress. I felt terribly betrayed and misunderstood. We tried to work out the relationship strain the next day, but weeks and even months went by without true unity being restored. Finally the husband of one of my friends initiated a meeting to talk through the fact that all of the relationships in our small community were being impacted negatively by the distance between me and the other wives.

I will always remember what my friends said to me at that meeting: "Judy, we love you. But we love you imperfectly. We aren't going to do a good job at times. But we're asking you to assume our love for you and view any disappointments and hurts we cause you through the certainty of our love." I was stunned. I realized that I had grown to doubt their love. I even doubted whether we had a relationship at all. I had been willing to let go of the relationships, convincing myself that they were not valuable and they did not matter. Because one man was willing to persevere through the painfulness of damaged unity, our friendships were healed that day. We reaffirmed our covenant with one another: *we do life together.* This experience of restoring broken fellowship has helped me learn what it means to persevere in friendship.

Establishing Relationships of *Shalom*

Some of the most common complaints we hear from women have to do with lack of relationship: "I'm so lonely." "I feel disconnected from people." "No one ever invites me over." "No one ever calls me or visits me when I am sick." "I don't have any real friends." Although it may be difficult to do so, we try to gently challenge them to consider whether *they* have been making relationships a priority. We ask, "What have you done to serve people?" "Krissy was in the hospital, did you visit her?" "I'm assuming that though no one's invited you over, you are persevering in reaching out?" Of course, it is hard to do so, especially when we feel lonely and hurt, but we are called to make relationships of *shalom* a priority. Instead of sitting back and saying, "There are no friends for me," we can take steps to use the gifts God has given us for the edification of the body through relationships (1 Cor. 12).

In the words of C. S. Lewis, "Friendship . . . is born at the moment when one says to another 'What! You too? I thought that no one but myself . . .'"[4] From that wonderful spark of knowing and being known, it takes time and effort to develop a relationship of *shalom*. The reality is, we will never *find* a friend, we can only *grow* a friend. Of all of our many friendly relationships that come and go over time, only a small number will develop into deep friendship. Friendships take a huge investment of time and energy, but they are worth it. Friends enrich our lives and keep loneliness at bay. Relationships of *shalom* are nurtured as we take the following steps.

Pray for friends. I (Tara) have a story of a miracle of friendship. As I shared earlier, I never felt like I fit in around other Christian women. Years ago, in a new location, intensely busy with work, I felt that there was absolutely no possibility that I could ever have true, intimate, female friends. Then my pastor gently confronted me one day by saying, "Tara, you need to pray for friends." A woman I respect greatly said, "Tara, you need to pray for friends." My faith was weak. I had no hope. But I did begin to pray. I must have made an offhand comment when I was teaching at a conference—something about praying for friends and wanting to get a small group of women together just for friendship—because months later a woman walked into my office and asked if I had ever gotten those women together to be friends. I did not even remember talking about this, but she did. And she said that it was time to do it.

That afternoon, I called up a woman that I had always wanted to get to know better and asked if she would be interested in meeting together in a small group of women for friendship—not to study the Bible or read a book together but just to be friends. Our hope would be that we would grow in love and go through life encouraging one another as friends. She said she would be there the next morning. Then I called a second woman. Later I saw my pastor and I asked him if his wife might be interested in meeting with a small group of women. He said, "Just last night she turned to me and said how much she could really use some true friends." She didn't want another Bible study or small group. She just wanted friends. We met the next morning, and we have been meeting once a week for years now. Two of us have had babies during that time, and the other friends were the babies' first visitors in the hospital. One has lost a young husband, and we helped to select the burial plot and write his obituary. Two are going through menopause, and we pray about struggles and treatment. Through it all, we are there for one another. We are imperfect in our friendship, but we are together. This is friendship, and you can experience it too. If you long for friends, *pray*!

Establish your friendships on the gospel and model them after Christ. Jesus spent a great deal of time with his disciples. He called them his friends: "I no longer call you servants, because a servant does not know his master's business. Instead, I have called you friends, for everything that I learned from my Father I have made known to you. You did not choose me, but I chose you" (John 15:15–16).

Living and working together, Jesus developed a rich community out of the most unlikely collection of people. During his years of relationship with his disciples, Jesus grew to trust them and be trusted by them. Jesus was transparent with his disciples, willing to reveal himself to them in order to be known as he really was. He also told them the truth even when they didn't want to hear it or were unable to understand it. Relationships filled with *shalom* are founded on the gospel and modeled after Christ's relationships. True friendships are products of invested time, trust, transparency, and truth.

To genuinely understand others and to be understood by others takes wisdom and effort. How do we learn to accurately understand people? Atticus in *To Kill a Mockingbird* said, "You never really understand a person until you consider things from his point of view . . . until you climb into his skin and walk around in it."[5] Only through the relational hard work of knowing another person so well that it is as though we are in her own skin can we begin to understand her. In having wisdom or taking the time to understand another person, we are like our great high priest, Jesus, who gives us the grace we need at the precise moment we need it: "Let us then approach the throne of grace with confidence, so that we may receive mercy and find grace to help us in our time of need" (Heb. 4:16).

Choose to love. The popular phrase "love is a decision" has much truth in it. Of course, love includes more than an act of the will; whole-hearted love also involves our thoughts and our affections. Yet the decision to love is one that honors God. In response to the question, "Of all the commandments, which is the most important?" Jesus replied, "The most important one . . . is this: 'Hear, O Israel, the Lord our God, the Lord is one. Love the Lord your God with all your heart and with all your soul and with all your mind and with all your strength.' The second is this: 'Love your neighbor as yourself.' There is no commandment greater than these" (Mark 12:28–31).

We are to love the people we enjoy, to be sure. But such love comes readily and easily. It takes no great effort to spend time with the people we enjoy after the church service. We are excited to see them. We want to hear about how they are. But God's grace and glory are shown when we don't just spend time with the people we naturally click with but choose to love people who are different from us. We seek out the visitor. We send a card to the new family. Even though we may not be interested in developing new friendships for our own benefit, we still take the time to bless, encourage, and love. For Christians there are only two real tasks on our task list: to love God and to love people. If we accomplish great things but fail at either of these tasks, we have accomplished nothing (1 Cor. 13:1).

The indwelling Christ enables our relationships to be filled with love (1 John 4:15–16). Love grows in us as we live in God and God lives in us. He grows us and he grows our love for others. God is making love complete among us (1 John 4:16–17). Take confidence in him and prayerfully seek to have all of your relationships model his love.

Sustaining Relationships of *Shalom*

The nature of our Triune God provides a clear pattern for not only establishing but also sustaining our relationships. Within the eternal fellowship of the holy Trinity, God loves and delights in himself (Luke 3:22), trusts himself (Matt. 26:39), and knows himself intimately (John 7:28–29). As we examine the relationship of the members of the Trinity with each other, we see qualities that apply to our own relationships—with Christ and others. God's love makes it possible for us to love him and others (Eph. 5:2; 1 John 4:19). God delights in us and sets us free to delight in him and in others (Ps. 147:11; Isa. 61:10). He reveals himself to us and makes it possible for us to reveal ourselves to him and to others (John 14:21; Ps. 139:23–24). Consider some of the ways that we can sustain relationships of *shalom*.

Be willing to sacrifice. Covenantal love always involves real sacrifice: time, money, energy . . . but few things are more costly than our emotions. The maxim "If it is worth having, it is going to cost something" holds true in the arena of *shalom*-filled relationships. This truth was demonstrated beautifully in the life of Amy. Amy attended a holiday party where one woman, Trish, monopolized much of the conversation. A younger Christian woman asked Amy about this after the party, and this was her reply:

> Trish really needed to talk, and it would have been offensive if I had started sharing about what is going on in my life. So I chose to focus on caring for her and drawing her out. She's not interested in anything about me. That's okay. My job is not to have her reach out to me but for me to bless her. Christ has all I need—he is my storehouse!

By faith, Amy chose to sacrifice in order to encourage Trish. Amy could have become angry and offended by Trish's self-centeredness, but instead she chose to serve her. Relationships always reveal our character—who we really are on the inside. Sometimes this is a comforting process; sometimes it shakes us to the core. In Amy's case, her relationship with Trish revealed a heart that truly placed others' interests above her own (see Philippians 2).

Do not look for repayment. *Shalom*-filled relationships are offered freely. When we give, we do not look for repayment. Instead, we are mindful of God's lavish love, and we strive to find ways to encourage and love our friends. We do not do so because we are expecting them to bless us but simply because we love them.

I (Tara) have a friend who did a generous thing for me years ago, and he has never let me forget it. I have grown so to dislike his bringing it up to me over the years that I have even offered to compensate him financially for the time he spent helping me. Contrast that with another friend, a true friend, who has helped me time and time again—with financial assistance, tangible help, encouragement—and has never once brought it up to me again. He lives out Jesus's teaching in John 15: "Greater love has no one than this, that he lay down his life for his friends" (v. 13). Jesus blessed his disciples who fed the hungry and visited those in prison, and he warned them against being like the Pharisees who broadcast their good deeds publicly (Matt. 6:1–4).

Develop proper expectations. We pray that you will experience the joy of deep and abiding friendship. However, even if you do have such good friends in your life, not every relationship will be intimate. One aspect of wisdom is realizing that because it takes so much time to have deeply connected friendships, we will only do so with one or two people. We just cannot keep many people up to date on all of the details of our daily lives—we simply do not have enough hours in the day. We pray for one or two friends to be our "Barnabas," and we understand that other relationships in our lives will not have the same level or frequency of contact and sharing.

Often our friendships emerge out of the external circumstances that draw us together. Working together, having children as friends or sports team members, or spending time together in ministry can unite us into deep relationships. However, circumstances change and the relationships rooted in those circumstances also change. I (Judy) truly grieve when my work brings me into close contact with others but then the circumstances around that contact come to an end. Working with clients, teaching multiple-day workshops or semester-long classes, and leading in women's retreats are bittersweet. They are sweet for the delight of connecting yet bitter with the knowledge that so many relationships come to an end—until eternity. Before I came to develop proper expectations about the nature of these relationships—that they will ebb and flow based on criteria other than mutual affection and respect—I felt an ongoing grief that prevented me from truly enjoying what the relationships provided. In addition, I sometimes committed to and invested in relationships that could not survive once the circumstances changed. Of course I am sorrowful when a close friend moves away or a dear co-worker is called to a new position in a different place. But with proper expectations, I am learning to love even in the face of the natural ebb and flow, trusting that in eternity I will again reconnect with those so dear to me.

Wisdom also helps us to develop proper expectations about when it is appropriate to share and what level of sharing is appropriate. For example, we learn that while a small group Bible study is a great forum for developing relationships, we ought not spend the entire study sharing all of the concerns and joys of our lives. We develop proper expectations, learn what level of sharing is appropriate, and act accordingly.

Demonstrate commitment and loyalty. The Old Testament heroines Ruth and Naomi demonstrate covenantal commitment in their relationship. Naomi's husband and her two sons, including Ruth's husband, had all died. Instructing her daughters-in-law to return to their homes of origin for care and protection, Naomi planned to return to her own people with whom she had not had contact in many years. Ruth refused to allow this older, widowed woman to return to her people alone: "But Ruth replied, 'Don't urge me to leave you or to turn back from you. Where you go I will go, and where you stay I will stay. Your people will be my people and your God my God. Where you die I will die, and there I will be buried. May the LORD deal with me, be it ever so severely, if anything but death separates you and me'" (Ruth 1:16–17).

Ruth's loyalty and faithfulness toward Naomi speak volumes about the God who is central to this relationship and volumes about the impact that God can have on our relationships and us. Relationships filled with *shalom* are relationships that reflect commitment, loyalty, and faithfulness.

Protect your friends. One of the greatest friendships in the Bible, that of Jonathan and David, demonstrates the importance of protecting your friends. When David was in physical danger, Jonathan sought to protect him: "Saul told his son Jonathan and all the attendants to kill David. But Jonathan was very fond of David and warned him, 'My father Saul is looking for a chance to kill you. Be on your guard tomorrow morning; go into hiding and stay there'" (1 Sam. 19:1–2). Jonathan's great fondness for David prompted him to warn David of the danger and compelled him to intercede on his behalf. Covenantal relationships are about protecting one another.

I (Tara) remember with fondness the many ways that my friends have protected me over the years. When I have been tempted to give in to my sin, my friends have rebuked and even restrained me. When I was falsely accused by a sister in Christ, my friends prayed faithfully, wept with me, and even felt the weight of my offense personally as they helped me to work through the conflict. Friends have protected me from financial, physical, and emotional harm. I simply cannot overstate the gratitude I have toward my friends for their loving and faithful protection. I pray that I protect them in the very same way, for we reflect the Lord—our strongest defender—when we defend and protect one another.

Perfecting Relationships of *Shalom*

We catch a glimpse of the perfection of heaven when our relationships are established and sustained according to the gospel of Jesus Christ. First John 4:10–12 illustrates gospel-centered relationships: "This is love: not that we loved God, but that he loved us and sent his Son as an atoning sacrifice for our sins [which is the gospel]. Dear friends, since God so loved us, we also ought to love one another [in gospel-centered relationships]. No one has ever seen God; but if we love one another, God lives in us and his love is made complete in us [which is a taste of heaven]" (explanation added).

Accept what is offered with hope for more. When we offer
our hearts and lives in a holy covenant to another person, we are
offering to them the best that we have. We are also calling for the
best that the other person has to give. Yet, because of our sinfulness and our fallenness, what we get often falls far below what we
hope to receive. Jesus himself experienced this disappointment. He
leaves behind a model for us to follow as we seek to navigate the
waters of our own covenantal relationships.

> When they had finished eating, Jesus said to Simon Peter, "Simon
> son of John, do you truly love [*agape*] me more than these?"
>   "Yes, Lord," he said, "you know that I love [*phileo*] you."
>   Jesus said, "Feed my lambs."
>   Again Jesus said, "Simon son of John, do you truly love [agape]
> me?"
>   He answered, "Yes, Lord, you know that I love [*phileo*] you."
>   Jesus said, "Take care of my sheep."
>   The third time he said to him, "Simon son of John, do you love
> [*phileo*] me?"
>   Peter was hurt because Jesus asked him the third time, "Do you
> love me?" He said, "Lord you know all things; you know that I love
> [*phileo*] you."
>   Jesus said, "Feed my sheep."
>
> John 21:15–17

Following Peter's denial of Jesus, Jesus asked Peter if he pos-
sesses the sacrificial and unfailing love of *agape*. Peter had previously committed his life and service to Jesus: "Lord, I am ready to
go with you to prison and to death" (Luke 22:33). In this passage,
however, the awareness of his failure and denial prevented him from
responding that the love he had for his Savior was the supreme
love of *agape*. Peter offered Jesus a lesser form of love, *phileo* love.
Phileo love is a brotherly love based on affection and kindness but
lacking a sacrificial component. Jesus again asked Peter for the
greater love, even while accepting and blessing the love that Peter
was able to offer. We too, in our covenantal relationships, are called
to accept the love offered by others, even if it is of a lesser quality
than we desire, while maintaining the hope that an even deeper
relationship will grow.

My (Judy's) friend Kelly has been patient with me in our friendship. I have had a difficult time accepting her love for me. At times I have been stunned by how much and how powerfully she has nurtured me with her love. At other times I have felt disappointment that I have been a lower priority to her than I thought I should be. During one of those times I felt hurt because she was not treating me the way I felt I deserved. Kelly said to me, "Judy, you can have all my love. I just don't have much to give right now. But what I have you can have." She helped me to see that at times, the most loving thing we can do is be grateful and appreciative for the love offered to us, even if it falls below what we want or desire. True friendship compelled me to ask Kelly for her best love, even though she could not give it all the time or to the extent I felt I deserved. True friendship made it possible for me to accept, not reject, the quantity and quality of the love she had to give.

Work through conflicts. Just as Jonathan brought David and Saul together when they were severely conflicted, true friends are peacemaking friends. "So Jonathan called David and told him the whole conversation. He brought him to Saul, and David was with Saul as before" (1 Sam. 19:7). Jonathan sought to promote unity between those he loved.

Although avoiding involvement in conflicts may be easier, we are called to get involved. Just as Jonathan risked himself by seeking to make peace between his friend and his father, *shalom*-filled relationships promote peace even more broadly than between the principal parties. True friends help one another to remember that God's glory and unity in the body of Christ are of paramount importance. As such, they prayerfully strive to live out all of the biblical peacemaking principles summarized in chapter 4.

I (Tara) will never forget the painful kindness of two friends who helped me to work through a conflict with another Christian. I wanted to run away and avoid the conflict. But these friends were true friends. Not only did they counsel and encourage me to obey all that the Lord commanded concerning biblical conflict resolution, but they even told me that they were praying *against* any possibility of me leaving the area. They prayed that my house wouldn't sell and that I wouldn't get a new job offer. They loved me enough to help me respond to conflict biblically.

Breathe grace. Grace is God's kindness and goodness to those who deserve the exact opposite (Luke 1:30; Eph. 2:3–5).[6] As we breathe God's grace *into* our own lives by reading the Word and growing in Christlikeness, we breathe *out* his grace into the hearts and lives of others. One of the main ways we breathe grace in our relationships is through our *words*. In every relationship, we are called to speak only in edifying ways. The biblical standard for what our speech ought to be is summarized in Ephesians: "Do not let any unwholesome talk come out of your mouths, but only what is helpful for building others up according to their needs, that it may benefit those who listen" (Eph. 4:29).

We are not just to avoid sinful speech. Our words are to be a balm of God's grace. We are to speak pleasant words that demonstrate charitable presumptions, humility, forgiveness, and healing (Matt. 7:12; Eph. 4:32). "Reckless words pierce like a sword, but the tongue of the wise brings healing" (Prov. 12:18).

Too often, however, our words show the judgment and unkindness in our hearts (James 4:11–12; Rom. 2:1–3; 14:4; 14:10). We grumble and complain (Phil. 2:14) and focus on the faults in others instead of the good (Prov. 11:27). We share private information for no legitimate purpose; we are gossips. This is a sign of our spiritual immaturity. "A perverse man stirs up dissension, and a gossip separates close friends" (Prov. 16:28).

At other times, we speak false and malicious words about another person even though the Bible gives repeated warnings against such slander (Lev. 19:16; Titus 2:3; 3:2). The Greek word *diabolos* (translated "slanderer") is used thirty-four times in the Bible as a title for Satan. Simply said, we imitate Satan when we falsely accuse others. "Do not slander one another. Anyone who speaks against his brother or judges him speaks against the law and judges it" (James 4:11).

For women especially, since many of us are quite verbal, one aspect of breathing grace is that we learn to keep a tight rein on our tongues: "If anyone considers himself religious and yet does not keep a tight rein on his tongue, he deceives himself and his religion is worthless" (James 1:26). If we have a rapid and intense communication style, we may make people uncomfortable or frustrated. Instead of blessing them, our words may box them into a corner or talk circles around them. We may win an argument because of our verbal prowess, but that makes us neither right nor loving. Even "quiet" women are called to keep a tight rein on their tongues. It only takes one or two well-timed and cutting words from a soft-spoken woman to tear others down. As Proverbs 13 reminds us, "He who guards his lips guards his life, but he who speaks rashly will come to ruin" (v. 3).

This is a serious issue! According to Jesus, we will give an account on the judgment day for every careless word we have spoken (Matt. 12:36). Learning to breathe grace is foundational to developing deep, intimate friendships.[7]

Dealing with Difficult People

As we strive to develop relationships of *shalom*, we may come across the uncomfortable situation of having to deal with a difficult or unpleasant person. It may be a family member, co-worker, or member of our church. Whoever it is, we have a great opportunity to respond to this unpleasant person in a way that sets us apart from non-Christians. After all, what other than faith in Christ would ever motivate a person to show kindness to people who are abrasive and unkind?

Destroy 'em. It is always shocking when we are attacked, especially by a Christian. Once I (Tara) received a telephone call from a professing Christian who was astoundingly rude to me. He verbally attacked me. I was frightened and angry and called Judy for advice on how to respond. Judy's advice was simple: "Destroy him. Take out the A-bomb of Christianity and blow him out of the water." My initially enthusiastic reaction showed that I did not know what she meant. But Judy's advice on dealing with difficult people is based on Romans 12, so she asked me to turn there with her. Together we read:

> Therefore, I urge you, brothers, in view of God's mercy, to offer your bodies as living sacrifices. . . . For by the grace given me I say to every one of you: Do not think of yourself more highly than you ought. . . . Love must be sincere. Hate what is evil; cling to what is good. Be devoted to one another in brotherly love. Honor one

another above yourselves. . . . Bless those who persecute you; bless and do not curse. . . . Do not repay anyone evil for evil. Be careful to do what is right in the eyes of everybody. If it is possible, as far as it depends on you, live at peace with everyone. . . . Do not be overcome by evil, but overcome evil with good.

verses 1, 3, 9–10, 14, 17–18, 21

As difficult as it was for me to hear, Scripture is clear. As Christians, in light of all we have received in Christ, we are bound to a different standard when it comes to relating with unpleasant people. The world may say, "He hurt you, so hurt him back." But God's Word says that we are to "destroy them" *with love*. In my case, this meant that although I *wanted* to use my verbal skills to defend myself and prove him wrong, I was instead called to consider diligently the truth in his accusations and respond in humility and love. I also looked for ways to encourage him through emails and calls, even though my preference would have been to avoid him. God's grace enabled me to speak carefully of him to others, even though in my pride I would have wanted to slander him and bring disrespect on him.

Fill the chasm between you with love. It may help to think of relating with difficult people in this way: *out of gratitude for God's love toward you, fill the chasm in the relationship with love.* Do your best to listen patiently. If you simply cannot reconcile your perspectives or even find common ground on which to stand, then you have a choice. Will you fill the gulf between you and them with bitterness, rage, malice, anger, and slander? Or will you fill it with love? God's grace enables you to remember that God sovereignly ordained that difficult person to be in your life, and he is working all things together for his glory and your good. God calls you to fill the chasm with the fruit of the Holy Spirit, beginning with love (Gal. 5:22–23).

Don't focus on being right. We may be tempted to verbally attack an unpleasant person in order to show that *we are right*. But even though she may indeed be much in the wrong, we are called to remember that *being right* is not the most important thing. As Christians, *being loving* is the most important thing. God cares that we have a holy heart and reflect his character in this world. One day, the Righteous Judge will reveal to us the truth—for he is Truth. Every wrong will be righted. Between now and that day, God's grace enables us to focus less on defending ourselves or our position and more on testifying to God's mercy and greatness. Being treated rudely is stressful. Often we do not know why God allows tension in our relationships. But one day it will all become clear and what will have mattered is this: Did we love God? Did we love others? Did we focus on being right, or did we walk in mercy, grace, and love?

Always rely on the Lord. We easily love people who love us (Matthew 5), but it takes a work of God's Spirit within us to enable us to love those who intentionally hurt us. When we love our enemies, we are radically obeying God. Whole-hearted biblical love involves our thoughts, emotions, and wills. As fallen people in a fallen world, our love for others is never fully whole-hearted. That is why we sometimes have a difficult time *liking* (engaging our affections and emotions) difficult or annoying people while at the same time we are committed to *loving* them (with our minds and wills).

Praise God that he will one day transform our half-hearted love into whole-hearted love. Until then, out of obedience to Christ, we are called to rely on the Lord and persevere in doing good to the difficult people in our lives. We may not call them up every day or hang out with them regularly, but we are called to be patient with them (just as God is patient with us), suffer well, and love them (out of gratitude for God's love to us).

In Conclusion

Intimate friendships are important because we are commanded to be in relationship. Relationship is a hallmark of what it means to be a human being. When we live in relationship, we live out the second greatest commandment to love our neighbor as ourselves (Mark 12:31). Friendship is part of the essence of how we are made. We are not called to go through life on our own—it is not good, and it is not God's way (Gen. 2:18). Friends encourage (*pour courage into*) our hearts. We are vulnerable when we feel alone, but our lives are enriched by regular, sincere, and loving encouragement. We also benefit greatly from the accountability people provide, for only our true friends love us enough to call us on the carpet and tell us that we are out of line. True friends stay with us and help us risk again when we have been betrayed, rejected, or hurt by others.

In this life, we are easily misunderstood, and people easily give up on us. Friends understand us, delight in us, and show forbearance and grace toward our "areas in need of further sanctification." True friends accept us and love us just the way we are, but they also love us enough to help us to grow to be more like Christ. True friends give us grace.

I (Tara) remember a time that I misspoke to a friend's husband at church. I meant to say something encouraging, but days later I realized that what I had said, which sounded somewhat mean, was the opposite of what I meant. I immediately called up my friend, who laughed a little as I retold what I had done. She promised to talk with her husband and call me back. Listen to the grace my friend's husband gave me as he said,

> Yes, Tara did say that at church. But I knew what she meant, so I translated what she said into what she meant *and I gave her credit for that*—because I know Tara and I know she didn't mean to say it the way it came out.

Such grace! Such love! "Beloved, let us love one another, for love is from God; and every one who loves is born of God and knows God. The one who does not love does not know God, for God is love" (1 John 4:7–8 NASB).

Shalom-filled relationships are gospel relationships. When we were enemies of God, he showed us kindness. The extent of his love was demonstrated in Jesus's incarnation, perfect life, substitutionary death, and resurrection. Out of gratitude for this love, we are called to live in genuine relationships and love the people God sovereignly places in our lives. Instead of giving up on each other, we speak the gospel to one another and encourage our mutual faith in Christ. We cast ourselves on his grace and trust that he is changing us. Instead of preaching a message of doom ("Get your act together or I'm out of here!"), we exhort one another to go to the cross and patiently trust in God's ongoing sanctifying work in each of us. Just as God doesn't give up on us, we do not give up on one another.

As you reflect on all of this information on relationships, you may be thinking, *That sounds accurate, but that sure doesn't sound realistic or describe my relationships.* If so, be encouraged. God is at work in us, and he will be faithful to conform us to Christ and help us in our relational struggles. Three qualities of God's character are essential ingredients for change: grace, truth, and patience. The process of growing to be like Christ is not a process of "quick fixes." God gives us time to change and grow. We need to give others and ourselves the same.

Personal Reflection

Questions for Reflection

1. If you had to describe most of your relationships, what words would you use? Check those that apply.

☐ shallow	☐ entertaining
☐ nonexistent	☐ redemptive
☐ superficial	☐ God-centered
☐ uncomfortable	☐ genuine
☐ conflicted	☐ safe
☐ unpleasant	☐ other: _____
☐ gracious	

2. Review the list of obstacles to relationships on pages 122–28. Do you put up any of these obstacles in your relationships? If so, which ones? Why do you think you do this? Pick one obstacle from the list that impedes your relationships and look up three Scriptures that speak to this situation. Write a "memo to self," confronting and encouraging yourself with your selected Scriptures.

3. Would you describe yourself more as a "relational" person or a "task-oriented" person? How much of a priority are your relationships and friendships? Read Leviticus 19:18. What does it mean to "love your neighbor as yourself"? In what ways are you successful and in what ways do you fail to love others this way?

4. Describe the type of friend that you are attracted to. Why are some people unattractive and unappealing to you? Are any of the things you dislike in people the very same weaknesses and sins *you* struggle with? List ten characteristics of God. What aspects of God's character do you most wish described you? What promises of God encourage you to continue becoming the kind of friend you want to be?

5. The nature of our Triune God provides a clear pattern for our relationships. Within the eternal fellowship of the holy Trinity, God loves and delights in himself (Luke 3:22), trusts himself (Matt. 26:39), and knows himself intimately (John 7:28–29). How do you see these qualities reflected in your own relationships? What acts of self-sacrifice did you make in the last week for your friends? In the last month? How is God calling you to serve the people in your life?

6. Do you breathe grace through your words? What is the nature of your speech? Read Ephesians 4:29. How do you fail to meet this standard? In what ways would your relationships change if *every* word you *ever* spoke met God's standard for your speech as summarized in Ephesians 4:29?

7. Who is a difficult person in your life? What makes it difficult to relate well with him or her? Write out three *good* things about this person. Meditate on all of Romans 12. What sincere actions could you take this week to show love to this person?

8. As you read chapter 5 on relationships and friendships, what did you underline? What thoughts jumped out at you? Why is that so?

9. Read John 15:9–13. Meditate on what this passage teaches about love. In three sentences, summarize how the Lord loves you. Do you love the people in your life as the Lord loves you? Write a prayer asking God to help you to live a life of love.

Praying Scripture to God

Lord God, please help me to put off my old way of living, to be renewed in the truth, and to put on my new, righteous, and holy self. Please, God, enable me to slander no one, to be peaceable and considerate, and to truly show humility toward the people in my life. Dear God, please enable me to speak only edifying words that are always full of grace. I lift my eyes to you, Lord, for my help comes from you. You do not slumber and you will keep me safe in your hands. Father, I thank you that in your unfailing love you lead and redeem me. Lord, I ask you to provide me with friends. May you cause me to be a redemptive friend, experiencing the joy of intimate friendship—all for your glory. Thank you, God.

(Prayer based on Eph. 4:22–24; Titus 3:1–2; Eph. 4:29; Col. 4:6; Ps. 121; Exod. 15:13.)

Recommended Resources for Further Study and Consideration

Ajith Fernando, *Reclaiming Friendship: Relating to Each Other in a Frenzied World* (Scottsdale, PA: Herald Press, 1993).

Susan Hunt, *Spiritual Mothering* (Wheaton: Crossway, 1992).

C. S. Lewis, *The Four Loves* (New York: Harcourt Brace & Company, 1960).

Alan Loy McGinnis, *Friendship Factor* (Minneapolis: Augsburg Publishing House, 1979).

Alfred Poirier, *Words That Cut: Learning to Take Criticism in Light of the Gospel* (Billings, MT: Peacemaker Ministries, 2003).

Paul David Tripp, *War of Words: Getting to the Heart of Your Communication Struggles* (Phillipsburg, NJ: P&R Publishing, 2000).

6

ROMANTIC LOVE

Love each other deeply, because love covers over a
multitude of sins.

1 Peter 4:8

Love is not love
Which alters when it alteration finds,
Or bends with the remover to remove:
O, no! it is an ever-fixed mark,
That looks on tempests and is never shaken.

Shakespeare, Sonnet CXVI[1]

First love. Puppy love. The "crush." All are precursors to a special love—*eros*—that romantic, intimate love between a man and woman. Nothing is quite like it. Throughout human history, art and literature have been devoted to communicating the thrill and tragedy of *eros*. Movies and television shows almost always have this romantic, intimate form of love as a prominent theme. While the Bible does not use the actual term *eros*, it does give numerous examples of romantic relationships—Adam and Eve, Jacob and Rachel, David and Michal, and the lovers in Song of Songs. Romantic, erotic love captures the imagination. God himself de-

147

scribes his love for his people in intimate, romantic terms (Hosea 2:14–23; Eph. 5:25–33).

The majority of women, even from their preteen and teenage years, spend a great deal of time thinking about "that special guy." Some of them plan their weddings before their first dates! As we enter into adulthood, our dating and courtship years are filled with thoughts and dreams of romance. Finally, after years of waiting and hoping, we may experience the excitement of becoming engaged and finally getting married.

For most married couples, that initial anticipation and excitement eventually fades as day-to-day demands drain away the energy required to maintain and preserve the feelings of romance. Frustrations increase and conflicts begin to surface. Ironically, our worst conflicts often come in this, our most intimate relationship. Of all the mediations we (Judy and Tara) do as Christian conciliators, marital mediations are the most difficult. Husbands and wives have often spent years perfecting the art of hurting one another. Such conflicts in marriage damage the fabric of the one-flesh design that God intended (Mark 10:6–9). Only God's grace can bring repentance, forgiveness, and reconciliation—*shalom*—to our marriages. Marriage teaches us about God's character: God loves us and pursues us, even when we reject him (see the book of Hosea). God pays a dear price to reconcile us to himself by offering his Son as the sacrifice for our sins. God continually works in the church to purify her as a spotless bride. Our vulnerability and safety in our relationship with God is unparalleled, and God designed marriage to be a reflection of our relationship with him. Our marriages should be the *most* peaceful, intimate, and fulfilling relationships in our lives.

In this chapter we will look at some of the most common *eros*-related conflicts by examining the *expectation-experience gap* that underlies many of these conflicts. We then will reflect on how to address that "gap" when *eros* is not returned and when *eros* shifts to contempt and hatred. Next we will discuss temptations related to romantic love. Finally, we will provide encouragement for those dark situations when *eros* has been distorted through addiction, perversion, and abuse.

The Expectation-Experience Gap

From the first inkling of romance to the golden anniversary of an *eros*-filled relationship, the common element is desire. As we discussed in chapter 2 on idolatry, our desires, even legitimate desires, may quickly become demands that we place upon others. When our expectations are not met, we have a choice: we can abstain from sinful desires which war against our soul, or we can sinfully insist that our demands be met (1 Peter 2:11). If we sin by making our expectations into demands, conflict will inevitably erupt (James 4:1–3).

Often the first clue that we have these potentially lethal expectations is when we feel hurt or disappointed because our experience falls short of our expectations. While some expectations are legitimate, many of our expectations are unrealistic because they require far more than anyone can give. We look for people to say, do, or be something specific—and then they fail to meet our expectations. We encounter a "gap" between what we hope for and what we actually experience. In those uncommon situations where our experience *exceeds* our expectations, we are pleasantly surprised. Most of the time, however, the result of this gap is disappointment.

How do we wage war against these desires? We fill the gap between our desires and our experience with the supreme love of other-centered *agape*. Without the constraint of *agape*, *shalom*-based *eros* is not attainable. When *eros* and *agape* are found together, we experience a satisfaction and joy that foreshadows the intense, wonderful pleasure awaiting us when we stand face-to-face with Christ. In the absence of the sacrificial and pure love of *agape*, expectations associated with our romantic relationships can cause injury to the human heart in a number of different ways.

Unexamined expectations can ruin romantic relationships. Unexamined expectations are generally unseen and unexpressed, differing from those clear, mutually understood, explicit expectations that we have of others ("I expect you to be home by 10:00 p.m."). When people have *unexamined* expectations, they are often not aware of them even though they involve specific "requirements" of others. Unexamined and uncommunicated expectations can sink a relationship quickly.

Consider one example of uncommunicated and unexamined expectations from courtship. We have sometimes observed in the Christian community a rather specific but unspoken set of rules concerning courtship and dating. Some of these rules include ideas such as that a woman should not show any interest in a man because he must prove himself a leader by pursuing her in the absence of her interest. As the relationship progresses, a woman should not be the first to tell a man how she feels because for him to show proper assertiveness, he must be the first to express his feelings. Men must exhibit a high level of originality and creativity in planning dates and purchasing gifts; otherwise their ability to succeed romantically is in question. Although some of these "rules" may have their foundation in appropriate biblical truths of manhood and womanhood, when "rules" become paramount and the focus is taken off of *agape* love and placed on a set of expectations, the foundation for a romantic relationship becomes shaky.

Frequently conflicts arise when men do not understand the implicit rules they are expected to follow. A huge *expectation-experience gap* arises between what a woman *wants* and what the man actually *does*. The woman gets frustrated and pulls back; the man is confused and pulls back; and the very standards of conduct that ought to control *all* Christians, male and female alike, go out the window. Instead of filling the gap with gentle honesty, mutual respect, genuine authenticity, and abiding mercy, relationships end with no explanation. This ought not be the case.

Anna was a lovely seminary student who had been dating another seminary student for several months. She was in love with this man, whom she hoped one day to marry. In deep anguish, however, she informed me (Judy) that she had terminated their relationship because he had not "initiated" properly as a would-be Christian husband ought to do. Further probing revealed that she had been sending conflicting signals to him. She did not always return his telephone calls because she did not want to appear "eager." Even though they had dated frequently, when they were at parties she would not speak to him because she didn't want to appear "clingy." The reason? She felt the responsibility for the relationship must rest on him; he must be the one to show the initiative despite her seemingly indifferent and unwelcoming response. When I (Judy) challenged Anna about her lack of honesty with him about her true feelings, she was shocked that I would suggest that she behave any differently. After all, her behavior was approved by her closest friends, who understood what it took to catch a "real Christian man who would lead a home and family well." I encouraged her to make her real feelings known in an appropriate way and to seek his forgiveness for sending him such conflicting, confusing, and hurtful messages. She did. Today, Anna is his wife and they have two beautiful children.

Filling the gap with sin will never satisfy. At the other end of the courtship spectrum is the woman who aggressively pursues men. Instead of actively choosing to fill the expectation-experience gap with patience and grace, these women seek to control the men in their lives in an attempt to satisfy themselves. Premarital sex is a common way for a woman to manipulate a man to get her own desires met. The price for fulfilling such desires is high. Many women sacrifice sexual purity to guarantee a relational outcome; they long to feel loved, valued, cherished, and beautiful. Promiscuity is their way of purchasing what they believe will meet their needs: a counterfeit form of affirmation, security, and commitment.

Kate, a leader in her church for over twenty years, appears to be happily married and raising three well-adjusted children. Although you would never know it from looking at her, Kate is unhappy with her life. Even though the outward trappings indicate that all of her expectations have been met, Kate feels unfulfilled and unappreciated in her marriage. She has a huge gap between her expectations and her experience. How does she fill the gap? She regularly indulges her sexual temptations by watching R-rated movies and masturbating in response to her physical arousal. She has hidden these thoughts and behaviors from her husband, children, and friends for years. Tragically, the result of this indulgence is only a temporary feeling of pleasure, and even that level of pleasure has diminished over time. What lasts is a deep-seated feeling of self-loathing and disgust because Kate feels that she is a fraud. Her spiritual life suffers because she never fully confesses her sins or repents. Her heart is less open to her husband; their friendship and intimacy suffers each time she fantasizes about other men. Instead of humbly talking to her husband and putting her lust to death as part of living in Christ (Col. 3:4–5), Kate continually fills her expectation-experience gap with sexual indulgence, feeding it so that it grows stronger.

Other women choose to marry unbelievers and become "unequally yoked." In clear violation of Scripture, they sinfully desire to fill the gap of loneliness with an ungodly marriage (2 Cor. 6:14). Consider Cathy's reflections on her marriage to Todd:

> I badly wanted to be married and have a family. When Todd came along, I thought it could work. He said he was a Christian, but he never read the Bible and only occasionally went to church. I knew in my heart that he was not a believer, but he wanted children and I thought he would be a good parent. After we were married, it became painfully obvious that Jesus was not the Lord of his life. He did not make wise decisions concerning the people he hung out with or the way he spent our money. Instead of the romantic boyfriend who had wooed me, I found myself living with a man who would rather watch television, work late, or be out with "the guys" than spend time with our children or me. We live like strangers. I thought it was hard to be lonely and single—but loneliness in marriage is worse. What have I gotten myself into?

Whenever the expectation-experience gap is filled with sin, our souls are left emptied and damaged. God gives us boundaries and commandments because he loves us, not to spoil our fun or deprive us of happiness. When we sin, the emptiness and damage can last a lifetime. But, of course, we can be forgiven and restored in Christ.

Expectations can become idolatrous. Expectations are actually desires. And just like any desire, those associated with romantic relationships can easily become idolatrous. When our expectations begin to consume us and we sacrifice our walk with the Lord, our relationships with other people, and even our health to them, they have crossed the line into idolatry. Idolatrous expectations can doom romantic relationships. In the words of David Powlison, "The Lord of all the earth often seems to put people together in marriage who are wired differently. As a result, either we grow to complement each other by learning to give intelligent love, or we incinerate the marriage on the battlefield of insistently different demands."[2]

During engagement, the desire for the "perfect wedding" often turns into an idol. Instead of focusing on prayerful preparation for a lifetime together, couples can find the engagement filled with constant bickering because huge gaps exist between a woman's desire for a "Hollywood wedding" and the financial resources needed to have such a lavish affair. Instead of quiet contentment, we often fill the gap with selfish greed that demands to be satisfied, even at the cost of relationship. Every year at the counseling center where I (Judy) work, we receive calls from parents whose children are soon to be married. When asked if we offer premarital counseling, we begin to describe our program for the soon-to-be-married couple. After a few seconds, we are interrupted by the words, "Not for them—for us! They are driving us crazy!"

Lauren was a young musician who had been planning her wedding for *years*—even before she had a serious boyfriend. Her desire for a lavish affair was so great that when her parents began to put unreasonable demands on her and her fiancé, she readily gave in to them because she needed their financing. I (Tara) talked with her about the true importance of her impending marriage—not the event of the wedding. She would not be dissuaded from her intense focus on the wedding celebration, despite many tearful fights with her fiancé. Sadly, she was willing to sacrifice *shalom* to have the perfect wedding on a beach with lobsters, fine china, and dancing under the stars. Years later, Lauren looks back with regret on these conflicts in their engagement and how her desires became idolatrous idols. "If I had to do it over again," she said, "I pray that God's grace would help me to turn away from what had become an idol to me—the 'perfect wedding'—and instead focus my energy on loving and serving my (then) fiancé and family well."

The gap continues into marriage. The expectation-experience gap can continue into marriage—especially in the sexual relationship. We may have high hopes for sexual fulfillment with our husband, but reality can leave much to be desired. Instead of rapturous bliss, our sex life can be unsatisfying and unpleasant, even if our husbands love us and try to please us.

Sexual frustrations provide wonderful opportunities for us to lay down our lives and seek to serve our husbands. We fill the gap between our desires and our experience with beautiful love as we pray for them, encourage them, and seek to find creative ways to experience God-honoring sexual pleasure with one another. Sadly, such a selfless response is missing in many marriages.

For example, we have counseled with many women who have listened to some well-meaning expert on marriage teach that if a woman's husband wants to have sex with her, he had better start getting her ready when the alarm clock goes off in the morning. Some women hold to this idea with rigid expectations and unloving demands. If a husband "does the right thing" (indicates romantic interest, helps with the dishes, spends time with the children), then his wife may be willing to have sex that night. But if he doesn't do these things, then she may not be inclined to respond to him. Her pre-romantic expectations must be met for sexual intimacy to occur. If they aren't met, the expectation-experience gap is filled with coldness and rejection—a far cry from the biblical notion that a woman's body is to be shared freely with her spouse, the co-owner of her body as she is of his (1 Cor. 7:4).

Expectations concerning biblical manhood and womanhood can lead to conflict. Another common area of conflicts associated with expectations in Christian marriage has to do with biblical headship and submission. Many excellent books on biblical manhood and womanhood help us to understand what Scripture says about how men and women ought to relate. Yet somehow our experience fails to completely live up to the beautiful model of marriage described in Ephesians 5 and 1 Peter 3.

While it is beyond the scope of this book to explore this topic fully, we do want at least to mention this conflict-prone area and encourage you to study it further (see the Recommended Resources at the end of the chapter). We have counseled many women who are angry because their husbands refuse to lead their households and many men who are angry because their wives refuse to support and follow them. Many times conflicts arise because the beautiful, biblical views of headship and submission have been warped into unbiblical chauvinism and abuse where the husband devalues the wife or unloving rebellion where the wife absorbs cultural notions of self-sufficiency and independence.

Conflicts arise when husbands and wives do not understand the distinction between roles and responsibilities and when they do not cultivate selfless love—*agape* love—toward one another. Roles in marriage are established by God and never change, regardless of the situation. Husbands are called to the role of servant-leader and wives are called to the role of helpmate. We are to help each other fulfill our roles in God-honoring ways. How we do this will differ dramatically from situation to situation, but we must always act with love and respect. Many excellent books have been written to instruct us about the beauty of marriage, and we commend them to you. All will remind us that when we are faced with disappointment in the expectation-experience gap, as Christians we are called to seek God's glory and serve others rather than promote ourselves or harbor bitterness.

Our families of origin can affect our expectations. Sometimes the expectation-experience gap in romantic relationships can be complicated by the values and communication styles of the family in which you grew up. Heather, a woman who grew up in a home where problems were not discussed, was married to Bill, a man who grew up in a home where problems were dealt with openly and quickly. Their early life experiences were the basis of two different sets of ideas on how to handle conflict. When her expectations were not met, Heather would withdraw into silence. Bill, however, would pursue her to try to get her to talk it through. Of course, the more he went after her, the more Heather withdrew because "married couples were not supposed to talk about hurt, they were supposed to get over it."

Both Bill and Heather were called to challenge the basic beliefs that lay beneath their expectations. Heather learned that instead of withdrawing, Ephesians 4:25–32 describes a different way of relating and communicating. Bill, on the other hand, had to let go of his conviction that his marriage relationship was solely his responsibility. He had to recognize that he could not be responsible for his wife's silence but must be willing to patiently encourage, help, and warn her (1 Thess. 5:14). This type of expectation-experience gap is painful, but this pain can be the motivation to seek maturity and wisdom, turning to Scripture's truth and direction.

The little things matter. In addition to the weightier issues of sexual intimacy and biblical manhood and womanhood, expectations are often frustrated in the simple tasks of ordinary, daily, married life. For example, I (Tara) used to be frustrated by my husband's failure to wipe down a countertop. He keeps the house neat and even takes the time to fold the towels just the way I like. However, for some reason he is usually oblivious to the crumbs he leaves on the counter and table. I (Judy) used to be irritated by my husband's repeated failure to put his shoes in the closet. Jim changed diapers and washed dishes but never remembered to pick up his shoes from under the coffee table before he went to bed at night. Fred and Jim are great men and wonderful husbands. We, Tara and Judy, are free to choose how we fill our expectation-experience gap. We can fill it with rage and attack, or we can fill it with understanding and consideration.

What a sense of joy I (Judy) felt when I discovered that it took less energy and brought about much more peace to carry Jim's shoes to the closet than to throw them into the backyard or stuff them into the trash. And I (Tara) had a similar epiphany when I began to count it a joy to wipe down the counters as I reflected on Fred's helping with dinner, cleaning up, taking out the trash, and caring for our daughter. We have the power to choose how to fill this gap when our expectations are not met. We can and should learn to fill the expectation-experience gap in such a way that *shalom* results. As in all things, contemplating the grandeur of what God has blessed us with, rather than nurturing our disappointments, is a key aspect of *shalom*.

Eros Unrequited

Some of the most powerful emotions and colossal conflicts arise when *eros* is unrequited. Rejected lovers have wept oceans of tears because of their broken hearts. Many a harsh word has been written in letters or shouted aloud when love is not returned. We quit jobs, stop attending Bible studies and churches, and even leave marriages over unrequited love—all to avoid the hurt associated with the other person's lack of love for us.

Although both men and women have been created for relationship, women are uniquely made to complement and complete men and to be completed by men. Women long to be loved, protected, and cherished as they live in partnership with men. Often we assume that if there is an *eros* connection in courtship—complete with sexual and emotional energy—then the other person really understands us and loves us. He seems to be a "soul mate" who "completes us." We mistake sexual attraction and emotional connection for intimate knowledge because we long to be understood and loved at a deep level. If this *"eros* connection" does not develop into *"agape* intimacy" either during courtship or marriage, the result is usually great pain.

The level of pain is tied to the level of intimacy. When *eros* is unrequited, the depth of pain and the severity of the conflict associated with that pain are both directly tied to the level of investment made in a relationship and the expectations that result. When we invest ourselves deeply, we experience true injury when our love is not returned. We suffer when our expectation is that the other person desires the same intimate *eros* as we do but we are sorely mistaken. This emotional investment in desiring intimacy from another leaves the heart vulnerable. A woman hopes that her desired lover will *choose her*. She holds out her heart and soul and says, "Please love me. Be my friend. Be my lover. Let me care for you, and you care for me." There is bliss when the answer is yes, "Come away, my lover" (Song of Songs 8:14). Grief occurs when the answer is, "No, I do not choose you. I do not want you."

The book of Proverbs reflects on the pain and struggle of "an unloved woman who is married" (Prov. 30:23). According to this Proverb, a marriage relationship "trembles" and "cannot bear up" when a wife is unloved by her husband. Of course, the same is true of men. Marriages groan under the weight of sorrow when a wife fails to love her husband. A lack of love looks like disinterest, disgust, and disapproval. "I just don't love him anymore." This standard seems to be the test of true love according to secular society. "Oh? You don't love him anymore? Well, you'd better get out of *that* marriage and find one where you love him and he loves you."

The results may be traumatic. Unless our hearts are firmly fixed on Christ and our identity is rooted in him, such rejection can be traumatic. This is particularly true if we have a history of being rejected—especially if the rejection was from our father. In this situation a woman may be looking to a romantic relationship to fill empty spaces in her heart left by her father's lack of love for her. When her lover also rejects her, she can easily feel condemned and worthless. She may lash out at the man and others. She may act as though everything is fine, but her internal conflicts may lead her to escape through sleeping, eating, sex, shopping, or other diversions. In extreme cases, she may even consider taking her own life—such is the power of unrequited love.

Only God's grace enables us to respond well. I (Tara) look back on my teenage and college years with much regret when I consider my responses to the various unrequited romantic relationships I experienced. I am ashamed by the way I led men on—often very kind, godly men who had beautiful hearts. I was flattered by their attention and gifts, and I felt "built up" by their attraction. But when they wanted a deeper relationship, I broke their hearts because my deceptive actions had led them astray. I am also ashamed by the way I responded when *I* was the one being rejected. I cringe when I think of the embarrassing letters I wrote to men who spurned me. Those letters were filled with rage, hurt, and accusation. They did not reflect grace and, sadly, they went on for page after page. I can only hope they have been burned or thrown away.

How I wish I had responded as a woman of faith and *shalom* when *eros* was unrequited in courtship. What might I have done differently? How can we respond in a more godly manner when romantic love is not returned?

We must never use romantic relationships to meet our felt needs. First of all, we should never use men to answer those basic questions of who we are and whether or not we are valuable. In Christ, those questions have already been answered. Also, to "lead someone on" is to use them in an attempt to convince ourselves that we are desirable and lovable. In Christ, we are deeply desired and loved. We must never use a man who desires an intimate relationship in an attempt to answer questions that have already been answered for us. This theft of emotion and affection is unloving and contrary to how our Lord calls us to treat one another.

We are called to respond with loving honesty. During courtship, when we become aware of a man's romantic interest in us and we do not return it, we are to take steps to communicate gently this hard truth. Cold distance never substitutes for honest and respectful communication. We may genuinely believe that treating our potential suitor with kindness will cause further unwanted pursuit. However, we are still called to speak the truth in love (Eph. 4:15). As we gently and honestly express our boundaries, we may cause hurt feelings, but we will not cause actual injury. Drs. John Townsend and Henry Cloud, in their book *Boundaries*, make a helpful distinction between hurting others and harming others. Real love requires us to be willing to hurt others by speaking the truth even while it forbids us from ever harming them—which often occurs when the truth is not lovingly communicated.[3]

This call to loving honesty continues into marriage. When troubles arise and conflicts come—and they will come—we must not treat our spouse in ways designed to encourage him to withdraw. Instead, we are called to communicate humbly and lovingly, to *breathe grace* to one another just as we described in chapter 5.

God's grace enables us to suffer well. When *eros* is unrequited, we are called to live out all of the truths elucidated in chapter 3 on suffering. A compelling illustration of this from literature is found in the character Lawrence Wentworth in Charles Williams's book *Descent into Hell*.[4] Wentworth falls in love with Adela Hunt, who never acknowledges him as a suitable romantic figure. Instead of grieving his loss, accepting the situation, and moving on, Wentworth develops an imaginary fantasy world in which he and Adela are intimately, romantically involved. As the real world dissolves into grayness, Wentworth's fantasy world comes to life. False hopes and dreamy fiction appear to give him meaning and self-definition. His friends and acquaintances see him fade more and more into a shadow of his previous self—withdrawn, uncommunicative, and haggard.

Instead of suffering, Wentworth chooses to bring himself pleasure—false pleasure, rooted in fantasy. *Unrequited romance is an opportunity to suffer and, in this suffering, to reflect the glory of God.* To waste this opportunity, to choose as Wentworth chose, is to create a world where delusion spreads and artificial peace anesthetizes. It matters not whether an illusory world is constructed of dreams, drugs, or promiscuous sex; it is an illusion and does not honor God.

We can respond with agape love. During my college years, I (Tara) had a wonderful friend, John, who developed romantic feelings for me. I loved John as a brother in Christ but not as a lover. When I told him how I felt, John was hurt. Our friendship cooled for months—almost a year—but then we gradually began to spend time together again as friends. Years later, I asked him why we were still friends since friendships rarely survive when romantic love is unrequited. John explained to me that although he felt *eros* for me, once he knew that I did not feel the same, he had a choice: either our friendship was over (because his desires were not met) or he would, by faith, grieve the rejection and *allow* agape *love to transform his feelings.* Today, Fred and I consider John one of our dearest friends. When I think about the *shalom*-based relationships in my life, my friendship with John is at the top of the list. It *is* possible to respond to unrequited love with grace and abiding, *agape* love.

We can't rely on feelings. Feelings of romance grow cold in most marriage relationships as the challenges of maintaining a home and raising a family drain off emotional and physical resources. Romance takes energy and work. Those times that we feel "in love" are those times that we are investing a great deal of energy into a relationship. When those romantic feelings cool, only through an investment of energy and commitment is *eros* revived. When *eros* is not reciprocated for long periods of time, a relationship begins to die.

I (Judy) see many couples that come in for marriage counseling about two years after their wedding. Their main complaint is that the romantic feelings in their relationship have cooled. They are afraid that they will live in an unhappy relationship forever. Many young couples begin to wonder if they have made a terrible mistake in the choice of their mate. What an opportunity exists when couples hit this "wall" of disinterest and doubt! While *eros* is exciting and energizing, *agape* love brings depth and meaning to a relationship. I think of the relationship between the two like an Oreo cookie—*eros* is the crème filling, and *agape* is the chocolate cookie. Together they make a great combination. Romantic, *eros*-based marriages are made and remade regularly through *agape*-motivated discovery, sacrifice, and commitment. *Eros*, to be deeply rewarding, must be safely nestled in that other-centered, sacrificial love—*agape*. Only the rich and renewable resource of *agape* flowing through the marriage can maintain the health and vibrancy of the relationship.

We are called to persevere in love. As Christians, even when love is unrequited in marriage, we are called to *continue to love.* We persevere in love. We must remember the important fact that love has little to do with the object of the love. Love has everything to do with the subject *doing* the loving. For instance, in the sentence "Jane kicked the ball," Jane is the subject. Jane is the one who acts by kicking the object. The object did not deserve to be kicked, nor did it command Jane to kick it. The ball had little to do with the act of kicking other than to provide Jane with the opportunity to act. The act of kicking had everything to do with Jane—her desires and motivations. *It is the same with love.* Love has everything to do with the subject who loves and little to do with the object of the love. God is love (1 John 4:16). God loves us—because he is love, not because we deserve or command his love. A woman who loves her husband speaks volumes about who *she* is, not necessarily about who *he* is.

Barb is married to an alcoholic, self-centered man who rejects her faith in Christ. Her friends and family would not blame her for leaving her husband. Most who know them believe that Barb would be better off without her husband. Even Barb's best friend shrugs her shoulders when Barb tells her that she *chooses to love* because she knows that not loving is a sin. For Barb, love means staying in this disappointing relationship—speaking truth, serving, and offering affection.[5] Barb understands that when a woman says of her spouse, "I don't love him anymore," it is a self-indictment, not an indictment of her husband. God commands us to love. To not love is a violation of God's calling to love him and to love one another. When love in marriage grows cold, our highest priority should be to repent, rebuild, and restore. *Shalom* in marriage is only possible when *eros* is revived by, constrained by, and reinforced with *agape.*

Eros Changed

No story in Scripture more clearly reflects the change of *eros* into contempt than the story of Tamar's rape by Amnon in 2 Samuel 13.

Amnon "fell in love" with his half-sister Tamar. The Bible describes Amnon as being consumed with longing—even to the point of illness. To satisfy his desires, Amnon devised a plot to rape his sister. He even brought his father, King David, into his plan in order to provide a level of credibility. When Amnon pretended to be sick and had Tamar come to cook for him, he attacked Tamar and overpowered her. Tamar's pleading proved useless. Following his rape and dismissal of Tamar, Amnon was filled with an intense hatred for Tamar—hatred greater than his previous feelings of desire for her.

Eros unrestrained by *agape* often becomes contempt. How can romantic love shift so quickly into hurtful hatred?

Insincerity. Love, in order to be love, must be sincere (Rom. 12:9). The word "sincere" is a fascinating word. The literal translation of this Greek word—*anypokritos*—is "without hypocrisy." In other words, love must not be feigned or pretended. Our English word "sincere" comes from the Latin phrase *sin cere*, meaning "without wax." In the marketplace during biblical times, inferior and worthless pottery was sold with cracks that had been filled with wax. When used, these pots proved useless because the wax would melt; the cracks that had been covered were now obvious, and the vessel was unworthy. "Sincere" means that something ought to be as it appears. *Eros* that appears to be love but in reality is something else (such as selfishness, greed, or lust) quickly becomes contempt and hatred.

Lust. Lust is a common counterfeit of romantic love. Lust demands satisfaction. *Eros*, constrained by *agape*, protects. Lust takes; love gives. Anything that leads to lust is not rooted in true love at all. Romantic love is often transformed into contempt through sexual sin during courtship.

I (Tara) was in a romantic relationship in college where the young man, a Christian, wanted to kiss passionately. I had been sorely tempted in the past with too much kissing, and I really wanted this relationship to last. So I asked him if we could *not* kiss just to avoid the temptation and be able to grow our relationship and true friendship. He broke up with me the next week. His passionate "love" for me changed quickly to contempt and rejection—he really wanted to take and not give. (As an aside, one of the ways I knew that Fred was the man for me was because *he* took the lead in us not having a physical relationship during our courtship—our passionate marriage is a wonderful fruit of that godly decision.)

Sexual sin. Giving in to sexual urges can often transform *eros* into contempt. We have counseled with many young men and women who have felt so overcome by their sexual urges that they have indulged in sexual actions such as heavy petting, oral sex, and intercourse outside of marriage. As soon as their desires are met in this ungodly way, however, they are shocked by the lack of love or even attraction they feel for the other person. Often their own guilt clouds their consciences and they seek to get away from the other person simply to avoid their own conviction. They hate the other person for their weakness while also hating themselves. At other times, individuals blame the other person for seducing them, in an attempt to justify their contempt and hatred.

Criticism and annoyance. Even when sexual sin is absent from the relationship, *eros* can still be transformed into contempt simply because of our sinful hearts. Our feelings can change. We may become attracted to someone else. Little habits and quirks that used to amuse and delight us suddenly make our stomachs tighten. Where we used to find him witty and charming, we are now embarrassed by his lack of social grace and chivalry. Instead of treating him respectfully, we begin to disdain him and treat him rudely.

The daily stresses of married life. All too often, the daily stresses and challenges of married life bring out our worst sins and fallenness. Instead of love, we find our marriage filled with tension and frustration. We make demands on each other and punish each other when our demands are not met. When emotional and physical resources run low, we attempt to force our mate to fill us. As illustrated by the telling phrase, "They act like two ticks with no dog," married couples often drain one another in selfish attempts to meet their own needs. Instead of making ourselves vulnerable to one another and seeking to serve one another, we put our own desires and demands ahead of our spouse. We can even begin to hate our spouse over time.

Rejection. Michal's contempt for her husband, King David, is a biblical illustration of the tragic truth that love can quickly change to contempt in the presence of rejection. In 2 Samuel 6, King David has returned to Jerusalem with the ark of the covenant.

As he enters the city, he is "leaping and dancing before the LORD" (v. 16). Observing her husband-king conducting himself in a way she thinks unbecoming, Michal despises David in her heart. Upon returning home, Michal rebukes him with words filled with disgust and condemnation. Her hatred for him drips from her words. David's response is equally contemptuous. What is the result of this hatred? Michal experienced a lifelong humiliation—she "had no children to the day of her death" (v. 23). Why did she have no children? Because David and Michal profoundly rejected each other in their contempt. Although we may have different results today, many Christian marriages flounder with similar rejection.

There is hope. Even when our sin warps beautiful love into ugly contempt, God's grace is greater than our sin. Instead of bitter hatred, we can enjoy the progression of maturing love. God's divine love enables us to repent of our sin and learn to serve with genuine compassion. The love that covers over a multitude of sins is pure grace. And God's love and mercy enable us to give grace to one another instead of contempt.

We grow in *agape* love by nurturing the friendship element in our romantic relationships. When distance creeps into the relationship, God's grace enables us to build a bridge of solid communication to draw us closer together. Instead of attacking or avoiding one another, we learn how to practice biblical peacemaking. We humbly learn from one another. We pray and worship together. Common activities and mutual interests knit us together, and appropriate separate activities keep our relationship vibrant and growing. By breathing grace, we intentionally interact with one another in polite and kind ways that demonstrate deep affection for one another. Speaking well of one another and building each other up helps provide a strong foundation of friendship and companionship for the times when conflicts arise.[6] When we lack the resources we need in order to mend the relational gashes that arise, we seek the help of appropriate third parties to assist us.

Temptation

No discussion about *eros* would be complete without some focus on the biblical notion of temptation. Much confusion about temptation exists in the church. Many in the church believe that temptation is sin. We know that temptation is not sin; otherwise Jesus would have been a sinner since he himself was "tempted in every way, just as we are—yet was without sin" (Heb. 4:15). Temptation can *lead* to sin, but temptation in and of itself is *not* sin. Temptation to sin urges us to go astray and walk outside of God's will. Temptation is filled with powerful desires and emotions. To choose obedience rather than self-indulgence is to experience genuine suffering. Our perfect Savior Jesus Christ himself experienced suffering in the face of temptation and consequently "is able to help those who are being tempted" (Heb. 2:18).

Why is it so important that we fight the battle of faith against our temptations?

Giving in to temptation hardens our hearts. Our hearts can often deceive us when we are struggling with sexual and emotional longing. How many times have we been convicted by the Holy Spirit that a certain feeling, action, or thought is leading us toward sin? Yet instead of acknowledging the temptation and turning in faith to God to help us, we often try to manage our temptation by convincing ourselves that our desires are acceptable. Or we seek to numb the temptation by shutting down our emotions. Or we wrongly believe that the temptation means that the sin has already been committed. Believers have little motivation to turn away from temptation if they believe in their hearts that they are already guilty when they experience the temptation. We wrongly believe that the act of satisfying the temptation is no additional sin beyond what has already been experienced. Therefore, we eliminate the temptation quite effectively—by giving in to it. Of course, when we do so we act just like unbelievers. This is to our own peril. Our hearts are hardened and we risk God's loving discipline when we allow the temptations of *eros* to control us.

Giving in to sexual temptation hinders true intimacy. Counseling offices are filled with couples, married and unmarried, who gave in to sexual temptation during their courtship. Counselors have found that couples who engage in sexual relations prior to marriage often struggle later on with broken trust, damaged respect, and unresolved guilt. In those weeks and months when dating couples are supposed to build intimacy rooted in trust and respect, they are instead experiencing the false intimacy of sexuality. The outcome is often a shallow marriage in which both people have little understanding of one another. True love, however, grows larger and deeper in "knowledge and depth of insight" (Phil. 1:9). When couples give in to the temptation of sexual desire, they effectively shut the door on deepening the knowledge and understanding that helps love to abound.

A couple came to me (Judy) for premarital counseling. As Christians, they knew that their sexual activity was wrong, and they had discontinued intercourse two months previously. Yet they continued to live together, sleep nude in the same bed, and shower together. They explained that they were committed to not acting sexually until their marriage, which was six months away. I gently explained that they were damaging their ability to establish true intimacy because they were spending their energy fighting temptation rather than knowing, understanding, and developing emotional and spiritual intimacy with each other. They refused to listen and insisted on living together in the same manner. Six months after their marriage, I received the expected call from the newlywed wife: "I can't stand for him to touch me. I have no interest in him at all. I don't even like him. What are we going to do?"

Temptation is not only sexual. Nearly every married person, at some point, is faced with temptation to infidelity. But temptation has many footholds and takes many forms. Loneliness invites temptation to seek intimacy with people other than our husbands. We may justify our actions by saying, "We are only friends. Nothing has happened." But deep in our hearts, we know we are being emotionally unfaithful. As we age and grow insecure about our appearance, we may be tempted to make idols out of clothing, jewelry, and even plastic surgery. Even though we may never sin with another *person*, Christians often indulge their temptations as they "escape" through R-rated movies and illicit television shows. Women are often tempted by "romance" novels—particularly the sensuous sex scenes—and may even go so far as to fantasize that they have a different lover when they are intimate with their husbands. Internet pornography, online gambling and shopping, and even addictions all find insidious and tempting footholds in the lives of countless believers.

The answer to temptation is not stoicism. Individuals who have "steeled" themselves against feeling temptation—because of the idea that the righteous do not feel temptation—are often emotionally stoic and withdrawn. When faced with a temptation, they deaden their hearts to what they feel. The desires and feelings are themselves viewed as the enemy. A beautiful part of how God has made them becomes damaged and sometimes destroyed. In addition, when emotions become disconnected and hard to identify, identifying the danger of temptation is more difficult. Emotional stoicism causes us to lose the necessary feedback that helps us flee from danger. Stoics are often the proverbial frogs in the pot; they cannot feel the water heating and so will boil to death before they jump out of the pot to safety. Instead of stoicism, we are called to live in faith, turning to God and his people for help. "Therefore let us draw near with confidence to the throne of grace, so that we may receive mercy and find grace to help in time of need" (Heb. 4:16 NASB).

Eros is powerful. In order to effectively battle against our temptations, we must first acknowledge the powerful urges that *eros* creates within us.

Sexual attraction and pleasure are a large aspect of the cement that holds one woman to one man for a lifetime relationship. *Eros* is a powerful force! Thus, we must not "arouse or awaken love" prematurely or unwisely (Song of Songs 2:7). Instead, when *eros* exists in our lives, we pray for the grace to choose obedience to God's Word and adherence to his standard of purity. Therein lies *shalom* and joy in our romantic relationships.

God's grace is more powerful still. As Christians, we are not called simply to figure out a way on our own to resist our temptations. Instead, we can trust that God's commands are good and rely on his grace to enable us to obey all that he commands. As Rick Warren writes, "God doesn't owe you an explanation or reason for everything he asks you to do. Understanding can wait, but obedience can't. Instant obedience will teach you more about God than a lifetime of Bible discussions. In fact, you will never understand some commands until you obey them first. Obedience unlocks understanding."[7]

Resisting temptation will entail suffering. The book of Hebrews helps us understand how to respond to temptation in a

Christlike way. Jesus suffered when he was tempted (Heb. 2:18), and he was tempted in every way but was without sin (Heb. 4:15). It is vital that we help one another understand that the godly response to temptation is neither denial nor indulgence but genuine suffering as God enables us to choose obedience. To suffer when we are tempted is to choose to *fix our thoughts on Jesus* (Heb. 3:1) rather than on our desires. To suffer when we are tempted is to choose to *hold on to our courage and the hope of which we boast* (Heb. 3:6) rather than allow ourselves to become discouraged and defeated by our thoughts and emotions. To suffer when we are tempted is to *turn to our fellow Christians for encouragement and help* so that we will not "be hardened by sin's deceitfulness" (Heb. 3:12–13), living isolated lives largely unknown by our family in Christ.

Joy and delight come from resisting temptation. Lest we give the impression that resisting temptation brings no earthly blessing but is simply a necessary and unpleasant task to be endured while we wait for our heavenly reward, we are reminded that joy is deeply embedded in suffering (James 1:2). How can that be? To break free of the power of temptation is to experience exhilarating delight.

For example, I (Judy) have struggled all my life with being overweight. When I successfully resist the temptation to eat wrongly, I soon begin to experience the joy of feeling physically and emotionally free. Few things are more enjoyable than being able to wear clothes that fit comfortably while also having greater energy to enjoy the opportunities of life. Refusing to indulge my sinful desires frees me to experience my deeper and truer desires. Having worked with many people who struggle with sexual temptation, I once heard it described that successfully resisting sinful inclinations felt like "a hot air balloon released of its ballast—I was free to rise up and float in the heavens." What a view!

Eros Distorted

We live in a licentious and hypersexualized society. I (Judy) am shocked by the emails and pop-up ads to which my young daughter is exposed on a regular basis. As I talk with her friends, I am amazed at the terminology they know about sexual acts and behaviors—things I did not know until I was well into my college years.

Clearly we need to teach our children to be wise as serpents and harmless as doves in a culture that distorts and twists *eros*. Open and early communication is necessary to make this topic a safe one for discussion so that we can walk alongside of our children, helping them think through and make decisions for themselves that are God-honoring and for their good.

Sexual abuse is common. For many of us, however, distortion has already happened. We have experienced sexual abuse in the form of actual physical assault, exposure to pornography, or simply being treated as a sexual object at a young age. We may have been harmed by the traumas of others, such as a sister who was raped. These distortions of *eros* affect our lives. The injury we experience has a profound impact on us. Instead of viewing our sexuality as a God-given gift, even our legitimate, God-ordained sexual relationship with our husband may be viewed as dirty, bad, or unpleasant.

Anne's life illustrated this distorted *eros*. Anne and her husband came to me (Judy) because they had not been able to enjoy their sexual relationship for over fifteen years. Initially, she simply complained, "All he wants is sex." As we talked, it became clear that her understanding and experience of *eros* had been distorted as a result of inappropriate treatment she had received from her obstetrician during previous pregnancies and deliveries. As she acknowledged what happened, began to understand how those experiences impacted her now, and grieved the damage done to her in light of God's sovereignty and love for her, Anne's attitude toward sex changed dramatically. A year after counseling, Anne sent a letter expressing her joy at the lasting changes between her and her husband as their sexual relationship had been transformed.

Past abuse sometimes lingers. Sometimes our past exposure to distorted *eros* may linger in our hearts and minds. I (Tara) was exposed to pornography at an early age. The images warped my view of men, women, and sexual intimacy. Even to this day, I will sometimes experience a "flash" of an image, photograph, or sexually explicit literary passage. I hate that this garbage is inside of me, but I trust that God will give me the grace to turn away from it and not to dwell on it. I also rejoice that over time God is removing these images from my mind, and one day they will not exist at all.

God is with us. I (Judy) was sexually abused between the ages of four and six. This abuse had a huge impact on me. I developed deep, irrational fears that expressed themselves through many different kinds of controlling behaviors. In order to create a sense of peace within me, I turned to reading books. I never really had a childhood as many people do, but I had a relationship with the public library, where I would read ten to twenty books a week. After more than ten years of living in books, I realized that I had little common ground with anyone. The loneliness and fear were almost unbearable. Driving perfectionism and ambition were my way of filling the gap between my experience of isolation and my hopes for loving relationships.

I was forty years old before I was able to make peace with God and myself over this abuse. In a pilgrimage to my past, accompanied by my dear friend Kelly, I visited all of my childhood homes. At each place I was able to remember how God had protected me and prepared me for his purposes. I began to learn that trusting God, even in the dark areas of my heart, was not about understanding God's purposes but about understanding him—his character, his love, and his passions. I was comforted because I knew that God was with me.

God is sovereign. God is sovereign even over the distortions of *eros* in our lives. In order to forgive those who have sinned against us, we must remember how much we have been forgiven and how much mercy we have been shown by God. As we live in a rich understanding of God's forgiveness of our sins, we are able to extend forgiveness to others: "Be kind to one another, tenderhearted, forgiving one another, even as God in Christ forgave you" (Eph. 4:32 NKJV). For those of us who have been hurt, we are comforted by the fact that God is just. We can trust that he will right every wrong more completely than we ever could: "Do not take revenge, my friends, but leave room for God's wrath, for it is written: 'It is mine to avenge; I will repay,' says the Lord" (Rom. 12:19).

If you have been a victim of a sexual sin, you may be tempted to hate your abuser.[8] Victims of sexual abuse often struggle with depression, unbearable shame, and horrible fear. Apart from Christ, victims of sexual abuse are often caught in a life devoid of *shalom*.

And yet *shalom* is possible even for those of us who have suffered great abuse. God enables us to not give in to anger, depression, or fear. Rather, *shalom* comes on the heels of forgiveness. *Shalom* flows from trusting in a just, forgiving, and loving Savior, whether or not our abuser is ever punished.

We are free to forgive even if our offender never repents. All unrepentant sinners will be punished. That punishment is eternal, severe, and awful. We do not need to take revenge, because God will vindicate us. Even Christ entrusted his cause "to him who judges justly" (1 Peter 2:23). The person who has wronged us will either be condemned to hell or made our brother or sister by Jesus's death on the cross. Whether our abuser is condemned or set free, *shalom* replaces our bitterness when we trust in God's justice as judge over all and God's mercy in Christ's death on the cross.

Marriage can be a safe and healing refuge when eros is distorted elsewhere. We can help others experience *shalom* when we demonstrate grace and forgiveness to them concerning their past. In many marriages, either the husband or the wife has experienced the harm of distorted *eros*. Perhaps one or the other has been sexually abused or has even perpetrated hurt and pain on others through their words or deeds. We have an opportunity to be used by God to help our mate experience peace as we demonstrate God's forgiveness and love. If sexual sin is involved and the person has repented, it is crucial to affirm the truth that those sins are covered by the blood of Christ and fully forgiven. We are called to remind one another of the truths of 1 Corinthians 6:9–11: "Do you not know that the wicked will not inherit the kingdom of God? Do not be deceived: Neither the sexually immoral nor idolaters . . . will inherit the kingdom of God. And that is what some of you were. But you were washed, you were sanctified, you were justified in the name of the Lord Jesus Christ and by the Spirit of our God."

God's grace frees us from our past guilt. We do not have to carry any regrets into our marriage bed because our sins have been covered. "There is now no condemnation for those who are in Christ Jesus" (Rom. 8:1). "Blessed is he whose transgressions are forgiven, whose sins are covered. Blessed is the man whose sin the LORD does not count against him" (Ps. 32:1–2).

Shalom-Based *Eros*

In all of life, but particularly in our romantic relationships, mature Christians are recovering "expectaholics." The *expectation-experience gap* creates a tension that demands to be filled with something. We have the opportunity and responsibility to decide with what we will fill our expectation-experience gap. Do we fill it with grace or anger? Do we fill it with patience or judgment? Do we fill it with kindness or criticism?

Marriage should be the one relationship in our lives that provides us with a constantly safe harbor. Friends, even close friends, will not live with us each day. Our children will grow up and one day leave our home. As long as both spouses have breath, marriage should be a daily celebration of lasting *eros* where we enjoy a thriving relationship with our truest love.

I (Tara) remember with grief (because it was painful) and gratitude (because God's grace was evident) the worst fight that Fred and I have had. I had been hurt and rejected by people I trusted, and I expected Fred to be as hurt and angry as I was. After all, he was my *husband*! Although Fred was injured by how I had been treated, he made the comment, "When they hurt *you*, Tara . . ." I blew up. "Do you mean that they didn't hurt *you*, Fred? They didn't hurt *us*? Our *family*? Are you saying that they only hurt *me*?" It was our worst fight to date because I felt utterly betrayed by Fred. I felt as though I had been physically kicked in the stomach and rejected *again* because he didn't hurt as much as I did over what had happened. I felt unloved and abandoned by the one person in my life who had *always* loved and wanted me.

With my expectations so completely unmet, how did I respond? I closed down emotionally. I pulled away, feeling sick and angry. I turned my back on Fred in bed, inching as close to the edge as I could. And there we lay—separated by a gap that felt too huge to cross. Yet the gospel of Jesus Christ was at work in our hearts, and my beloved husband would not let us rest. "Tara, I will not allow our relationship to have distance in it or this hurt to get a foothold. We *must* persevere and work through this. Our friendship and love are just too important." It was a long night but a good one as our miscommunication was resolved and our hearts were reunited because Fred chose to fill the gap with love, even when I initially failed to do so.

When our expectations become demands (see chapter 2 on idolatry), the only answer is repentance. If legitimate expectations are not met, we may need to be willing to confront others and forgive their failures. Yet many times, expectations should be open to discussion and negotiation. The husband who has worked all day wants to watch TV and rest when he gets home. The stay-at-home wife and mother who has labored all day with small children craves conversation and connection. Their expectations are at odds. What an opportunity to lay down our own desires, consider the interests of the other person, and compromise to meet as many expectations as possible.

As you reflect on this chapter and consider the many challenges associated with romantic love, you may feel like giving up in frustration. "Why even try? Isn't it just too difficult to have a beautiful, *eros*-filled relationship?" No! The beauty of *shalom*-based *eros* is profound and worthy of our effort. To give yourself to another and to receive his love in return is a pleasurable, God-honoring gift to be prized. When all of who we are comes together with all of who our husbands are—physically, spiritually, emotionally—we reflect the union of Christ and the church (Eph. 5:21–32). As we give ourselves fully to one other person for life, our love reflects a picture of eternity in heaven to come. The tension of the expectation-experience gap brings the opportunity to lay down our lives for one another, reflecting Christ to the world.

Yes, it takes concentrated effort to work through the conflict, pain, and disappointment associated with romantic love, but it is worth it. May God grant us increasing peace in our romantic relationships.

Personal Reflection

Questions for Reflection

1. In what ways do you think that your boyfriend, fiancé, or husband fails you? Describe your expectations and your experiences. Is there a gap? With what do you tend to fill that

gap? At your next opportunity, ask him the following question: "How do you think I treat you when I feel disappointed because I don't get from you what I hope to get?"

2. How would you complete the following sentence? "If only my husband/fiancé/boyfriend would _____, then I would be happy and our relationship would be great." What does your answer indicate is your perceived need? Review chapter 2 on idolatry. Are you elevating desires to idolatrous demands?

3. If you are single, what expectations do you have for a future boyfriend or spouse? How can you prepare yourself now for when those expectations *will* (not might) be disappointed? Think about how expectations have been harmful to your past relationships. In what ways might you have filled the expectation-experience gap differently? How does Christ's love for you impact your experience of singleness?

4. If you are married, how satisfying is your sexual life? Read the entire book of Song of Songs. In this book, the husband and wife are delighting in their marital and sexual intimacy. Over time, their intimacy progresses and their joy increases as they spend time learning about one another. Is your sexual and relational intimacy increasing with your spouse? If not, what steps can you take this week to grow this aspect of your relationship?

5. In the Bible, non-marital relationships are described in familial terms (1 Tim. 5:1–2). Can all of your relationships with men other than your husband be described by "absolute purity" (1 Tim. 5:2)? If not, how would you describe them? Where is repentance needed to make your relationships more God-honoring? Who can you ask to pray for you and hold you accountable for sexual purity?

6. We suffer when we resist temptation. What temptations do you experience? Write a personalized sentence summarizing 1 Corinthians 6:18–20. What do these verses teach about the momentary pleasure associated with sexual immorality?

7. Are you struggling with sexual sin? What do you expect your sexual behaviors to produce in your life? How do your sinful actions affect you? Read Ephesians 2:1–5 and 2 Peter 1:4.

What do these verses say to you? What actions can you take today to begin to turn away from your sexual sin?

8. Describe any ways others have sinned against you that may be contributing to conflict in your romantic relationships. Where have you forgiven, and where does forgiveness need to occur? Pray and ask God to show you what you might do in order to experience healing or restoration. Are you willing to pray about these experiences until God brings healing? If so, consider scheduling on your calendar three additional times for specific prayer. You may also want to pray with a spiritually mature person whom you respect and trust.

Praying Scripture to God

Gracious God, I thank you that you love me and have a perfect and good plan for my life. Dear God, I pray that you will help me to guard my heart and my mind in Christ Jesus, especially concerning sexual purity. May I persevere in honoring marriage as the one-flesh design you intended. May my marriage honor you by reflecting the relationship of Christ and the church. Father, may I relate with my boyfriend, fiancé, or husband in a way that is edifying and ministers your grace. May I never know the pain and struggle of an unloved woman who is married, but may our love always be sincere—without hypocrisy. Father, I draw near with confidence to your throne of grace, for in you I find mercy and help in my time of need. Please do not allow me to arouse or awaken love prematurely or unwisely. Instead, may I fix my thoughts on Jesus rather than on my desires. God, please cause me to hold to the courage and the hope of which I boast. In my romantic relationships, as in all of my relationships, please help me to be kind, tenderhearted, and forgiving toward others, just as you are kind, tenderhearted, and forgiving toward me.

(Prayer based on Jer. 29:11; Ps. 25:20; Mark 10:6–9; Eph. 5:22–23; 1 Peter 3:1–12; Eph. 4:25–32; Prov. 30:23; Rom. 12:9; Heb. 4:16; Song of Songs 2:7; Heb. 3:1; Heb. 3:6.)

Recommended Resources for Further Study and Consideration

Jay E. Adams, *Marriage, Divorce, and Remarriage* (Grand Rapids: Zondervan, 1980).

Dan B. Allender, *The Wounded Heart* (Colorado Springs: NavPress, 1990).

Dan B. Allender and Tremper Longman III, *Bold Love* (Colorado Springs: NavPress, 1992).

Linda Dillow, *Creative Counterpart* (Nashville: Thomas Nelson, 1986).

Elizabeth Dodds, *Marriage to a Difficult Man* (Philadelphia: Westminster Press, 1971).

Elisabeth Elliot, *Passion and Purity* (Grand Rapids: Revell, 1984).

Susan Hunt, *Your Home a Place of Grace* (Wheaton: Crossway, 2000).

Diane Langberg, *Counseling Survivors of Sexual Abuse* (Wheaton: Tyndale, 1997).

Diane Langberg, *On the Threshold of Hope: Opening the Door to Hope and Healing for Survivors of Sexual Abuse* (Wheaton: Tyndale, 1999).

Kevin Leman, *Sheet Music: Uncovering the Secrets of Sexual Intimacy in Marriage* (Wheaton: Tyndale, 2003).

Robert Lewis and William Hendricks, *Rocking the Roles: Building a Win-Win Marriage* (Colorado Springs: NavPress, 1999).

Wayne A. Mack, *Strengthening Your Marriage* (Phillipsburg, NJ: P&R Publishing, 1999).

David Powlison, Paul David Tripp, and Edward T. Welch, *Domestic Abuse: How to Help* (Phillipsburg, NJ: P&R Publishing, 2002).

David Powlison, *Pornography: Slaying the Dragon* (Phillipsburg, NJ: P&R Publishing, 1999).

Ken Sande, "Church Discipline to Preserve and Heal Marriage." Presentation, Building Strong Families in Your Church Conference, sponsored by the Council on Biblical Manhood and Womanhood and Family Life Today, March 20, 2000.

Ken Sande, "Pastoral Responses to Domestic Violence." Presentation, Building Strong Families in Your Church Conference, sponsored by the Council on Biblical Manhood and Womanhood and Family Life Today, March 20, 2000.

Ken Sande, *Peacemaking for Families* (Wheaton: Tyndale, 2002).

Harry W. Schaumburg, *False Intimacy: Understanding the Struggle of Sexual Addiction* (Colorado Springs: NavPress, 1997).

R. C. Sproul, *The Intimate Marriage* (Phillipsburg, NJ: P&R Publishing, 1975).

Paul David Tripp, *Marriage: Whose Dream?* (Phillipsburg, NJ: P&R Publishing, 1999).

7

FAMILIES

Jesus said, "Let the little children come to me, and do not hinder them, for the kingdom of heaven belongs to such as these."

Matthew 19:14

Family solidarity strengthens the church. . . . Church and family must be driven by an unswerving commitment to Christ's crown and covenant.

Susan Hunt[1]

Families matter. When families are filled with *shalom*, the world sees Jesus in a powerful way. God shows himself to the world through our familial relationships. Having already briefly looked at marriage in the previous chapter, we now turn our attention to our parenting relationships. For some of us, no relationships cause more consistent conflict than the relationships we have with our own children or our parents. We invest much of ourselves in these relationships, and we are vulnerable to great pain when conflicts arise.

When we parent, we pour an incredible amount of who we are—our prayers, hopes, and energies—into our children. The resulting opportunity for joy and satisfaction, as well as disappointment and hurt, is profound. Our parents have invested much of themselves in *us* as well. The resulting adult relationships can reflect beautiful fellowship as brothers and sisters in Christ. Sadly, they too often entail strife and suffering. The challenges we experience in relating to our children, our own parents, and our spouse's parents can make life miserable when the investment seems to bring poor returns. We may long for friendship and relationship with our parents and children, but ongoing pain with no apparent likelihood of resolution can lead to broken relationships over time.

The impact of children and parents on our lives cannot be overstated. God's commandment concerning parents is so important that it is tied to a promise: "Honor your father and your mother, as the LORD your God has commanded you, so that you may live long and that it may go well with you in the land the LORD your God is giving you" (Deut. 5:16). In light of the importance of these key family relationships, how do we live as peacemaking women when conflicts in the family arise?

Raising Peacemakers

All parents hope that their children will experience great joy and peace throughout their lives. We pray that Isaiah's words will be true in our lives and "great will be [our] children's peace" (Isa. 54:13). Of course, living in a fallen world, surrounded by sinners—some redeemed, some not—we know that peace is not automatic. In fact, the opposite is true: conflict will inevitably be a part of our children's lives. Therefore, a key responsibility as parents is to raise our children to be peacemakers as part of rearing them to fear the Lord.[2]

Many of us, however, fail to teach our children the skills they need to lead lives of *shalom*. We invest time, money, and effort encouraging them in academics, music, and sports, but too often we fail to invest in one of the most worthy pursuits—helping them to be at peace in all their relationships. Raising children to be peacemakers is not easy. But the good news is that children learn biblical peacemaking principles faster and apply them better than most adults. Have faith that your children can learn and change;

it is never too late to start. We can trust that God will give us the grace to help our children to live out these biblical truths.

We are called to start with the gospel. How do we encourage our children to be pure, peace loving, considerate, and full of good fruit (James 3:17)? We are called to address all conflicts on a heart level—both our conflicts with them and their conflicts with others. It is not enough to merely constrain or require certain behaviors in order to have the illusion of peace. Instead, we are to prayerfully start with the gospel of Jesus Christ. When conflicts arise, our tendency may be to teach our children a series of rules and enforce their compliance. This would be applying the law. The law is good and necessary and must be emphasized in our children's lives, especially when they are very young and unable to comprehend complex concepts such as sin, grace, and redemption. But the law does not change hearts. Only the gospel changes the human heart. Conflicts in our children's lives provide a window into their hearts. Instead of merely forcing outward compliance to a set of rules—even good rules—we are called to show them Christ, the true help for their heart struggles.

To illustrate this, think of a little girl who pays no attention to traffic on a busy street and willfully disobeys your instruction to stay in the yard. In that situation, the law is necessary and good to bring about immediate compliance. But what if she throws a temper tantrum at the park and the family has to leave earlier than planned? When this happens, you may be tempted to reprimand her, tell her that her behavior is wholly unacceptable, and send her off to sit somewhere for a "time out" until she can act better. This would be an application of the law: "The rule is that you are not to behave selfishly and throw tantrums, and you are being punished for doing so. Once you stop misbehaving and apologize, we will move on." Contrast that approach with a gospel-centered approach. Instead of merely scolding her in order to force outward compliance, you might get down on your knees in front of her, look her in the eyes, and say something like this:

> Joanna, do you ever feel really bad inside because you know that you are acting wrongly, but you don't know how to stop? I feel that way sometimes. I want to do the right thing, but I can't. And I end up making people mad and ruining a fun day, and I feel terrible. Well,

the Bible calls this acting wrong *sin*. The good news is that Jesus
came to save us from our sins. Instead of being stuck, we can ask
Jesus for his forgiveness and his help to change. Jesus uses moms
and dads to help children grow and learn. I want to teach you how
to apologize to the rest of the family so that we can all be at peace
with each other. I also want to help you to ask Jesus to forgive you
for acting wrong and change your heart to be more like his. Let's
pray together.

As the gospel penetrates the heart, our children are helped
to turn away from false worship of idols ("I want to stay at the
park . . . I will stay at the park . . . If you don't let me stay at the
park, I'm going to punish you by stomping around and saying all
sorts of mean things") and turn to the Lord instead ("I want to
stay at the park, but in this situation I am not going to get what
I want. How can I honor God and my family even though I am
disappointed?").

How we raise peacemakers changes over the years. Our
relationship with our children changes drastically over time. When
they are young, our control over them is great. We choose what they
wear, what they eat, and where they go. Over time, however, as they
grow in wisdom, control gives way to influence. They choose what
they wear, what they eat, and where they go—with their choices
hopefully being guided by loving, godly parental influence. When
children are first learning to take control over themselves and their
environment, we have a great opportunity to model peaceful relationships to them as well as train them in the art of peacemaking. Loving parenting adheres to the 2 Timothy 3:16 model that
involves requiring certain concrete actions (teaching), confronting
wrongdoing (rebuking), enforcing rules that encourage obedience
(correcting), and coaching on how to act (training in righteousness).
As parents, we must pray for wisdom to know what is appropriate
for each child based on age, temperament, and the present situation. Our hope is that we will continually be relying on the Word,
no matter their age, and helping to instill this same reliance and
obedience into their lives.

We are sinners helping sinners. One reason teaching our
children to be peacemakers is particularly challenging is because
we are not perfect peacemakers ourselves. With all of our conflicts,

how can we instruct our children? Simply said, we humbly acknowledge that we are sinners saved by grace. In the words of Dr. Dan Doriani, "Discipline is the process in which bigger sinners attempt to convince little sinners to mend their wicked ways."[3] We pray for and work toward lasting change so that our own hearts and lives model *shalom*. As we study and obey the whole counsel of God ourselves, our instruction to our children becomes stronger. Even our peacemaking failures provide opportunities to model repentance and humility to our children. Instead of training our children to be hypocritical liars in their confessions ("Say you're sorry." "Okay, I'm sorry. Now can I go play?"), we can model genuine repentance in our own confessions as we pray for their hearts to be convicted by sincere sorrow (2 Cor. 7:10).

God calls us to keep the real goals of our parenting in mind. As we delight in our children and long to see them become happy, successful adults, we are called never to lose sight of the big picture—the real goals of parenting. As Christians, we are to do our best to help our children grow into mature, God-loving adults by impressing the truth about God on their hearts (Deut. 6:6). We seek this goal so that God would be glorified as we do our part in his work to conform our children to the image of Jesus Christ. If we become distracted by lesser goals, we will continue to be embroiled in conflicts with our children even into their adult years.

Sharon experiences frequent conflict with her preteen daughter, Kate. Kate loves her mother intensely but has a difficult time expressing her frustrations and fears. She sometimes says hurtful things like, "I hate you, Mom!" even though she does not in fact hate her mother. She does, however, lack the maturity and skills to communicate well and appropriately deal with her own sin. Sharon frequently loses sight of the big picture—God's glory and our conformity to Christ—and instead fixates on her daughter's unkind words, further fueling the conflicts. The ensuing hurt leads her to stop persevering as she loses sight of the goal of ministering to her daughter. Instead of counseling her daughter from Scripture or seeking to understand better her daughter's heart, Sharon simply shuts down emotionally and closes the door on the relationship.

In order to work through this conflict and work toward restoration of the relationship, I (Judy) reminded Sharon of the truths of 1 Peter 3. Although broadly directed to all relationships, these verses provide excellent reminders of certain principles to follow in parent-child relationships: "Live in harmony with one another [purpose]; be sympathetic [perspective], love as brothers, be compassionate and humble [passion]. Do not repay evil with evil or insult with insult, but with blessing, because to this you were called so that you may inherit a blessing [patience]. . . . Who is going to harm you if you are eager to do good [priority]? But even if you should suffer for what is right, you are blessed [perseverance]. . . . But in your hearts set apart Christ as Lord [prayer]" (1 Peter 3:8–9, 13–15).

As a Christian parent, Sharon is called to cling to the *purpose* of pursuing peace as she develops a clearer *perspective* of what is happening in her daughter's heart and in their relationship. Like all parents, Sharon is called to grow in *passion* (love) for her daughter as she patiently strives to be conformed to Christ—all the while helping her daughter do the same. Despite the pain she feels, this Christian mother is to *persevere* through the difficulties as she reminds herself that it is Christ who ultimately changes the heart. As she continues in *prayer*, God's strength enables her to live out her main *priority*—to love God and others.

God chose us for our children. When Sharon came to counseling, her thinking led her to despair and emotional flight: "My daughter doesn't respect or love me," "Kate's life is ruined because of me," "I'm a bad mother," "My daughter is better off without me," and "It hurts too much to be close to Kate." What does scriptural truth say to these thoughts? Sharon is not perfect, but God has sovereignly ordained that she mother this child. God chose to put Kate in this particular family; it was not an accident. This means that God will work in Sharon to do what is necessary to bring honor to himself through her parenting, and Sharon is called to do her part to rise to the occasion. Instead of shutting down and pulling away when she feels hurt, Sharon is called to engage Kate and help her to talk through her frustrations. She can help Kate look at life differently and bring her thinking more in line with biblical truth.

I (Tara) prayed for years that I might *not* have a child like me— driven, slightly compulsive, a real "go-getter." I was afraid that I would not be able to wisely shepherd such a little one. I prayed only for children that were just like Fred—kind, patient, gentle, easygoing. Before my first child was born, I was confronted by dear friends who helped me to see that each person is precious and that God delights in the way that *he* designs his children. No matter what personalities our children develop, I can trust in God's grace to help me to enjoy and wisely shepherd them.

When Parents Don't Agree

A common area of family conflict is disagreement on how to parent children. Considering all of the possible variations in background, childhood experiences, communication styles, and learning preferences, we really should be amazed to imagine parents agreeing on much concerning their children. So what is important to understand when parents don't agree?

Unity, not uniformity. As Christians, we are called to have unity even if we don't have uniformity. Often we are frustrated with our spouse and we try to demand that he see things and respond just like we do. We try to force our husbands to parent like us. One young mother remembers many fights with her husband when their first child was born because he did not hold the baby "correctly" and forgot to "wipe front to back" when changing a diaper. Sometimes we try to control our husbands because we are afraid that if they don't do things just the right way, something bad will happen ("The baby will slip out of his arms and fall." "The baby will get an infection."). At other times we do not feel secure in who we are, and we feel validated when others are like us. Our thinking might go something like this: "If you don't agree with the way I educate my children, then I must be wrong. If I'm wrong, then I'm bad. If I'm bad, then that means that I am not loved and accepted and there's no place for me to belong." In this situation, the problem is not how we parent our children; it is a heart issue about our craving for approval.

God has graciously ordained that even though we are one family and members of one body, Christian parents have different gifts, talents, and functions. This diversity can help us to develop a good parenting team where each part functions differently towards a common goal (1 Corinthians 12).

Disputable matters. One can find many wise ways to view and respond to various situations. Although we might prefer for life to be "black and white," in reality much of life is filled with the "gray" of disputable matters (Romans 14). A disputable matter involves an issue that is neither forbidden nor required in Scripture. To respond well to these somewhat confusing issues, we need to look to biblical *principles* to guide us, especially when no clear biblical *precepts* are present. Applying principles rather than being guided by direct and clear precepts in Scripture requires great wisdom, especially when differing perspectives can apply the same principle in the same situation in very different ways.

God's grace enables us to realize how much we benefit from parenting from the perspectives of our mates. We can learn to trust one another, not as perfect people but as people gifted and called by a perfect God to the task of co-parenting.

Faithful obedience. Maryann is dissatisfied with Tom's approach to child discipline. Both Tom and Maryann agree that disrespecting adults is wrong, but Maryann wants their children to be spanked when they are disrespectful, whereas Tom wants to coach and counsel their children instead of spanking them. When Tom fails to spank the children and instead sits with them and kindly talks through the conflicts, Maryann becomes furious. She feels that Tom and the children are not honoring her and that Tom "allows the children to get away with murder." She says bad behavior needs to be punished with spanking; he says it needs to be dealt with through discussion. She thinks he's wrong; he thinks she's wrong. She thinks he's too soft and wishy-washy; he thinks she's too harsh and critical. What help is there for Tom and Maryann?

As Christian parents, Tom and Maryann are called to understand that they will stand before God and give an account *to him* for how they fulfilled *their own* parenting responsibilities. When we recognize that we will give an account not to each other but to a holy God for the decisions in our lives, we can better partner with each other to help one another live in such a way that we both might one day hear the words "Well done, good and faithful servant!" (Matt. 25:21). God does not evaluate us on the results of our parenting efforts but on our faithful obedience to him during our parenting years. It is our faithful obedience to God's Word, not the outcome of our parenting (which is ultimately beyond our control), for which we are held accountable.

The great "watchman" passage in Ezekiel comforts us with the truth that God does not hold us accountable for the disobedience of others—even that of our children or spouses. Ezekiel's story is solemn. He spoke God's Word clearly and powerfully to his people. He pleaded, he exhorted, and he pleaded again. But few listened. Ezekiel was to experience the horror of watching those he knew and cared about be destroyed by their own disobedience.

> The word of the LORD came to me: "Son of man, I have made you a watchman for the house of Israel; so hear the word I speak and give them warning from me. When I say to a wicked man, 'You will surely die,' and you do not warn him or speak out to dissuade him from his evil ways in order to save his life, that wicked man will die for his sin, and I will hold you accountable for his blood. But if you do warn the wicked man and he does not turn from his wickedness or from his evil ways, he will die for his sin; but you will have saved yourself."
>
> Ezekiel 3:16–19

This passage in Ezekiel can make us feel sad as we grapple with the truth that no matter how hard we try, no matter how concerned we might be, ultimately we cannot force our children or spouses to do anything. God himself has given people the freedom to make their own choices—even choices that lead eventually to eternal death. God does, however, hold us accountable for our personal obedience to him even in the bleakest of situations. And yet we can find great comfort in the story of God granting the people of Nineveh repentance following Jonah's preaching (Jonah 3). Jonah reminds us that God can change even the hardest of hearts.

Issues, positions, and interests. In parenting as in all of life, we are particularly helped by remembering the distinction between "issues," "positions," and "interests."[4] An *issue* is a problem that needs a solution. An easier way to think of issues is to view them as questions requiring answers. For instance, an issue might involve an effective way to discipline a disrespectful child. Put in the form of a question, the issue might be, "Is grounding our ten-year-old son appropriate discipline when he is disrespectful?" Because disputable matters exist, even devoted Christians can arrive at different answers on the same question. Let's call these *positions*. We know in Scripture that children should be disciplined. Yet how a child should be disciplined in a given situation may well fall into the category of a disputable matter. Dad's position on the issue of grounding their ten-year-old for disrespect is "yes." Mom's position on the issue is "no." Most parents get stuck right here. Some parents divorce because they are never able to move past the issue/position impasse.

It is at the level of *interests*, however, where disagreements are resolved. Interests are the reasons and motivations supporting the position. An interest can be understood as "that which is valued and drives our positions." Dad's true desire is to see his son make good choices. This is mom's true desire too. They have shared interests in this regard. Dad, however, believes that grounding is appropriate because it provides a strong incentive for his son to be respectful. He thinks that his son will be motivated to change by having to stay home instead of going out and having fun. After all, it worked for dad while he was growing up. Dad believes that this form of discipline will help his son learn the painful cost of sin. Mom's interests on the question of grounding are different. She believes that grounding their son will unnecessarily anger him because the punishment does not fit the crime. She too wants their son to make good choices, but she fears that increasing his anger will make their son disrespect his parents more. In her view, the best way to correct his disrespect would be to require him to do unpleasant chores. She thinks that when her son experiences immediate consequences, he will recognize that it is far better to avoid the inconvenience and embarrassment of the consequences by choosing to speak kindly.

The level of interests is where unity is found and preserved. A wife who understands the heartfelt goals and perspectives of her husband has the opportunity to affirm the value of these hopes, gently challenge less worthy desires, and minister to him by helping him grow in trust and faith in God. Husbands have the same opportunities to minister to their wives. Parents who value each other can often risk "experimenting." Together they can try plan A to see if it is effective. If not, they can try plan B. Or perhaps together they can develop a new and creative plan C. The advantage of a mutually agreed-on plan is that no person loses if the plan fails, because it is not "his" idea or "her" idea but "their" idea. If the plan succeeds, success is shared. Poor plans can be reevaluated without hurt feelings when parents are connected and committed to pursuing the same goals (shared interests). Getting locked into a battle of positions drains energy and commitment. The child eventually gets less attention and discipline as parents divert their energy into a battle of wills.

Compromise. Is it ever okay to compromise your position? Isn't it sinful to step down from your position—especially in parenting? It depends. When a position is not specifically required in God's Word, a willingness to move away from one's own position to accommodate a different position (which is not specifically forbidden in God's Word) may be an act of mature faith. To refuse to pursue or do what is right, or to pursue what one knows is wrong, is sin. To refuse to pursue one right answer *in order to pursue another right answer* may be to "make every effort to do what leads to peace and to mutual edification" (Rom. 14:19). While Romans 14 and 15 speak specifically to eating meat sacrificed to idols and drinking alcohol, a broad principle expressed in this passage is that we are called to do what leads to peace and mutual edification when we are dealing with disputable matters. One person can possibly have a perspective that is completely different from another person's view, and they both can be worthy of respect so long as they do not contradict or ignore scriptural commands. The whole counsel of God must be considered in order to know how to proceed in our responsibilities to live in a Christian manner.

If the question we are attempting to answer is not disputable, then the answer will most likely be clear from Scripture. Otherwise, when our perspectives, preferences, convictions, and values lead us to diametrically different conclusions, we are called to pursue peace while we help others grow in their faith. We are not to insist that our position be followed if it causes another to go against their conscience. To persuade someone to take a course of action contrary to what they *prefer* is a far cry from persuading someone to take a course of action contrary to what they believe is right. Of course, in matters where our own conscience calls us to a particular position, we have been called to model humility, gentleness, and a willingness to learn and grow even as we stand on our convictions.

For example, caring for our children and providing for their physical needs are indisputable matters. We cannot allow them to go hungry or unclothed if we have the means to care for them (1 Tim. 5:8). Murdering our children with harsh words or unkind remarks (Matt. 5:21–22) is indisputably wrong. Scripture states clearly that we are not to harm others, especially children: "Fathers, do not exasperate your children; instead, bring them up in the training and instruction of the Lord" (Eph. 6:4).

Of course, not many parents argue over whether their children should be neglected or abused, but we do argue over things like whether to give our children an allowance for doing chores or just because they are in the family. This is not clear from Scripture. To handle such a disagreement, we must first ask, "Will following my position cause my spouse to believe he has done wrong and therefore interfere with his relationship with God?" (Rom. 14:14–15). If the answer is no, then perhaps it is acceptable to ask my husband to consider my preferences on the issue. However, if the answer to this question is "yes, it would make him feel as if he is doing something wrong," then I need to rethink my position and consider a course of action that is acceptable to both of us. Even though I may feel it is appropriate to give an allowance without requiring chores, if my husband believes strongly that it encourages sinful irresponsibility on the part of the child, the loving thing may be to require chores for an allowance because of my husband's convictions.

When different convictions exist on a given issue that falls into the category of disputable matters, in order to promote unity, we best begin by addressing the issues underlying each position with gentle and biblically informed counsel. In those instances where one person is unable to change his position, even though we have tried to find a mutually satisfying agreement and have sought biblical guidance, our freedom in Christ allows us to model Christlikeness by "giving up" our position in an attempt to "please [our] neighbor for his good" (Rom. 15:2). I am not being loving toward my spouse if I am not willing to set aside my own positions in those "gray" areas not explicitly dealt with in Scripture. In the words of David

Powlison, "Relationships have been destroyed when even minor preferences become life-ruling demands."[5]

Divorce and Remarriage

Almost always, divorce destroys any sense of peace and unity in the family. Without going into a biblical analysis of divorce—an important topic to be sure—we would be remiss if we did not at least speak to a few of the conflicts associated with parenting, divorce, and remarriage and how we can walk in *shalom* in these situations.

Keep your eyes fixed on eternity. Whether personally going through a divorce or dealing with its aftereffects, we can easily begin to focus only on the other person and the sad circumstances. Such a focus usually leads us to despair. We forget the gospel and live out of our own hurts and weaknesses. As Christians, we are called to prayerfully keep our hearts and minds fixed on Jesus, "who for the joy set before him endured the cross, scorning its shame" (Heb. 12:2). Christ's suffering on the cross is our hope in any pain, even pain as excruciating as divorce. A willingness to suffer well with heaven as our goal is a real alternative that God's grace enables us to choose by faith.

Mindy demonstrates how precious this mindset can be in the trauma of divorce. After Mindy developed a degenerative disease in her thirties, she and her husband could not enjoy many of the outdoor activities that had drawn them together initially. Mindy felt terrible and did all she could to regain as much strength and health as possible, but she still struggled daily with debilitating pain. Fed up with the inconvenience of caring for an invalid wife, her husband left her and moved in with a younger, healthy woman. Of course Mindy was devastated—rightfully so. But instead of growing bitter, she consecrated this horrible offense to the Lord and prayed for wisdom and strength to respond in a Christlike manner. Her church rallied around her, and in their loving care, Mindy persevered in doing good to her ex-husband, speaking well of him and even blessing him when opportunities arose. Her heart attitude and her actions all gave a glorious testimony to her children and provided them with love and stability even after the divorce.

We wish we could report that Mindy's husband was so moved by her testimony that he repented and came to faith in Christ and they were reconciled. We cannot. But Mindy is comforted in this life by the hope and assurance that in the next life, God will right every wrong and that in some miraculous way her testimony of grace in this life will give glory to God *forever*.

Be honest. Like all conflicts, conflicts associated with divorce are painful. In our zeal to promote peace, we may be tempted to hide or deny our hurts. But God's love is bigger than our pain, and we can find comfort in him. Helping children experiencing divorce to acknowledge their hurt honestly and learn to work through their pain faithfully is also important.

In addition to how we handle our suffering and pain, we are called to be honest about our sin. Divorce reveals sinful hearts. Instead of denying our contribution, we have a rich opportunity to model genuine humility, repentance, and confession. This goes for both parents and children alike. Divorce brings many opportunities to help others honestly acknowledge sinful anger, unbelief, and destructive actions as they are taught to cast themselves fully on God's grace for deliverance. Although it is difficult, we are to honestly admit our sin regardless of whether anyone else—even our spouse—ever does so.

Rest in the Lord and trust in him. One of the most frightening aspects of divorce is the complete lack of stability that often results. Stay-at-home wives lose their financial security. Children lose their homes. Husbands lose their children. As Christian children or adults, one of the key ways that we can walk through the conflicts of divorce is by taking proactive steps to rest in the Lord and trust in him despite the intense fears and difficulties that come from the instability of the divorce. In our pain and suffering, we may need help to bring those fears and hurts to the Lord. But such trust in the one true, immutable, unchanging, eternal God carries us through even the darkest of times.

When I (Judy) was fifteen, I attended a youth group regularly and studied the Bible often. I was growing in the knowledge and love of the Lord until my parents divorced a year later. The devastation I felt soon became a rejection of God because I blamed God for not preventing this tragedy. Over the course of a few weeks, I lost my home, my financial security, and my family.

No Christian adult ministered God's comfort and hope to me. My mother, although a believer, was too broken over my father's abandonment to help me deal with my grief. My youth group leader was preoccupied with other things and did not realize the extent of my suffering. My Christian friends were only teenagers and did not understand or have the resources to help me. My own faith was immature and unable to sustain my doubts and despair. Because I did not receive the help of others, I walked away from the Lord for more than ten years. And yet, even though I still feel some pain twenty-five years later, God has done a miraculous healing in my heart. My parents' divorce and the resulting pain and loss motivate me to work with marriages in conflict. Having not benefited from help in my time of need, I deeply desire to see others encounter the grace and wisdom of the almighty God who uses even divorce as he "works for the good of those who love him" (Rom. 8:28).

Work through conflicts. A genuine commitment to working through conflicts is the only way that divorced families have any hope of living in harmony (1 Peter 3:8). If we fall off the "Slippery Slope" of conflict" (see chapter 4) into flight or attack, we have little chance of experiencing God-honoring relationships. Only as we cast ourselves on the Lord and earnestly seek to obey his commands concerning conflict resolution can we experience peace.

Of course, the only way we can truly work through conflicts is if we understand our hearts and the idols that might be ruling us and leading us to sin. Many divorced families become severely conflicted when one parent remarries and chooses to value the new spouse over the children and grandchildren. I (Tara) used to work in the area of estate planning. A person's will can often show this unhappy scenario: the mother remarries and immediately leaves her inheritance to her new spouse—a virtual stranger—instead of her children of thirty or forty years. Other situations also cause children to feel hurt and devalued. For example, if a child's father takes a vacation with his new wife instead of coming to visit her, she feels the pain of believing she is a low priority to him. As Christians, we may rightfully be disappointed when a parent does not value us as highly as we desire. And yet if we make a good desire (like being valued by our parent) into an idolatrous demand, we will often live with bitterness and resentment.

Do good—even to your "enemies." Romans 12:21 gives a strong command: "Do not be overcome by evil, but overcome evil with good." The phrase "be overcome" can also be translated as "conquered." In this light, this command reveals a startling truth—nothing can cause an individual to be or to feel conquered the way that evil can. But nothing can conquer evil like good. The power of evil is real. In this life, when evil strikes, we can either overcome it or be overcome by it. We have no other choice.

Few life experiences have the power to defeat us like divorce. Divorce causes two people who know each other intimately to focus their hate in particularly damaging ways. The harm done through divorce is often all the more devastating because spouses use intimate knowledge gained through trust and tenderness to overcome their adversary. The one who once was a partner, sharing hopes and dreams, is now the enemy causing destruction and the one who must be destroyed. No defeat, however, comes to those who fight evil with good. The greatest good of all, the ultimate good of love, overcomes evil.

Sheri was shocked when her husband abandoned her and her two-year-old daughter, but God's grace enabled her to raise her precious child in the Lord. With the help of her church, Sheri went to school, worked multiple jobs, and provided for her family. Years later, Sheri's ex-husband approached her about having a relationship with their daughter. Of course, Sheri's initial inclination was to refuse. After all, she had done the hard work of raising this child. And now *he* wanted to come in and enjoy the good fruit of all of her labors after giving up his parental rights years ago. Truly, apart from faith in Christ, Sheri never would have permitted her ex-husband to develop a relationship with her daughter. Sheri understood not only that her daughter would benefit from knowing her father but also that Sheri would provide a testimony of grace to her ex-husband by granting his request. And so, by faith, Sheri demonstrated how the Lord would have us to respond to an "enemy." Instead of dismissing or intentionally harming people who hurt us, our obligation and joy as Christians is to pray for them daily, beg God for his mercy to soften their hearts, and remember that apart from Christ we too would be enemies of God. Only God's grace saves us and makes us alive—nothing we do merits God's love. In view of the gospel, we are to do good especially to those who wrong us.

Don't give up. Continue to hope. Hope is like the atmosphere surrounding us. It is like the air we breathe. We have an abundant supply close at hand, but it does little good until it is drawn in. The problem with hope is not that we do not have any but that we fail to access the hope that is present and available.

The most tragic marital dispute mediation I (Judy) have ever participated in involved a family where the parents had spent nearly $500,000 in legal fees in repeated attempts to hurt and control one another. From dad's refusal to allow mom to see the children to mom's attempt to control the children with threats of calling the police, the hurt and devastation were immeasurable. Their teen-aged children turned to self-mutilation (cutting themselves), drugs, alcohol, and sex to cope with their pain and anger. The situation seemed hopeless, especially as the father faced a prison sentence for failure to pay child support. The mother, however, had begun to be transformed. She learned to hope. Through support groups in her church and the prayer of a small group of people she enlisted to pray for her, this devastated woman eventually rebuilt her relationships with her children, began to heal the relationship with her ex-husband, and sought the Lord's wisdom as she made many difficult decisions. At last I knew, this mother was planning on pursuing graduate school in order to help others benefit from the pain of her own experiences, especially her experience of learning to persevere in hope.

It *is* possible to walk in hope regardless of the circumstances. Consider the divorce experience of two dear friends of mine (Judy's). Jeannie and Derek, both Christians, each brought two children from previous marriages into their new marriage. Despite the pain of their divorces, they committed to witnessing for Christ both to their unsaved ex-spouses and to their children. Jeannie and Derek have granted Jeannie's ex-husband a gracious welcome into their new home by providing him a copy of their house key to use when he picks up the children on "his day" or when he needs to stop by to pick up forgotten clothing or sports equipment. God's grace enables Derek and Jeannie to extend courtesy and genuine kindness to Derek's ex-wife by welcoming her at holiday celebrations involving the children. Family meetings between parents and stepparents are a common occurrence as they work together to parent the children.

Although saddened by their parents' divorce, Derek and Jeannie's children never fear that their parents and stepparents will make them "choose" between one or the other. Jeannie and Derek are precious reminders to all divorced families to keep hoping in the Lord and not give up. By God's grace, fragments of families can be redemptively restored into beautiful vessels full of grace.

Families formed after divorce or remarriage are often referred to as "blended" families, but I (Judy) am not sure that is the best term. My daughter loves to make smoothies. Strawberries, bananas, milk, and ice thrown into the blender form a delightful, delicious treat—with a consistent texture and color. Having counseled many "blended" families, I have wondered if "stir-fried" is a better adjective. Each child and parent brings their own unique flavor and texture into their new family, and those differences may never change. To expect a smoothie when you are served stir-fry is to encounter disappointment and frustration. But great peace and even joy can come when we have realistic expectations about the "stir-fry" nature of our new family dynamics.

Parents and Adult Children

Even as adults, we are linked to our parents. And as parents, we are linked to our adult children. Where honor exists, *shalom* is often present. Sadly, the relationships between many parents and their adult children are filled with conflict and strife. Why is this so? And what can we do?

Changes in the parent-child relationship. As children become adults, the parent-child relationship changes profoundly. A frequent source of conflict between mothers and their adult children comes when mothers, so involved in their mothering role for decades, lose sight of their role as Christian women apart from motherhood. Instead of living to serve the Lord and using their gifts for his glory, these women have centered their lives around their children. When their children break away to begin their own adult lives, the mothers frequently become frustrated and feel lost. This can lead them to become controlling and manipulative. They may insist that their children give them time and attention and may view other interests in their children's lives as a competition for their affection. When nurturing goes awry in this manner, parents lose the ability to celebrate their children and delight in them as they become gripped by the idol of their children.

I (Tara) saw this in an intense conflict between a mother, Rose, and her adult son. The mother was distraught over her son's treatment of her. Although he tried to encourage her, spend time with her, and show her love, it was never enough to satisfy her demands. Her expectations were putting a huge stress on his relationship with his wife and children, and resentment was beginning to build. As the mother and I talked, I began to observe that this mother was making her son's love an idol. She said things like, "If only he would love me as he ought, then I would be happy," and "All I want is for him to make me a priority like I made him a priority all those years." We prayed together and looked at Scriptures but did not seem to make much progress. Then I pulled my chair around so that I could look her right in the eyes, put my hands out in front of me, and said, "Rose, if God's love, attention, and care for you were in my right hand, and your son's love, attention, and care for you were in my left hand, and you could only choose one, which would you choose? What is more important to you—God's love or the love of your son?"

She froze. Her eyes darted back and forth from hand to hand. And then she looked at me with tears in her eyes and said, "That I'm even hesitating means I have a pretty big problem, doesn't it?" Clearly, she was looking to her son for her fulfillment instead of to the Lord. And her son would never be able to satisfy her. Instead of growing their friendship and love, the weight of her expectations and idolatrous demands was crushing her relationship with her son (see chapter 2).

Failure to leave and cleave. Peace is threatened when parents and their adult children fail to understand the biblical admonition to "leave and cleave" (Gen. 2:24 KJV). This does not mean we are to end our relationship. Instead we are to care for our parents, sharing in a loving relationship as much as it depends on us. A sign of true religion, the kind that pleases God, is caring for our parents and grandparents (1 Tim. 5:4). As children, we should be attached to our parents, but not in a way that deprives our new family of their appropriate priority in our lives. "Leaving" our parents means we are no longer dependent on them.

The fact remains that separating from our families of origin is hard. In one sense we never can. We take our values and experiences with us wherever we go in life. But we do need to renegotiate and reestablish a relationship as adults. We stop relating as "dependent child to adult" and learn to relate "adult to adult." Sometimes this means that we will all have the maturity to give and receive love and our relationships will deepen into intimate friendship. At other times we will have to learn to bear with one another and do good to one another when one or more of the people involved is emotionally, socially, or spiritually incapable of having a good relationship.

Abbie was a woman who had failed to leave her parents and cleave to her husband. When hard things happened in her life, her first call was usually to her mother, not her husband. When she needed something done around the house, her dad was always there with his tools to help out. Of course, a close friendship with a mother and father *can* be a blessing. But in Abbie's life, the relationships were interfering with her relationship with her husband and causing conflict. Abbie had to learn how to develop an intimate friendship with her husband and affirm his headship in their home by turning to him with her requests and accepting his provisions.

Lack of sympathy. Many conflicts between adult children and their parents arise from unsympathetic and uncharitable hearts. Instead of taking the time to get to know one another and prayerfully develop a sympathetic perspective on each other's lives, we respond with harshness and a graceless lack of love. Many times our parents simply do not make us, or our children, a priority. They may not be Christians. In that case, we may more easily understand why they would put their own happiness and comfort ahead of us—taking lavish vacations and rarely visiting their grandchildren, spending money on luxuries and comforts instead of helping us with our daily needs, expecting us to drop everything for a visit when it suits them instead of taking our schedule into consideration. We may understand, but it still hurts. It hurts even more so when they are professing Christians yet do not delight in our children or in us. We may long for intimate relationships with our parents and sadly find that conversations are awkward and shallow. In these as in all disappointments, we are called to suffer well and continue to do good, even in the face of sorrow and pain.

If you struggle with a lack of sympathy toward your adult children or your parents, we encourage you to pray for the grace to change and the courage to take practical steps to get to know one another. Whether they are Christians or not, we are called to suffer well (see chapter 3) even as we grow in sympathy toward them. We may even be called to love them as a "difficult person" (see chapter 5).

Love thrives in an environment of understanding. Consider talking with your parent or adult child about the circumstances and people that have impacted you the most. How were your parents' relationships with *their* own parents? Could that be where your mother learned to speak harsh words to you now? What was your child's experience in college truly like? Do you know her successes and failures, struggles and victories? What influenced your father to make the decisions he has made in life? Understanding backgrounds does not provide excuses for sin, but it can help us sympathize so that we might patiently minister to them out of godly compassion. As we get to know and accept one another, we learn to hold tightly to the agenda of glorifying God as our priority in life.

Critical and judgmental attitudes. We are called in Scripture to speak words that build up others according to their needs: "Do not let any unwholesome talk come out of your mouths, but only what is helpful for building others up according to their needs, that it may benefit those who listen" (Eph. 4:29). As adults, we may be called to deal with overbearing parents or adult children who might give criticism without encouragement. It is helpful to remember that critical behavior reflects on the speaker, not on the object of the criticism.

I (Tara) once taught a workshop on the topic of "Healing the Conflicts between Mothers and Daughters."[6] To prepare, I interviewed over one hundred fifty mothers and daughters. I heard comments like, "Do you have any idea how much I have sacrificed and suffered because of my mother? It's hopeless!" "My daughter is a codependent, whiney, immature, and disrespectful person. How could I have raised someone who is so mean?"

Critical words do not necessarily portray accurately another person's strengths or weaknesses. Instead of reacting in hurt and anger, we pray for grace to respond in a God-honoring way. Consider how Jesus confronted the woman caught in adultery (John

8:2–11). First he demonstrated his care for her; then he exhorted her to change. When people reverse this order, exhorting change before demonstrating care, the exhortation is felt as graceless criticism. Receiving this feedback is particularly difficult when it comes from our own parents or children. Only God's grace can enable us to overlook, forgive, and patiently persevere in relationships with critical and judgmental people.

Forgetting the gospel. It is easy to forget the gospel when it comes to parents and adult children. Recently I (Tara) went through a painful family conflict over the name that my daughter would call my stepfather. As I reflected on the situation, instead of mercy and blessing, I was tempted to respond with selfishness and bitterness over past hurts. In light of some recent offenses, I initially did not *want* to give him the gift of being called "Grandpa." As I reflected on my behavior, I began to despair as I considered what a terrible witness I was giving to him and to the rest of my family. But then I remembered—yes, God is holy. He does expect and require that I respond in a way that honors him. God is also merciful—he gives me all that I need to live by faith and respond with love.

In the past, I might have defended my position or redoubled my efforts to "be better," but by God's grace, this time I remembered that although I am a sinner, I have a great Savior. That is my hope. As I remembered the gospel and cast myself on Jesus, he graciously enabled me to do good even to family members who had hurt me. As I repented of my sin, I began to see anew all the wonderful ways that my stepfather had been a loving and supportive part of my life for years. I also saw with crystal clarity the many ways that I had been selfish and petty. Eager to repent and live a life of love, I took great joy in encouraging Sophia to call him Grandpa. Apart from the gospel, we have no hope. But in Christ, we have all we need for life and godliness, even in these sometimes difficult relationships (2 Peter 1:3).

Families of *Shalom*

God's standard for how we treat one another in all relationships, including families, is quite clear: "If you have any encouragement from being united with Christ, if any comfort from his love, if any fellowship with the Spirit, if any tenderness and compassion, then make my joy complete by being like-minded, having the same love, being one in spirit and purpose" (Phil. 2:1–2). We are to honor one another, respect one another, and love one another. "Above all, love each other deeply, because love covers over a multitude of sins" (1 Peter 4:8). Yet sometimes this can be so difficult! Our children may try to manipulate us or may say hurtful words to us. Our parents may compete with us or try to control us because they are living their lives vicariously through us. And yet God calls us to love them well! Out of gratitude for his love toward us, we are to love them.

Whatever your conflicts with your children or parents, we pray that your families will have such unity and love that you will reflect Christ to a watching world (John 17:20–23). I (Judy) can honestly say that I have been blessed abundantly in my relationship with my mother, Nadine, as have my husband and children. My husband, Jim, praises my mother frequently, grateful for the role she has played in all of our lives. My children have received a great gift in knowing their grandmother as few in our society today will ever know theirs. My mother has lived with us for over fifteen years, helping to raise our children and physically caring for us. She knows us intimately. She makes coffee just the way we like it. She reminds us to feed the dog. She is always willing to run out to the store for something we forgot. She insists that we take vitamins. She is our confidant, encourager, and friend. My children have felt her delight and her respect over the years. She is a huge part of helping them grow into mature and confident adults, and her ministry in our home testifies to the grace and power of Jesus Christ.

I (Tara) remember when God impressed upon my heart that I am my mother's daughter. I did not want to believe this! I had felt so estranged, hated, and rejected by her that I simply could not even imagine that I came from her. Yet the truth of God's sovereignty was vividly communicated to me with a picture. It was as if I could see my mother standing with God's hands placed behind her womb. I had the strongest sense that I was called to submit not to my mother but to God's providence in choosing my mother for me. Every sorrow and hardship I would experience in my family? God knew them all. God knew that he would be with me and would save me as his precious daughter. I was not called to trust my *mother* but to trust *God*. I am my mother's daughter because God himself chose her for me and me for her. Realizing this was the beginning of healing in my relationship with my mother.

When dealing with difficult family relationships, we may need to get help from a pastor or trusted friend to be sure that we remain biblical in our thinking and obedient in our interactions. When tempted to give in to anger or idolatry, nothing can compare to a mature, godly friend lovingly confronting us and reminding us of God's will for our life. God has chosen our families for us. We rest in the assurance that he is with us and that he will enable us to live in our families as peacemaking women.

Personal Reflection

Questions for Reflection

1. Meditate on 1 Peter 3:8–17. Then consider carefully the conflicts that you typically experience in the parent-child relationship by answering the following questions:
   - Have I determined or committed in my heart to live at peace with them?
   - Have I done the hard work of seeking to understand their perspectives?
   - Am I passionate about loving and caring for them with a humble spirit?
   - How can I change to be more patient?
   - Have I failed to follow through on my God-given priorities? Am I more concerned with lesser goals?
   - Am I persevering through this conflict, or am I giving up?
   - Have I brought my concerns to the Lord in prayer?
   - Am I believing God's promises?
2. Write out a two-sentence summary of your strongest desires for your children (or grandchildren). In what ways have your children failed to meet your expectations? Have these desires

led to conflict? In what ways have you elevated any of these desires to demands?

3. How have your parents disappointed you? List three of the greatest disappointments you have experienced. What is your attitude toward your parents? Read Ephesians 4:22–24. Can you identify any attitudes that need to be "put off"? What might God be calling you to "put on"?

4. Read Colossians 3:1–14. What three ideas do you gather from this passage that apply to you in your family relationships? You might consider completing the following sentence in three different ways: "According to Colossians 3:1–14, I am to_____ . . ."

5. What conflicts are you currently having with your parents? Your children? Review the peacemaking principles in chapter 4. What steps are you called to take to work through those conflicts in a biblically faithful manner?

6. Read Philippians 4:19. When you consider the stresses in your family, what meets all of your needs? Write a response to the Lord based on the message of Philippians 4:19.

Praying Scripture to God

Lord God, you are awesome in glory! I thank you that you redeem and lead me by your strength. Please strengthen me according to your Word and keep my heart set on you. Father, please help me to love my children and parents deeply. By your grace, may I cover over a multitude of their sins with love. May I live by faith in you, Lord God, and may I serve like Jesus served. Please help me to work through our family conflicts in loving and biblical ways that honor you. May I humbly keep my heart fixed on eternity and entrust my parents and children to you. In all things, may I hope in you, for you are good and you work all things together for your glory and my good.

(Prayer based on Exod. 15:11; Exod. 15:13; Ps. 119:28–31; 1 Peter 4:8; Heb. 10:38; Matt. 20:28; Gal. 5:13; Matt. 18:15–17; Rom. 8:28–29.)

Recommended Resources for Further Study and Consideration

Ross Campbell, *How to Really Love Your Child* (Wheaton: Victor Books, 1977).

Ross Campbell, *How to Really Love Your Teenager* (Wheaton: Victor Books, 1987).

Elisabeth Elliot, *The Shaping of a Christian Family* (Nashville: Thomas Nelson, 1992).

Kevin Huggins, *Parenting Adolescents* (Colorado Springs: NavPress, 1989).

Susan Hunt, *By Design* (Wheaton: Crossway, 1994).

Susan Hunt, *Heirs of the Covenant—Leaving a Legacy of Faith for the Next Generation* (Wheaton: Crossway, 1998).

Susan Hunt, *The True Woman* (Wheaton: Crossway, 1997).

Susan Hunt, *Your Home a Place of Grace* (Wheaton: Crossway, 2000).

Kevin Leman, *Bringing Peace and Harmony to the Blended Family* (Dallas: Sampson Ministry Resources, 2000).

Kevin Leman, *Keeping Your Family Together When the World Is Falling Apart* (New York: Delacorte Press, 1992).

Elizabeth Prentiss, *Stepping Heavenward* (Amityville, NY: Calvary Press, 1993).

Corlette Sande, *The Young Peacemaker* (Wapwallopen, PA: Shepherd Press, 1997).

Ken Sande, *Peacemaking for Families* (Wheaton: Tyndale, 2002).

Paul David Tripp, *Age of Opportunity: A Biblical Guide to Parenting Teens* (Phillipsburg, NJ: P&R Publishing, 1998).

Tedd Tripp, *Shepherding a Child's Heart* (Wapwallopen, PA: Shepherd Press, 1995).

H. Norman Wright, *The Power of a Parent's Words* (Ventura, CA: Regal Books, 1991).

8

THE CHURCH

They will become one in my hand.

Ezekiel 37:19

How Christians resolve their conflicts, theological and otherwise, speaks loudly of the faith they profess to believers and unbelievers.

Ted Kober[1]

After coming to faith in Christ as a teenager, I (Tara) was confirmed into membership in a conservative church. The men, women, and children became a family to me. They gave me rides to and from services, encouraged my involvement in Bible study and music ministries, and supported me on short-term missions projects. The year I started college, I returned to the area and visited a congregational meeting. I was shocked. The same people who had loved and encouraged me were at each other's throats. Being a relatively new Christian, I sat wide-eyed and silent as brutal words were flung back and forth over the pastor, theological issues, and the future of the church. I had never imagined that Christians would or could attack one another with such ugliness. Men and women yelled, accused each other publicly of terrible things, and demonstrated little humility, kindness, or love. After that meeting, the church split.[2]

A few years later I found myself embroiled in a terrible conflict when I directed the handbell choir at my college church. A young man in the choir began to miss some rehearsals because of other responsibilities. He was incredibly bright and a hard worker, but handbells are dependent upon one another, and his absence held back the entire choir. After seeking the counsel of my pastor and giving the young man many warnings, the sad day came when I was forced to ask him to step out of the choir. His father, a gifted musician himself, was furious with me. Again I was shocked by the venom that one Christian can direct at another Christian. I was shocked, that is, until years later when I saw the rage and hatred I had in my own heart when I was the one being hurt in the church. Suddenly I understood better the truth vividly portrayed in the entire book of Hosea that the ones we love the most are the ones who cause us the most pain. Frequently the pain inflicted on us becomes the pain we inflict on others. This sad cycle happens all too often in the church.

Addressing conflicts in the church is particularly important because the church is not an institution made by man. We do not join the church the same way we voluntarily join a community club or professional association. Jesus describes the church as his body (Eph. 1:22–23) and his family (Eph. 2:19). To be part of Christ is to be a part of his church. Scripture teaches that the communion of the saints leads us to deeper union with Christ: "My purpose is that they may be encouraged in heart and united in love, so that they may have the full riches of complete understanding, in order that they may know the mystery of God, namely, Christ, in whom are hidden all the treasures of wisdom and knowledge" (Col. 2:2–3).

Conflicts in the Church

Since the church is one of the God-created institutions against which Satan constantly makes war (Rev. 12:17), we have been called to understand the conflicts we face within the church and faithfully prepare to respond in a God-glorifying, peaceable manner. Of course, there is nothing new under the sun. Conflicts in the Christian church go all the way back to New Testament days. Almost every one of Paul's letters deals with misunderstanding and controversy in the church. These quarrels and divisions can be overt or hidden (1 Cor. 1:11), but even the absence of obvious conflict does not mean the presence of true *shalom*.

Idolatry. In church conflict as in all conflicts, we must examine our idols. Scripture commends the effort of opening our hearts to evaluation. Lamentations 3:40–42 sets the model for repentance of heart idols: "Let us examine our ways and test them, and let us return to the LORD. Let us lift up our hearts and our hands to God in heaven, and say: 'We have sinned and rebelled and you have not forgiven.'" Likewise, Psalm 139 leads us to examination of our motives: "Search me, O God, and know my heart; test me and know my anxious thoughts. See if there is any offensive way in me, and lead me in the way everlasting" (vv. 23–24).

One church experienced serious conflict when two women's ministries—one a Bible study for retired women and the other a mother's-day-out ministry—wanted access to the fellowship hall at the same time on the same day of the week. Both were important ministries, of course, but the room was simply not big enough for both groups to meet simultaneously. Instead of working together to resolve the conflict, the members of the two ministries began competing with one another, arguing why *their* ministry should have access to the room and the consequences that would occur if they didn't. Some families actually threatened to leave the church over the controversy. The desire for access to the room escalated to a demand, and when the demand was not met, the church's unity and fellowship were sacrificed on the altar of securing space in the fellowship hall.

Defensiveness. In church conflicts, we often become defensive—which can be viewed as one way we "claim to be without sin" (1 John 1:8). We refuse to take responsibility for our words, motivations, and deeds. We *insist* that people listen to us and understand us as we explain, over and over again, our position. Our demanding insistence that *we* explain and *others* listen and understand is one of the most common—and hidden—forms of defensiveness. Once conflict breaks out, it grows wider as we grow further apart. We set our hearts on defending our positions and ourselves. We insist on being "right." It is easy to try to deny our pride, selfish ambition, and vanity, but the truth is that we often value our own opinions—our "rightness"—over love and unity. This is particularly true in the church where so often we feel passionate and even biblical conviction on many matters.

Consider a church conflict that grew because two women were defensive about their children. Sarah and Rhonda began to dislike each other when their teenage children had a falling out. Instead of talking with one another and encouraging their children to do the same, both women became defensive and suspicious of one another. They began to think uncharitable thoughts about each other ("She is only doing this to hurt me!") and criticize each other's looks, parenting, marriages, and even ministries. They forced people to listen, over and over again, to their explanations of why *they* were right and the other person was wrong. Long after the children had forgiven one another, Sarah and Rhonda's defensiveness grew to such a level that their husbands and friends knew that to even infer that the other woman might have a good point on any aspect of the conflict would bring about wrath. Thankfully, the church loved these women enough to get involved and help them. It took over two years of mediations, meetings, and a lot of prayer—but the women are now reconciled. The wounds of defensiveness can be deep, and only God's grace can deliver us.

Core issues. Sometimes church conflicts are related to our deepest beliefs and convictions. Conflicts flare and grow when they touch on core issues. When the deity of Christ and other essential beliefs come into question, theological truth is at stake. Even related to these crucial matters, we are called as Christians to discuss them and even disagree in a respectful manner: "And the Lord's servant must not quarrel; instead, he must be kind to everyone, able to teach, not resentful. Those who oppose him he must gently instruct, in the hope that God will grant them repentance leading them to a knowledge of the truth" (2 Tim. 2:24–25).

I (Tara) once helped a church that was going through a serious transition over core issues such as the ordination of women, the gifts of the Holy Spirit, and the purpose of the church. As the church leaders and members wrestled with these weighty matters, conflicts eventually arose. But the leaders set a wonderful example for the rest of the church members in how to discuss even these important, foundational matters with mutual respect and abiding love. At the end of the day, some members and church leaders did end up leaving the church because their consciences constrained them to do so. But the personal relationships were not destroyed. Sadly, examples of such wise and gracious dealing with conflicts over core issues are rare.

Preferences. Most church conflicts do not revolve around foundational or core theological issues. Instead, they often grow from personal preference and opinion and generally demonstrate spiritual immaturity. A question arises or a criticism is expressed, and we personalize the issue as an attack on us. Instead of responding graciously, we close our hearts to the person who has hurt us.

Common conflicts over preferences include conflicts over worship styles, allocation of budget dollars, and Christian education curricula. We know of one church that experienced heated disagreement over the color of the geraniums that would line the church driveway. Some members saw the folly in this and begged the pastor to intervene. One person aptly captured the key issue by writing, "What will we say to God to explain why the color of the geraniums was more important than modeling love, joy, peace, and patience in front of our children and neighbors who are watching this conflict worsen?"

Looking to church to meet our felt needs. Church conflict escalates when we look to the church to meet our felt needs and something happens to disappoint us. For example, a common cause of conflict in the church involves the mind-set many people have that church is like a cruise ship. When we have this view of the body of Christ, we expect everything in the church to be conveniently tailored to our wants and desires. Our expectation is that we will be served, cared for, and entertained by professionals whose sole focus is our happiness. Of course, this misguided mind-set leads us to view people in the church as resources for our comfort rather than valuable members of one body who both need us and are needed by us. As a result, we neither love nor serve them well. In fact, when our expectations are disappointed, we engage in destructive gossip, criticism, and bickering. Instead of keeping careful confidences and protecting fellow members, we often speak ill of others. Church conflict—a terrible witness to the watching world—is the frequent result.

Often when I (Tara) teach on biblical peacemaking, someone will get excited to bring these truths from Scripture back to her church, approach her church leadership, and . . . nothing happens. In her motivated conviction about biblical peacemaking, she is expecting her church leaders to immediately rally around the biblical peacemaking materials and transform their church into the "culture of peace" that Peacemaker Ministries encourages. But for whatever reason, her church leaders do not act to implement the material. The irony is just how often conflict results when a church does not act fast enough to meet the expectations and felt needs of someone desiring to implement biblical peacemaking. Even zeal for peacemaking and "needing" our church leaders to implement biblical conflict resolution can become a source of conflict in the church.

People fail us. I (Tara) remember the time I received a phone call from a member of my church. I was hoping to hear an apology—she had hurt me previously and the ramifications in my life were ongoing. It seemed as though she was beginning to see how her actions affected me, and I truly thought that the call might contain an apology from her or even some offer of help. Instead, she began to confront *me* and list all of the ways that I should have handled the situation better. Just as she had done previously in our conflict, she emphasized *my* faults (of which, I admit, there are many). I was so hurt and angry that I asked if we could end the call and talk again the next week because I needed time to compose myself and pray. The real challenge arose that night when I had to attend a church event. I did not want to see *her,* and I surely did not want to be around other "so-called Christians" who might be similarly cruel and insensitive. Yet I had an obligation to be there, so, filled with misery, I went.

When I arrived at church, I was still replaying her words over and over again. The fellowship felt phony. I had difficulty worshiping. Then a miracle occurred. Seated with true friends, my heart began to soften. I looked into the faces of people who had faithfully, lovingly stayed by me over the years and put up with my many weaknesses and failings. I realized that I could never deserve their love or kindness. I had failed them and they had failed me. But I also realized that the deepest friendship in all of life is only possible within the body of Christ. The only way I could truly be a part of the body was if I was willing to risk being hurt. No one can befriend us like a Christian, and no one can hurt us like a Christian. Such is the risk of living and loving.

Comparison. A comparative mind-set is a fertile breeding ground for conflict, and women in the church are particularly susceptible. We (Judy and Tara) have both experienced the pain of having women compare themselves to us. Regardless of whether we "win" or "lose" in the comparison, *we lose.* We lose relationship and love. When evaluated and assigned "winner" status, we are robbed of the depth of connection and understanding that we long for. Once I (Judy) tearfully challenged a woman who worked for me to repent of her comparison of herself with me. (She had communicated to me that she felt intimidated by me because she could "never be as good in counseling.") I said, "When I win the comparison game, you set me up on a pedestal that is just high enough so that you don't have to relate to me or love me. I don't want to be idolized; I want to be known and loved. You can't do that if you keep me out of arm's reach." On the other hand, to be assigned "loser" status—to be judged as unacceptable and worthless by another person—is to receive another wound that can take a long time to heal.

When we are the ones comparing ourselves to other women, someone also must lose that game. When we feel strong, beautiful, and in control, we have confidence—we "win." When we fail to measure up in our own eyes—we "lose." Instead of keeping our eyes on Christ, we become focused on the people around us. We think:

My life seems so much better than theirs—I must be doing something right.

She is so much prettier, smarter, and more successful than I am. She wouldn't want me for a friend.

I always seem to suffer more than they do.

They don't have the right personality, way of expressing themselves, or ability—I don't want them serving on this committee.

I can never measure up—my past is spotted and my family roots are
   dishonorable.
It's no wonder they don't have friends; they are so shallow.

Such comparisons inevitably diminish love and lead to conflict.
Jesus spoke to our tendency to comparisons when he reminded
Peter to focus on the important things rather than on others: "Peter
turned and saw that the disciple whom Jesus loved was following
them. . . . When Peter saw him, he asked, 'Lord, what about him?'
Jesus answered, 'If I want him to remain alive until I return, what
is that to you? You must follow me'" (John 21:20–22).

A common but subtle way we play the comparison game may be
revealed by our passionate affiliation with some group or individual
that seemingly confirms our value because we "belong" to them.
Whether politics, sports, or the common saying of grade school children, "My dad can beat your dad!" the idea exists that those to whom
we belong somehow enhance our status. In 1 Corinthians 1, Paul has
devastating words for those who caused division amongst the body
of believers through their affiliation with Paul, Apollos, or Cephas.
Seeking to appear better than our neighbor by flaunting "our group"
always results in division. Therefore, Paul redirects the Corinthians
back to Christ in verses 18–31 and concludes with the powerful
"leveling" statement: "Let him who boasts boast in the Lord."

Competition. Similar to comparison, another common experience in the church that diminishes our experience of *shalom* is
competition. We compete against one another like orphaned street
urchins, scrambling for the last crumb of moldy bread. We forget
that our God is the God of the universe, the One who owns the
cattle on a thousand hills, and the One who knows even the number of hairs on our heads. Instead, women in the church often
compete against other women and try to impress one another by
being smarter, thinner, more disciplined, more godly, and more
"together." Instead of supporting one another, women compete
against each other for respect, relationships, and resources. The
church can be a breeding ground of competition—especially when
it comes to "our" ministry.

We are not saying that Christians should be passive people who
do not push themselves to excel by working hard to serve the Lord

and his people. We are suggesting, rather, that together the body of Christ is called to develop a unified vision for servant-hearted ministry within the church. Otherwise, in our pride, we will bicker and fight over the value of "our" ministries—instead of remembering that we have only one ministry: that of the Lord Jesus Christ.

I (Judy) once viewed some aspects of "women's ministries" as shallow, so I avoided participating in them. I felt superior in some sense because I was involved in the "serious" ministry of counseling. I was at a women's conference sponsored by Covenant Theological Seminary when I became sickened at the sight of my own arrogant and competitive heart. The seminar facilitator revealed to me my sinful attitude as I watched how graciously he related to these bright and hardworking women. He clearly valued and appreciated these women and actively encouraged them in their ministering roles.

I realized that I had been putting "my" ministry of biblical counseling above other important ministries, and I was wrong. I should have been supporting and encouraging the ministries of other women. God is graciously turning me away from my competitive mind-set. I have changed a great deal since that day when I saw the ugliness in my heart. Today I delight in the ministries of others and I actively seek to encourage everyone, especially women, to pursue the opportunities God offers to them. While not all are called to be pastors, teachers, and evangelists in the church, all of us, men and women alike, are called to ministry as members of the body of Christ (1 Peter 2:9).

Male-female relationships. A great deal of confusion can sometimes occur over the nature of male and female relationships in the church. While we cannot do justice to this topic here, our hope is that engaging, biblically accurate books will continue to be available to guide all of us in this important relational area.[3] In our ministries, the topic of male-female relationships frequently arises in response to the tensions and frustrations that are experienced. For a church to be filled with *shalom* and for us to enjoy that same peace, we are carefully to consider Scripture's teaching with regard to male and female relationships.

Sometimes conflicts arise when male leaders fail to have good relationships with women in the church. At other times, however, the women of the church create problems where no problems previously existed. For example, in one church conflict, the female leaders in the church were strangely silent during the meetings and mediations. Although they were intelligent and knowledgeable, having many questions, ideas, and thoughts that would aid in the ministry of reconciliation, they refused to speak up in front of the men. While there was no indication that the male leaders did not value these women, the women had adopted a wrong view of themselves and withheld their help and wise counsel to the detriment of the entire church.

Consider one real-life church conflict having to do with the male-female relationship. Patricia called her senior pastor, Ed, to ask for help regarding a conflict that had arisen at the missions committee meeting the previous night. Apparently two of the women on the committee had been discussing their "concern" that it was inappropriate for Patricia to work as an assistant to the pastor of missions, Larry. As the conference coordinator, Patricia was making numerous telephone calls to Larry to get his direction on how certain planning issues ought to be handled. Email messages commonly went back and forth as well. Mary and Sue thought that Larry should have a male assistant because "everyone knows what happens when a man and woman work closely together." Devastated, Patricia offered to resign as coordinator, but Larry refused to accept her resignation. Mary and Sue then made veiled comments that it was too late, clearly these two had feelings for each other. Ed and Larry met to discuss the issue.

What should Larry do? Should he accept Patricia's resignation in order to "avoid the appearance of evil"? Or should Ed and Larry gently instruct Mary and Sue, hoping to help them to evaluate their uncharitable presumptions and understand that in some ministry situations it is appropriate for women and men to serve together, even as Paul served side-by-side with his female fellow workers (Rom. 16:3, 12)? Should a policy be prepared and presented to the church to educate the congregation on how men and women are expected to work together? Should a policy be implemented that prohibits men and women from working together in any capacity? Such important issues and questions can easily lead to conflict.

Developing Churches of *Shalom*

How do we become peacemaking women when we are part of a church body that engages in the "quarreling, jealousy, [and] outbursts of anger" (2 Cor. 12:20) that Paul feared? How can we let "the peace of Christ" rule our hearts (Col. 3:15) when we have been the recipients of and participants in slander and gossip? The following are just a few ideas for how churches filled with sinners can demonstrate the unity of the Triune God so that the world might see that the Father sent the Son and the Father loves them (John 17:23).

Walk in the light of the Lord. When we see our sin and repent, *shalom* in the church is deepened. "But if we walk in the light, as he is in the light, we [God and believers] have fellowship with one another, and the blood of Jesus, his Son, purifies us from all sin. If we claim to be without sin, we deceive ourselves and the truth is not in us. . . . If we claim we have not sinned, we make him out to be a liar and his word has no place in our lives" (1 John 1:7–8, 10, explanation added).

I (Judy) used to be troubled when I read passages where my fellowship with God seemed to hinge on my "walk." I had always been painfully aware of my own sin and felt confused because I had misinterpreted "walking *in* the light" to mean "walking *according to* the light." To walk according to the light is to live perfectly, just as Jesus lives—something none of us can do. Walking *in* the light doesn't require perfect living, but it does require truthful living. It is a rich concept that includes, among other things, a penetrating honesty about our imperfection. Light dispels darkness, and walking in the light allows us to see and honestly acknowledge the truth about ourselves. In fact, seeing our own sin can be comforting because we know that only the light of God reveals it. When we try to deny our sinfulness, we deceive others and ourselves. By walking in the light—and dealing with our sin through genuine confession—we experience the sweetness of fellowship with God and others. As John reminds us, "If we confess our sins, he is faithful and just and will forgive us our sins and purify us from all unrighteousness" (1 John 1:9).

Practice biblical peacemaking. While the way we live cannot create or destroy our *relationship* with God (he alone establishes and sustains our relationship with him), the way we live does impact our *fellowship* with God—that sweet sense of connection that is necessary for *shalom* to abound in our lives. One component of *shalom* in the church is the wonderful liberation that results from our willingness to live out "The Four G's" when we face conflicts in the church: Glorify God, Get the log out of our eye, Gently restore, and Go and be reconciled (see chapter 4).

As Christians we are called to pursue unity in the church with our hearts fixed on glorifying God. The love that covers over a multitude of sins is pure grace. As grateful recipients of such grace and love, we have the duty and joy of giving that same love to others, especially those who hurt us the most. With prayer and hope in Christ's grace, our relationships will continue to improve over the years, though we may have to wait until heaven to enjoy the fullness of *shalom*. In this life, God's miraculous grace gives us the determination to forgive one another over and over again so that the world sees Christ formed in us (Gal. 4:19).

Sometimes our relationships in the church become so conflicted that we are not able to work through the conflicts on our own. I (Tara) have been the blessed recipient of the peacemaking help of my church on many occasions. When I try to work through a conflict privately but am unable to do so, I reach out to a trusted friend in the church—especially someone who the *other person also trusts*—to prayerfully help us. And when needed, I will ask my elders for intervention and help. I sometimes refer to myself as my elder's "high-maintenance sheep" because he has had to help me with some difficult conflicts over the years. And yet I know that he delights in doing so. Helping church members work through conflicts in a way that glorifies God and promotes unity is one of the greatest blessings that a church leader can have. When we are in conflict, we should not be afraid to get help even though it may humble us to do so. God designed the church for peacemaking, and our work toward reconciliation honors him in many ways.

In addition to intervening in conflicts, church members can also help to proactively *protect* their churches from conflicts through loving and humble mentoring.[4] I (Judy) am grateful for the mentors that God has brought into my life, especially my long-term mentor Howard Eyrich. While all my mentors have loved me deeply and helped me profoundly, for over twelve years Howard has helped guide me through times of challenge and stress. He has promoted a godly perspective and helped when I have faced potential conflict. When we reach out to one another for help and mentoring, we find that in Christ we have wisdom, encouragement, and knowledge to impart to one another. Often we learn best by sharing from our failures and turning together to Christ.

Set your hearts and minds on things above. In Colossians 3, Paul gives a "paradigm of peace" for believers to consider and follow. He tells his readers, "set your hearts on things above, where Christ is seated at the right hand of God. Set your minds on things above, not on earthly things" (vv. 1–2).

Three things have changed me (Judy) the most: marriage, mothering, and ministry. Nothing in life has caused me greater joy or grief than these three life endeavors. Years ago, during an excruciatingly difficult time in ministry, I could not sleep and ended up curled up on my bathroom floor sobbing. Sometime before I returned to bed, I came to the painful realization that my suffering was in part a consequence of setting my heart on earthly things. My pain stemmed from the fact that I had become wholeheartedly committed to protecting my position in the ministry by doing my work perfectly in the hopes of pleasing others. The more I lived for this purpose, the emptier and more fearful I became. I had lost my focus on the two great purposes in life—to love God and to love others. True repentance comes as we turn our hearts from unworthy loves and set our hearts on things above. When we do so, we begin to care about the same things that God cares about.

When we are in conflict with others in the church, we can easily start to feel superior, mistreated, and even "more spiritual." Yet when the active thoughts of our minds are fixed on Christ and the glory of his holiness, the darkness of our sin humbles us before him. Instead of judging and disliking others, we begin to treat them with kindness and humility. When our minds are focused on Jesus, our hearts are set on the important matters of the Lord: justice, mercy, and faithfulness (Matt. 23:23).

Put pride to death. Once we have set our affections and our thoughts on the things of God, we are to prayerfully strive to "put to death . . . whatever belongs to [our] earthly nature" (Col. 3:5).

While the list of things we must put to death is long, one common aspect of our earthly nature is often at the root of many other sins and conflicts: pride.

Pride is an excessive focus on ourselves. Pride has two faces: the face of other-condemnation, and the face of self-condemnation. Pride says "I'm too wonderful for you," but it also says "I'm not good enough for you." The root problem is the focus on self rather than on God's truth. Truthful thinking—such as, "I'm forgiven, you're forgiven, and we're both being changed"—sets us free from pride. When pride flourishes within the church, the pain caused to others and ourselves is great.

Many years ago I (Judy) attended the wedding of a godly couple who came from families that were known for their love of God and service in the church. I remember the excitement of the event and the joy at the reception. The happy mood was broken, however, when a woman seated at my table began to criticize the mother of the bride. "She hasn't even made her way over here to say hello. We are supposed to be such great friends, but all she wants to do is spend time with all those other people. I'm going to give her a piece of my mind." Confronted by another woman who overheard the comments, the "friend" remained seated with a dark expression and eventually left the hall. As I was getting ready for church the next morning, I reflected on the situation and was struck by the realization that the self-absorption of pride eventually results in an "everything is always about me" mentality. Even at an event that was to be wholly a celebration of a new covenant family that would reflect Christ and the church, this woman would not lift her focus beyond herself. Knowing my own tendency to struggle with this kind of pride, I was grateful for God's gracious conviction to help me to focus my thoughts on the things of God instead of my own self-centeredness.

Walk our own paths. A lack of contentment creates an environment of conflict. A lack of contentment may best be understood not as a desire for something different or better but simply as ingratitude for what God has done. We choose neither the paths of our lives nor our talents and gifts—God does. We do not even choose our families or the opportunities that come our way. Some of our life paths will be steep and rocky, and some will be level and smooth. We may never know why our road is much harder than another person's road. But what is that to us? We have Christ, and he is enough.

Seeking ways to improve our lives in the context of trusting in the God who creates our circumstances is commendable. The apostle Paul encourages active effort to improve our material circumstances, but only in the context of understanding who we are in Christ and how he orders our lives: "Each one should remain in the situation which he was in when God called him. Were you a slave when you were called? Don't let it trouble you—although if you can gain your freedom, do so. For he who was a slave when he was called by the Lord is the Lord's freedman; similarly, he who was a free man when he was called is Christ's slave. You were bought at a price; do not become slaves of men. Brothers, each man, as responsible to God, should remain in the situation God called him to" (1 Cor. 7:20–24).

I (Judy) once counseled a teacher, Brad, on some career decisions he was facing. In listening to his story, I was surprised to hear that although he loved his students, enjoyed teaching, and thought that his faculty and administration were top-notch, he felt it was time for him to "move on." As we reflected on why he wanted to leave a career that provided a lot of satisfaction, Brad shared, "My father and brother are both attorneys, and my sister is a doctor. All I have is a bachelor's degree, and I teach middle school science. I need to do something better with my life." I asked if his family agreed with him. Brad was silent for a few moments before he answered. "They think I'm crazy for wanting to change careers. Even my dad says I was made to be a teacher. But they all drive nice cars and live in nice homes, and all I have is a middle-class lifestyle. I feel like I've been cheated and all I have to show is a stupid 'Teacher of the Year' award." Brad's discontentment continued to grow into deep resentment, and he eventually left his teaching career. Two years later, halfway through law school with a small mountain of student loan debt and a strained marriage, Brad returned to counseling to seek help for his depression. My heart broke as he told me, "I will never know why I traded happiness for misery. I wish I was a teacher again." Brad lost his peace because he failed to trust God and walk the path that God had laid out for him.

Clothe yourselves. In order to experience sweet *shalom* in the church, we are also called to clothe ourselves with the virtues that God graciously endows to us. Although we are growing in Christ, we are not yet perfect. Within the intimate boundaries of our church family, we will bump into one another and sparks will fly. That is why we have been called to bear with one another in love: "Therefore, as God's chosen people, holy and dearly loved, clothe yourselves with compassion, kindness, humility, gentleness and patience. Bear with each other and forgive whatever grievances you may have against one another. Forgive as the Lord forgave you. And over all these virtues put on love, which binds them all together in perfect unity" (Col. 3:12–14).

Without affection and compassion, we will have no hope of forgiving one another's inevitable failings and offenses. Genuine Christian fellowship begins when we let one another down, become disillusioned, but still choose to forgive and forbear. Until we actively clothe ourselves with the virtues of God, we behave no differently than the people of this world whose relationships are dependent merely on pleasure and enjoyment. As we remember and experience God's lavish love for us, we are empowered to love others even when such love is difficult and not reciprocated. As we do so, we can remember God's promise to us in Hebrews 6:10 that "God is not unjust; he will not forget your work and the love you have shown him as you have helped his people and continue to help them."

Consider an example from real life. Caryn had been insulted when someone in her church called her a "fat cow" who had "no business taking up space." As I (Judy) counseled with her, Caryn and I reflected on Philippians 4: "Whatever is true, whatever is noble, whatever is right, whatever is pure, whatever is lovely, whatever is admirable—if anything is excellent or praiseworthy—think about such things. . . . And the God of peace will be with you" (vv. 8–9). I encouraged Caryn to clothe herself in the fruit of the Holy Spirit in order to bring glory to God.

Caryn shared that she was tempted to remember over and over again those hurtful words—"fat cow"—and she felt increasingly hurt as she dwelt on them. These words would ring in her ears when she tried to sleep and return when she got dressed in the morning. She tried to silence them by telling herself that the man who insulted her had no business speaking to her in that way, but then she just felt angry. She wanted to hurt him as he had hurt her.

As we counseled together, however, we reflected on the truth that Caryn's debt to our holy God had been paid for her by his great kindness. We reflected on the amazing grace and mercy that she receives each and every day from the Lord. And with her heart and mind fixed on things above, she practiced *thinking* new thoughts toward this man so that her *emotions* might reflect Christlike concerns. Caryn began to consider that perhaps he had lashed out because of spiritual and emotional immaturity. Caryn mulled over the possibility that his sinful attack might indicate he himself was suffering in some way. What he had done was wrong and hurtful. He had sinned against her, and she needed to either overlook his offense by forgiving it outright or else go speak with him with the hope of encouraging him in faith and godliness. Caryn did not have to be captive to his words—she could experience a sense of *shalom* as she clothed herself with God's grace.

Asking for God's wisdom and help, she called the man to ask for a time to meet. Despite her fear, Caryn knew that the reputation of Christ was preeminent over her hurt. During their time together, Caryn graciously and humbly shared her thoughts and feelings with the hope of being reconciled to him. He was receptive and repentant. God even helped him to see how his harsh words hurt other people, not just Caryn. Because Caryn had clothed herself with compassion, kindness, humility, patience, gentleness, and love, God was glorified in a restored relationship. The church was strengthened, and at least two people grew in the likeness of God.

Remember that all believers are progressing in sanctification. Another thing that can prevent us from experiencing "the peace of Christ . . . as members of one body" (Col. 3:15) is that in many of our relationships, but especially in the church, we sometimes have a hard time "letting" people around us change. People are learning and growing, but we sometimes have difficulty being willing to see them in a new light. While we know that God is doing something wonderful and new each day in *our* lives, we forget that God is working in others as well, and therefore we doubt that others can really change. An attitude of "that's just the way she is" replaces an attitude of faith that says, "God is present; he is at work." We are suspicious. The way we relate to others does not change because we do not believe they have changed. We relate as we have always done, requiring them to relate to us as they have always done. We essentially refuse to allow those in our lives to be "new creation[s]" (2 Cor. 5:17). Deep hurts and past experiences blind us, keeping us from being the encouragement and help to others that we otherwise could be.

Carl and Mindy came in for marriage counseling. Carl had ended a three-year affair with another woman more than a year ago, had begun attending church, and had prayed to receive Jesus Christ as his Lord and Savior. The changes in Carl were astonishing. He stopped drinking alcohol excessively, he helped out more at home, he was willing to talk about his relationship with Mindy, and he frequently read his Bible and prayed. His children saw the changes and were amazed. Yet Mindy refused to believe that Carl had changed. She spoke about Carl's past as if it were a present, day-to-day reality. In tears he pleaded with her to see the difference in him and forgive him so that they could begin anew. Her response was "I can't. Even though it looks like you have changed, I know that deep down you are the same person." Mindy stubbornly refused to see Carl as a new creation and therefore failed to clothe herself in compassion and forgiveness.

Even as we begin to see others grow, we can become easily discouraged when old patterns manifest themselves from time to time. Instead of giving up, we then have the opportunity to pray and cheer them on as they travel the same journey of growth in Christ as we ourselves are on. We can rest in the fact that God is transforming them: "And we, who with unveiled faces all reflect the Lord's glory, are being transformed into his likeness with ever-increasing glory, which comes from the Lord, who is the Spirit" (2 Cor. 3:18). And it is a transformation that God promises he will complete (Phil. 1:6).

Learn to disagree peacefully. Isn't it interesting that unity can be experienced not only as the result of perfect agreement but also as a result of bearing with one another in love? Even in our differences we can have unity, because unity is a lot like "harmony." Harmony involves the playing of different musical notes or chords which, when performed together, create a pleasing and beautiful blend. Harmony is music where varying notes are unified under a set of principles. For us to have unity in the body of Christ, we have been called to be unified in our submission to the headship of Christ. In order to maintain charitable hearts toward one another, we are to remember that our unity comes from an understanding of the foundation for our unity: "There is one body and one Spirit—just as you were called to one hope when you were called—one Lord, one faith, one baptism; one God and Father of all, who is over all and through all and in all" (Eph. 4:4–6).

As we pursue unity as members of one body, following our one God and Father, "We will in all things grow up into him who is the Head, that is, Christ. From him the whole body, joined and held together by every supporting ligament, grows and builds itself up in love, as each part does its work" (Eph. 4:15–16). Just as God's love is given to us, the undeserving, let us give love to those around us who least deserve it. Otherwise, we open our lives and our churches to the influence of the devil (2 Cor. 2:8–11). We give Satan an opportunity when we give in to bitterness and refuse to forgive (Heb. 12:15). In contrast, we reflect the grace of God and live in peace when we bear with our brothers and sisters in Christ: "Finally, brothers . . . aim for perfection, listen to my appeal, be of one mind, live in peace. And the God of love and peace will be with you" (2 Cor. 13:11).

Graciously allow for different perspectives. In the church we are called to allow for differing perspectives. We are to maintain unity without uniformity in order to experience peaceful fellowship in the body of Christ. As a beautiful example of this, I (Tara) love to reflect on the young mothers in our congregation. Some are very rigid with naptimes, bedtimes, and feedings. Others are more laid-back and individually responsive to their infants. Some only feed their children non-dairy, organic, whole foods. Others have been known to share an ice cream treat or cookie with their toddlers. I *love* that women with different convictions on nursing, bottles, cribs, and family beds can all enjoy fellowship together without fear of rejection or compulsion to change. We have different opinions on education (homeschooling, public, private, Christian, classical education), but we share fellowship in Christ. We sit in the cry room at church and share our struggles, celebrate our joys, and point one another to the Lord Jesus. When it comes to the gospel, we live out Paul's admonition in 1 Corinthians to be united: "I appeal to you, brothers, in the name of our Lord Jesus Christ, that all of you agree with one another so that there may be no divisions among you and that you may be perfectly united in mind and thought" (1 Cor. 1:10).

We should be flexible on many things, but on those essentials that cannot be compromised, we must stand firm, though in a gracious and winsome way. For example, I (Judy) had an ongoing theological debate with my husband for years. We simply did not agree on a couple of theological points. I shared this with a woman I was counseling who struggled in the relationships in her family. She was shocked. "How can you be married to a man you don't agree with theologically?" I explained that Jim and I learned from one another. I did not require him to see everything my way, and he gave me similar room to grow. I even explained to her that the apostle Paul left room for others to be wrong, content that God would make the truth clear to them in his own time (Phil. 3:15). She was stunned. In her marriage and friendships, she saw no room for different perspectives. Eventually, she divorced her husband. When the church disagreed with her "right" to divorce, she left the church. When her daughter shared the viewpoint of the church, she terminated her relationship with her daughter.

When any of us reject the notion that people can disagree and still remain in a loving relationship, we will eventually become divided and separated from others. Scripture teaches that we can have relationships with others even when we do not share their perspectives. We may not agree on some issues this side of heaven, but we will certainly agree on them in heaven: "All of us who are mature should take such a view of things. And if on some point you think differently, that too God will make clear to you" (Phil. 3:15). In the meantime, I can wait for God to bring you around as you wait for God to bring me around, and our patience and gentleness with one another will maintain our unity.

Remember that we are one body. We have referred frequently to the body of Christ as we have discussed conflicts in the church.

The marvelous truth in 1 Corinthians 12 is that Jesus Christ is the Head of the church and all believers are members of his body.

Even if we don't *feel* it, the truth is that all believers belong in the body of Christ (v. 15). God has chosen to create us as we are, with different gifts for different types of service and for different purposes (vv. 4–6). God arranges the members of the body as he wishes them to be (v. 18). Furthermore, these true and obvious differences are intended to be for the common good of us all (v. 7). To call into question the varied uniqueness of the members of the church and the placement of each member in the body is to call into question God's sovereign and good work. We are all a part of the body: "Now you are the body of Christ, and each one of you is a part of it" (v. 27). Perhaps the way we most challenge God's sovereign goodness is in our refusal to live the truth that we do in fact belong in the church and our refusal to help others live the truth that they are a part of us and we are a part of them.

Different parts of the body will necessitate different treatment. We cut our hair, but we do not cut our skin. We stretch our muscles, but we do not stretch our bones. We remove cancerous lesions, but we do not remove our vital organs. It is impossible and unwise to treat every part of the body in the same way. Yet differing treatment must be rooted in the realization that we treat church members differently to prevent division in the body rather than to create it (vv. 24–25). What would happen in the church if we treated everyone as a wayward sinner? Or what if we treated everyone as a spiritually mature believer capable of teaching God's Word rightly? Or what if we treated everyone as a needy person requiring help and support? The members of the body would experience great frustration and become ineffective. Understanding what it means to be a member of the body of Christ advances *shalom*. We are each equally valuable members of Christ's body on earth.

I (Tara) love how my church handles our "new member Sunday." Once a year we have a formal ceremony where we welcome the new members into our church family. Toward the end of the ceremony, our pastor turns to us, the congregation, and points to the new members as he says something to the effect of, "These are the brothers and sisters in Christ that *God* has chosen for our church family. They did not choose us, and we did not choose them of our own volition. But God has sovereignly ordained them for us and us for them." It is a precious reminder to us all that we are bound together as one family and one body.

Recognize that it may be appropriate to move to another church. We must be careful that we do not slip off the Slippery Slope of conflict (see chapter 4) into flight when we think about leaving a church. Most of the common reasons for leaving a church are actually persuasive arguments for staying. The things that are bothering us the most about our church may be God's instruments of grace and change in our lives. The things I think I *need* may be hindrances to God's work in my heart. The things I want to *avoid* may be the distasteful medicine that my soul requires. The decision to leave a church is a serious one that requires solid biblical counsel and intense prayer.

If we are considering leaving our church because it is not "meeting our needs," we must be careful that we are not making an idol out of the church and expecting far too much from it. For example, Carrie wanted to leave her church because "the worship was dry as dust." As I (Judy) asked questions, however, it became clear that she was holding her church responsible to be her parent, husband, source of significance, and fount of spiritual life. When her life was not going well, she blamed her church. If her church could not inspire, challenge, help, and love her sufficiently, then the problem was with the church, not with her. As we studied God's purposes for the church, Carrie was convicted that her reasons for wanting to leave were reasons that she should, in fact, stay.

We do have a huge responsibility to our churches. We are to use our gifts for the edification of the body, speak the truth in love to build others up, and pray for our leaders and the other members. But in some circumstances, it may be appropriate to move to a new church. If, after much prayer and respectful appeals, your conscience still convicts you that the issue is a core issue and there is no room for compromise, separation from the church may be the only resort. In this case, *how* we leave our church speaks volumes about our love for God and his children.

Consider the disappointing example of the Smythe family. When their independent Bible church voted to join a conservative evangelical denomination, the Smythes were incensed. After all, their family had helped to found the church, and they considered independence to be one of the most foundational principles of the church. The Smythes voiced their disapproval at every congregational meeting and in private meetings with people from the church. They broke fellowship with the pastor and his family and even turned away from the other church leaders. After the church joined the denomination, the Smythes resigned their membership with loud complaining and much anger, and they began meeting in their home with a couple of other families as a "real" independent church. For years to come, the Smythes would show up at church social events as "guests of friends," but they refused to even visit with the church leaders. Numerous attempts by church leaders to work toward personal reconciliation with the Smythes were unsuccessful.

Contrast the Smythes with Jacquelyn, who also felt that she needed to leave her church. After prayerfully studying Scripture, Jacquelyn was convicted that a certain view of baptism was the most theologically accurate. The problem was, she had been raised in and attended a church where a different type of baptism was the theological stance. Jacquelyn knew that wise and biblical thinkers could arrive at different conclusions about such important topics as baptism. She also knew that it would be sinful for her to cause conflict in the body by trying to convince others to hold a view contrary to the teachings of the church, but she felt that she should not remain in her current church. Although everyone was sad for her to leave, the church leaders lovingly worked with Jacquelyn to find a church home where she could worship according to her convictions. At all times Jacquelyn has guarded the witness and testimony of her former church, and she enjoys rich fellowship with its members to this day. Jacquelyn is a gentle example of how to move graciously to another church.

Our Imperfect Leaders

To experience the precious joy of *shalom*, we have been called to submit to the God-ordained authority of our leaders, both civil and ecclesiastical: "Remind the people to be subject to rulers and authorities, to be obedient, to be ready to do whatever is good, to slander no one, to be peaceable and considerate, and to show true humility toward all men" (Titus 3:1–2). Many church leaders are amazing examples of sacrificial love and service even though they sometimes fail us. God commands us to submit to them in the midst of disappointment just as in the presence of delight.

As we pray for, support, and follow our leaders, our submission pleases the Lord because by this too we promote peace in the body of Christ. We can love and support our leaders in countless ways in order to promote peace, but we will highlight just a few.

Admit that submitting is sometimes difficult. Being subject to "rulers and authorities" can be difficult at times. Some leaders in the church may be theologically astute and yet lack "people skills." Men who are "type A," task-oriented personalities commonly take on the time-consuming challenges associated with church leadership while the more relational men hang back from church governance. When sensitive issues arise, people—often women—are hurt by the lack of kindness and sensitivity modeled by their task-driven leaders. Even if these leaders want to be loving, they simply may not know how.

An example of this involves a pastor who realized that he needed to grow in gentleness because, although he communicated accurately, his words were sometimes harsh. At a Wednesday evening prayer meeting, he requested prayer for a young couple whose child lived for only one day. He stated rather abruptly, "God has marked out the days for this child as one day only" and moved on to the next topic. While his statement was theologically true, the hearers were in shock. "I hope another elder comes to comfort us at the hospital if we ever lose a child," one young mother said to herself. She was tempted to harden her heart to him and began to struggle in her submission to his authority. But then she remembered how he had humbly stood in church on numerous occasions and asked for prayer to grow to be more relational. So she gently went to him and discussed what had happened. Not only was he grateful for her feedback but her counsel helped him to grow to be more like Christ.

Remember that our leaders are human too. Both of us (Judy and Tara) serve on mediation teams that go into conflicted churches, seeking to help bring reconciliation and restore unity. Precious little in life is more beautiful than church leaders humbling themselves before one another and before the congregations they serve. Sometimes leaders do not naturally relate in a loving, gentle manner. But they are nonetheless capable of change and growth.

In one church intervention the senior pastor resigned because he did not handle conflict well and had not succeeded in his relationships with other church leaders. The most painful aspect of this particular intervention was a meeting where person after person shared their strong feelings of anger and offense with the pastor. The charges? He did not seek them out enough. He did not know enough about them and their personal lives. He did not encourage them enough. In his confession he repented of "not loving well" and committed himself to living differently, placing a much greater priority on relationships with others. This pastor had no moral failure that brought about his downfall. He simply didn't give enough of what was wanted, needed, and expected by his flock—more of himself.

Of course, no one ever loves anyone enough, and the burden on church leaders is intense. They are called to love a great many people in powerful, life-changing ways. That is why we are called to afford pastors a special level of understanding and compassion as they shepherd us. We are exhorted to "respect those who work hard among you, who are over you in the Lord and who admonish you. Hold them in the highest regard in love because of their work" (1 Thess. 5:12–13). We pray for them. We do not give up on them as they too are growing in Christ. Instead of expecting and demanding perfection from them, we are called to show them grace. Rather than complaining about our leaders' shortcomings, we can help them. In so doing, we are also helping the whole body of Christ to function better.

Practice biblical peacemaking. As we have ministered to church leaders, especially pastors and elders, we have heard stories of incredible hurt experienced by them in their ministries. Most of these men verbalized how much they would have appreciated the opportunity to be confronted in a gracious way by those who felt offended or frustrated (Matt. 18:15–17). Those times when others failed to follow a biblical process of confrontation were when their greatest wounds were experienced.

One pastor came to an annual church meeting, expecting to share with the congregation budget matters and his vision for future ministry opportunities, only to discover that a vote had been secretly scheduled in order to oust him. Another pastor arrived at his office to find himself locked out and a note taped to his door informing him that his belongings would be shipped to his home later in the week. An elder once shared a story about how his fellow elders arrived at his workplace and demanded to be told the truth about his "affair" with his secretary. Not only did his "inquisitors" initially refuse to believe his story that he had never had an affair with his sixty-year-old secretary (he was thirty-five), this elder was never even given the opportunity to dispute the anonymous note that prompted the inquisition. The hurt and betrayal felt by our church leaders can be devastating.

As peacemaking women, our loving help, submission, and counsel can make a real difference in our leaders' lives and the life of the congregation. A young college student, Penny, was concerned about the amount of gossip in her church's singles ministry. As she attended social events and Bible studies, she was shocked by the sarcastic comments and joking (but unkind) words that the leaders used. Instead of judging them, however, God's grace enabled Penny to work through all of the biblical peacemaking principles summarized in chapter 4. She prayerfully sought wisdom on how she could best glorify God. She tried to overlook things, and when she felt she couldn't, she humbly and privately approached the leaders. She started out by encouraging them before sharing how she has struggled with her own speech over the years. She then gently confronted them about their words. Some were more open and responsive than others, but Penny did not give up. Over time, her faithful efforts to address the conflicts biblically and lovingly bore beautiful fruit as the singles ministry grew stronger and more unified.

Submit especially when we disagree. Our responsibility and duty is to submit to those in authority over us in the church—even as we seek to bring about God-honoring change. In addition to our heart attitude, we can take overt steps to model our submission to our church leaders. Submission is an act of love, character, and commitment. It is a willing, powerful response to the proper exercise of biblical authority by our servant-leaders.

In J. R. R. Tolkien's *The Return of the King* we see several stunning examples of submission.[5] At the foot of Mount Doom, Sam exerts his strength, love, and commitment by lifting and carrying Frodo up the mountain in order to help Frodo to fulfill his calling to destroy the ring of power. Sam did not usurp Frodo's authority to carry the ring; he instead served Frodo by carrying *him*. In another example, the men of Rohan willingly submit to the decision of King Theoden to ride to the aid of Gondor, even though this act would likely cost them their lives. Such submission is compelling, passionate, and beautiful. Submission is a true privilege that Jesus Christ models for us in his submission to the Father (see John 8:28; John 12:50), and he calls us to imitate him.

Of course, submitting to our leaders is easier when we agree with them and approve of their decisions. But we are called to submit to our church leaders *especially* when we disagree with them. If we only submit when we agree, then we are not submitting at all.[6]

Consider an example from the journals of explorers Lewis and Clark.[7] As you may know, the goal of the Lewis and Clark expeditions was to find the most efficient route to the Pacific Ocean. Somewhere in what is now Montana, the expedition reached a fork in the river. Each fork was equally large, and they had no idea which way to go. To a man, all of the enlisted men felt they should take the north fork. But the leaders of the expedition thought they should take the south fork. Much was at stake on the rightness of the decision because a wrong decision could seriously hinder the year's progress. As a tribute to their submission to authority, the enlisted men honored the officers' decision even though they strongly disagreed with it. In the end, the officers turned out to be correct. But even if our leaders are not correct, we are still called to submit to them and entrust the results to the Lord's sovereignty because God works out his will through authority.

Respectfully appeal. In those times when we disagree with our church leaders or when they mistreat us, we have a choice about how we will respond. We can rebel and fight against the apparent injustice, succumb to it and be controlled by it, simply quit and leave the church, or resist it in a gracious way and try to change it. Will we leave? Or, without growing bitter, will we respectfully appeal and sometimes suffer, all with the hope of redemptive change?

How do we seek to bring about growth and change in the church, all in the context of biblical submission to our leaders? We are to set our hearts and minds on doing what God's Word calls us to do. We speak the truth in love. We stay willing to ask, rather than demand, a hearing from our leaders. We gently, respectfully persuade with biblically informed positions. We willingly invest our own time and energy to help provide solutions, not just complain about problems.

Submission to our authorities may result in a degree of suffering for us. We may suffer when we support their preferred Sunday school curriculum, embrace disruptive people to whom they are ministering, or sacrifice financially to fund the goals they choose for our church. We always have the option of choosing to submit, even in the face of unjust suffering, because we are conscious of God: "For it is commendable if a man bears up under the pain of unjust suffering because he is conscious of God" (1 Peter 2:19). We may not particularly enjoy discomfort, but we can delight in the privilege afforded us to suffer—joyfully anticipating our future reward from our true master, our Lord Jesus Christ. We choose suffering for many reasons: because we are conscious of God's character and sovereignty; because we are called to do so; and also to inherit a blessing, for Scripture says, "Do not repay evil with evil or insult with insult, but with blessing, because to this you were called so that you may inherit a blessing" (1 Peter 3:9; see also 1 Peter 4:1–2).

Forgive our leaders. When we are hurt or disappointed by church leaders, we honor God by being willing to pursue reconciliation and being eager to forgive. A powerful truth is that God himself has chosen the pathway of suffering in order to reveal his glory. As we experience present suffering, even to the point of being mistreated within the church, we have the expectation of God's glory being revealed in us (Rom. 8:17–18).

I (Tara) once experienced hurt and disappointment in my relationship with a pastor in my church. During the months that we both worked toward reconciliation, I suffered terribly whenever this pastor led the worship service. Each word he spoke felt like a knife ripping through my heart. Sometimes I would just cry throughout the entire service. One Sunday I was prompted to go to him after the service and ask him to pray for me. I knew that such an action would humble me and allow me to reaffirm my submission to him even while we were not yet fully reconciled. Years later the pastor told me how much that act meant to him. Even though I did not enjoy making myself vulnerable to him, God's grace enabled me to obey God's mandate to forgive him. How grateful I am! Today this pastor and I enjoy true fellowship and trusting friendship. We both continue to grow in faith and godliness as we reflect on that painful season in our relationship and learn from our past sins and mistakes. By God's grace, our faith in God's unshakable, unmovable, bedrock faithfulness grows each day.

In Conclusion

One woman can make a huge difference in the peacemaking life of a church. Just as Abigail's humility and wisdom were used by God to turn around what otherwise would have been an overwhelmingly destructive conflict (see 1 Samuel 25), one peacemaker in the church can bring peace to a world of offenses and hurts. By the same token, one catty, competitive, immature woman can cause a chasm of divisiveness. We must never underestimate the impact that living a life of humility and peace within our church can have.

Lana's story shows the amazing impact that one person can have on a conflicted church. An elderly woman who had been born, baptized, and married in her southern church, Lana had raised her children in her church and had expected to be buried in her church's cemetery. So when her church began to experience serious conflicts, Lana was grieved to the point of weeping. She prayed. She read the Bible. And then one day she read *The Peacemaker* by Ken Sande and encouraged her pastors to call Peacemaker Ministries for help. They started a long process that involved teaching, mediating, and church-wide meetings, but all along the way, Lana was there. She encouraged, helped, prayed, watched children, taught on peacemaking, and even sat with people during mediations when they were too afraid to go alone. From her own peace in Christ, Lana helped to bring peace to her church. That church did not split and is now known in its community as a place where conflicted Christians can go for help.

Regardless of our circumstances or the people around us, Paul calls us to "conduct [ourselves] in a manner worthy of the gospel of Christ. Then, whether I come and see you or only hear about you in my absence, I will know that you stand firm in one spirit, contending as one man for the faith of the gospel" (Phil. 1:27). We have the power to build up and encourage or to cut down and destroy people. Our enduring relationships and abiding friendships provide victorious testimonies of God's saving and sanctifying grace. In the words of Thomas M'Crie, "He will establish unity on the solid and immovable basis of immutable truth and eternal righteousness."[8]

As redeemed children of God, let us commit to living at peace with our brothers and sisters. May *shalom* abound in our churches so that when Jesus returns, he will find us to be unified, eager to praise and glorify him as one body. "How good and pleasant it is when brothers live together in unity!" (Ps. 133:1).

Personal Reflection

Questions for Reflection

1. Generally speaking, what is your view of the church? How would you specifically describe *your* church? Read Ephesians 3:10–11. What do you believe may be one or two specific intentions that God has concerning your church?
2. In your own words write a definition of the church. Read Acts 20:28; Ephesians 1:22–23; and 1 Timothy 3:15. What relationship does Jesus have with the church? How does this impact your definition?
3. How do you understand the church's role in meeting your spiritual needs? What is the importance of corporate worship? List three things that, in your view, your church does well and three things that it does poorly.
4. Using at least one Scripture passage to support your response, answer the following question: "How important are relationships within the church, the body of Christ?"
5. Think about the relationships in your church. If you could only pick one word to describe the relationships among the

women, what would it be? What are some of the relationship strengths in your church? What areas still need further improvement to better reflect Christ to the world?

6. As you consider the various causes of conflict in the church listed at the beginning of this chapter (idolatry, defensiveness, conflicts over core issues, preferences, felt needs, people fail us, comparison, and competition), what conflicts do you observe most often in your own church? How do these conflicts detract from the ministry and testimony of your church? How do you contribute to these conflicts, and what can you do to promote peace and reconciliation in your church?

7. Do you struggle with submitting to authority? Describe conflicts you have had with people in leadership within the church. Read Ephesians 5:21. What does this verse say to you?

8. How does the cross of Jesus Christ offer you proof of God's love for you? Read Ephesians 5:2 and 5:25 and Revelation 19:6–9. How much does Jesus love his bride? Do you believe that as a member of his church, Jesus loves you this much?

9. How is God calling you to promote a culture of peace in your church?

Praying Scripture to God

Father, I thank you that you watch over my church and me as a shepherd watches over his flock. Father, please give me a true and abiding love for your church. Lord, I thank you that you are my safe haven and my refuge. By faith, may I serve my church leaders and faithfully administer God's grace to them. Lord Jesus, your love enables me to love others, especially the brothers and sisters in Christ in my church, for love comes from you. Please help me to appreciate each member of the body and delight in their differences as we seek the unity of the Spirit through the bond of peace. By your grace, I commit to loving my brothers and sisters in Christ, for this shows that I love you, Lord God.

(Prayer based on John 10:1–18; Ps. 26:8; Ps. 31:1, 3–4; 1 Peter 4:10; 1 John 4:7–8; 1 Cor. 12; Eph. 4:1–6; 1 John 4:19–21.)

Recommended Resources for Further Study and Consideration

Jay E. Adams, *Sibling Rivalry in the Household of God* (Denver: Accent Books, 1988).

Lawrence J. Crabb, *The Safest Place on Earth:Where People Connect and Are Forever Changed* (Nashville: Word, 1999).

Mark Dever, *Nine Marks of a Healthy Church* (Wheaton: Crossway, 2000).

Edward G. Dobsen, Speed B. Leas, and Marshall Shelley, *Mastering Conflict and Controversy* (Sisters, OR: Multnomah Press, 1992).

Horace L. Fenton Jr., *When Christians Clash* (Downers Grove, IL: InterVarsity Press, 1987).

Leslie B. Flynn, *When the Saints Come Storming In* (Wheaton: Victor Books, 1988).

Kenneth O. Gangel and Samuel L. Canine, *Communication and Conflict Management in Churches and Christian Organizations* (Nashville: Broadman Press, 1992).

Hugh F. Halverstadt, *Managing Church Conflict* (Louisville: Westminster/John Knox Press, 1991).

Diane Langberg, *Counsel for Pastors' Wives* (Grand Rapids: Ministry Resources Library, 1988).

John MacArthur, *God's High Calling for Women* (Chicago: Moody Press, 1987).

Wayne A. Mack and David Swavely, *Life in the Father's House* (Phillipsburg, NJ: P&R Publishing, 1996).

Frank Martin, *War in the Pews* (Downers Grove, IL: InterVarsity Press, 1995).

James Qualben, *Peace in the Parish* (San Antonio: LangMarc Publishing, 1991).

Ken Sande, *Managing Conflict in Your Church* (Billings, MT: Peacemaker Ministries).

Ken Sande, *Transforming Your Church: Cultivating a Culture of Peace* (Billings, MT: Peacemaker Ministries, 2003).

Marshall Shelley, *Leading Your Church through Conflict and Reconciliation* (Minneapolis: Bethany, 1997).

John Wecks, *Free to Disagree* (Grand Rapids: Kregel, 1996).

9

FEMALE LEADERS WITH POWERFUL PERSONALITIES

You know that the rulers of the Gentiles lord it over them, and their high officials exercise authority over them. Not so with you. Instead, whoever wants to become great among you must be your servant, and whoever wants to be first must be your slave.

Matthew 20:25–27

There is nothing wrong with having a strong personality. In fact, one of the things missing in our culture today is strong, ethical leadership—especially in our homes. . . . The issues that plague us cry out for people who make decisions from a position of power and strength rather than from the depth of their insecurities.

Tim Kimmel[1]

Whether at home or in the workplace, women with leadership gifts and strong personalities will be prone to conflict. I (Judy) remember the first time I ever met Tara. She was leading an advanced training event for Peacemaker Ministries, and the entire room was captivated by her intellect, charm, and obvious skill. I remember thinking as I watched her teach, "Tara is going to suffer in this life." I thought this because every woman I have ever known with strong leadership gifts and a powerful personality—including myself—has experienced *conflict*. Our strengths can be our greatest weaknesses, and strong women seem prone to attract attacks and cause offenses.

Of course, male leaders may struggle with the same tendencies to cause or increase conflicts. Yet sometimes it is worse for women. Most people expect women to be naturally relational and gentle, and when a woman is task-oriented and weak in interpersonal areas, people may not know how to respond to her. In addition, when a woman is both strong at relationships and driven to accomplish tasks, those around her may feel confused and wonder which "personality" will show up in a given day, so they may respond in fear and uncertainty. Our hope is that the advice in this chapter will be an encouragement and help not only to the female leaders with powerful personalities but also to the people with whom they relate. No matter what your personality is, the biblical principles in this chapter apply to you too!

When Our Gifts Are Our Downfall

As is so often the case, the leadership gifts and strong personality of many women can be both a blessing and a burden. By leadership gifts we mean the ability to encourage and motivate people to follow. By strong personality we mean that combination of vivaciousness and infectious enthusiasm that often accompanies bright minds and verbal prowess. How do these gifts cause conflicts?

Blindness. Sometimes a woman with a strong personality does not understand how she comes across to the people around her. We (Judy and Tara) both cringe when we consider how we related with people when we were in our twenties. Often we were decisive—and intimidating. We were determined—and disrespectful. Instead of understanding that some people thrive in more contemplative environments, we communicated with people in ways that implied we thought they were slow or weak. We were blind to how much our drivenness communicated that we believed others lacked passion and importance simply because they did not strive to accomplish as many goals or objectives as we did. Ironically, that same drivenness came from a desire to succeed and to bless the people around us. But our attitudes and our behaviors put people off and caused conflict. Our very gifts almost seemed to blind us.

As we have spent time with women leaders, we have seen clearly that some of the loneliest women we have ever met are women with powerful personalities and leadership gifts. They struggle to have good relationships, being either oblivious to the realization that they may offend the people around them or frustrated at their inability to refrain from doing so. Sadly, few people love powerful people enough to speak gentle truth to them. Instead of "perfect love driv[ing] out fear" (1 John 4:18), perfect fear seems to drive out love. Encountering fear rather than the love they so deeply desire, powerful women ache with loneliness experienced by few others.

A woman named Olivia was talented, successful, and had a great deal of credibility in her vocation of financial planning. Yet in her zeal she often appeared to have a self-serving agenda. Intending to be efficient, she would challenge people and dismiss them if they questioned her authority. Although quite competent, she did not communicate that she was listening to the people around her. When differences in opinion occurred, Olivia talked more loudly in order to be heard. Her employees viewed her as an unsafe leader, even though her corporate superiors found her to be more than acceptable because of the profits she earned. Olivia caused conflicts, in part, because she was blind to how she was coming across to people.

Arrogance. Women with leadership gifts can sometimes be arrogant and prideful. Instead of stewarding our authority and gifts for the benefit of the people in our lives, we can be tempted to wield our gifts for our personal goals—even good and godly goals. Because we are task-oriented, we take pride in succeeding at our tasks and can sometimes fail to demonstrate Christlike humility as we ought: "Do nothing out of selfish ambition or vain conceit, but in humility consider others better than yourselves" (Phil. 2:3) and "Whoever humbles himself like this child is the greatest in the kingdom of heaven" (Matt. 18:4).

A church-based women's ministry went through a season of conflict because one of their leaders, Paula, kept driving people away from the Bible studies. She was a great teacher and had a strong understanding of theology. But she unintentionally lorded her gifts over the other women. Paula used her biblical knowledge as a weapon instead of as a tool to help others grow. Rather than create an environment to encourage thinking and engaging the text, she would correct women at the Bible study by saying, "The Bible says . . ." Many verses later, she had proven her point. Unfortunately, the other women thought the point was that they were stupid and had nothing to offer. Without intending to do so, she communicated arrogance and a lack of love.

Lack of appreciation. Conflict is less likely to emerge and *shalom* is more likely to flourish when people feel valued and appreciated. But different people feel valued and appreciated in different ways. Leaders with strong personalities often fail to invest the time needed to discover how best to communicate respect and genuine care *in a way that is meaningful to the other person.* Instead of listening to, embracing, and engaging the people around them, they communicate a lack of concern or appreciation. Conflicts often erupt when people feel unappreciated.

Stacey was a successful attorney in the world's eyes, but she was a failure in the majority of her working relationships. She talked fast, walked fast, and did not accommodate people who could not keep up with her pace. Stacey's attitude was, "Meet me on my terms or not at all." She was decisive, direct, driven, and determined. Another woman, Sandy, described herself this way: "I just love being in charge of my engineering projects and delegating tasks. I love to organize, shepherd, and keep things moving along. I can perceive the twenty-five steps to get from A to Z, and I know just what it takes to get there. I'm not afraid to speak my mind. Some like it and some don't; that's their problem, not mine. But I guess I do feel bad about how people don't like to work with me." Even if we do not actually have such a dismissive attitude toward people, our failure to connect with people will cause conflict unless we consciously find ways to communicate value and appreciation.

Learning to Use Our Gifts with Grace

I (Tara) once had the joy and honor of working with a man of extraordinary success in life—professionally, academically, spiritually, and interpersonally, this man was *together*. I respected him immensely and was shocked when he shared with me his realization that I frightened him. In his words, he felt intimidated by "my gifts, my quick thinking and speaking, and the supersonic speed at which I used technology." Thankfully, he is a compassionate and gracious man who even to this day is helping me to grow and change. In conjunction with help from Judy, my husband, elders, and friends, I am learning to take the following steps in order to apply graciously my gifts and personality strengths for God's kingdom.

Develop understanding. Instead of rushing through life, task-oriented female leaders are called to grow in love and develop understanding. One way we can do this is to *redeem the time by becoming an observer of people and the world.* Beginning with ourselves, we can learn to become a student of others. Instead of being satisfied with accomplishing our substantive goals while being blind to how we are relating with people, we are called to understand and to serve others in love.

To understand others and ourselves better, we can quietly ask ourselves: *What nonverbal cues am I observing? Are they comfortable, or am I talking too fast? How often am I interrupting? Has everyone in the room had an opportunity to talk? Am I communicating genuine interest and care?*

Another way that we can grow in self-awareness and self-understanding is to ask the people around us for feedback. I (Tara) once asked a co-worker and good friend to help me during meetings if I began to talk too much or dominate the conversation. This kind man would gently raise one eyebrow or nudge my foot under the table if I began to relate in offensive and unloving ways. My husband, Fred, is constantly on the lookout for ways to encourage me when I am acting in gracious and humble ways and to help me when I don't realize that I am intimidating the people around me. I have every hope and confidence that God will continue to grow me in conformity to Christ and over time I will have less and less blindness as to how I relate with people. I will grow in understanding and love. My hope is in the Lord who promises to conform me to himself (Rom. 8:29).

Grow in humility. To paraphrase C. S. Lewis, pride is the national religion of hell.[2] In Matthew 18:4, Jesus explains that the chief kingdom characteristic is genuine humility, the opposite of pride. The world misunderstands and devalues humility. The abilities to exhort others and cast a vision are highly prized, but when was the last time we heard someone praised for showing compassion and patience toward others? One friend retells how at a recent women's conference for Christian leaders, each attendee was asked to complete a questionnaire to help identify and evaluate her spiritual gifts. Of all of the women present, over one hundred women leaders, *none* reportedly had the gift of mercy.

Women with powerful personalities tend to experience great tension because we know we are to be humble but deep in our hearts a war rages. Even though we would probably not admit it to many people, deep down we believe that compared to others, we often know more, understand more, and have the right way to do things. Such pride leads to conflicts and broken relationships. In the words of Susan Hunt, "Pride always divides, but the cross unites."[3] God's grace develops humility in us and enables us to show the world Jesus.

Terri was a highly educated leader who had to take an administrative job in an automotive repair shop because of some financial troubles in her family. Before Terri became the counter clerk, customers and employees alike had little regard for one another. Sharp words and careless acts were not uncommon. Terri, however, treated everyone with gentleness and consideration. Instead of communicating disdain and frustration over her "lowly" position, Terri humbly served as unto the Lord and sought to bless every person with whom she came in contact. Before long customers became "regulars" rather than one-time visitors. The mechanics, noticing the way Terri conducted herself, began to treat each other and their customers with the same grace. The owners of the shop frequently commented that while many could have done Terri's job, few could have transformed the culture of rudeness into one of consideration. Terri's humility and servant heart impacted all those with whom she related.

Value relationships. As we grow in grace, we must never be willing to break a relationship in order to achieve a goal. God's goal *is* relationship (love of God and neighbor). Consider Aimee, a homemaker with strong leadership gifts and positions in her homeschooling cooperative, the local crisis pregnancy center, and her church. Aimee prides herself on her careful stewardship of the family's finances. She keeps meticulous notes and knows where every dime is spent. When she hired a friend from church to do some repairs on her garage, she was shocked at how long the man took to complete the task. It just seemed to drag on and on, and so the cost was higher than he had originally estimated. At that point, Aimee had a choice. In her own words, "I knew that my tendency would be to push and nag to get the job done and then to haggle over the cost to save money. But as I reflected on the importance of relationship—especially within the church—and on my own tendency to focus too much on accomplishing tasks, I knew that I had to let it go. In that circumstance I was called to humble myself and entrust the delays and cost overruns to the Lord in order to preserve the relationship."

So how does a woman with strong leadership gifts and a powerful personality learn to value relationships? Years ago, I (Tara) was greatly helped in this area by Judy. She gave me a word picture that has stayed with me for years. She said that I needed to change from living my life as a mountain *climber* to living it as a mountain *guide*. I had approached life as a sure-footed mountain climber whose sole task was to get to the top of the mountain. I had all I needed to make it to the top, and I climbed hard and fast. I often viewed myself as one of the best climbers around. Whatever it took, I put my head down and did the job. Of course, the problem was that as a Christian leader, my job is not simply to get to the top of the mountain. Rather, my goal is to help my entire *team*—the people around me, especially my brothers and sisters in Christ—get to the top of the mountain. My job is to come alongside others to serve, encourage, and help them. Granted, some are out of shape or wearing the wrong shoes. Some like to go slowly and sniff every wildflower, while others are frightened of the wilderness. But these are not excuses for leaving them behind. I am to educate, protect, equip, and guide them. In fact, I learned that I will fail at my job if all I do is accomplish "my task" but forget the people around me.

Turn away from perfectionism and control. We grow in grace when we realize that sometimes the Lord approves of work that fails to meet our ideals. What can arguably be referred to as one of the greatest sermons ever given was written with a finger in the dirt (John 8:1–6). Excellence is important, but we can get caught up in minutiae that keep us from spending well the limited amount of time we have. We are especially prone to focus too much of our energy and time on the *task* and have nothing left for the *people* around us. When I (Tara) was frustrated because I didn't have the funding I wanted to do a great job with a project at work, Judy taught me a helpful phrase. "Memorize it!" she told me, "And repeat it often." It is: "In view of my present circumstances, this is the best I can do. It is not *the* best, and it may not be *my* best given different circumstances, but it is the best I can do *right now*."

This simple phrase reminds us that God is in control and we are merely stewards. We are to work faithfully and strive to do our best, but the outcome belongs only to God. As we trust in God's sovereignty and goodness, we learn to turn away from perfectionism and enjoy peace regardless of our circumstances.

Listen well. Another important aspect of growing in grace has to do with our communication style. To develop better relational skills, a helpful model that I (Judy) developed and teach often is the L-U-A-U Model of Communication:

- ***Listen*** carefully, with the intention of really understanding the other person, regardless of whether or not you agree with them.
- Seek to ***Understand*** the other person's perspective—uncovering the real issues at the heart of the matter—so that you are able to restate their position as completely and convincingly as they can.
- ***Address*** the issues lovingly, seeking a biblical and godly resolution, remaining open to considering not only your own interests, but also the interests of others (Phil. 2:4).
- Strive for ***Unity***, the fruit of *shalom*, by consciously committing to God's purposes in building peaceful community in your relationships.

Instead of mowing over people by the sheer force of our personality and enthusiasm, we are called to develop the skill of listening—not just for the next idea to debate or discuss but out of an earnest desire to show love. This may not be native to our strong personalities, but God's grace enables us to grow in this area. Paula, the formerly dominating Bible study leader we introduced earlier in this chapter, is a great illustration. Once taught the L-U-A-U model, Paula quickly realized that she tended to dominate conversations and give far too much information. Now Paula has learned to ask probing, insightful questions that engage her study members and often elicit the same insights that she wanted to offer herself. Because she was loving and humble in confessing her wrongs, the other women have warmly forgiven and embraced her. Learning to listen well has been key to Paula's growth in using her gifts with grace.

I (Tara) have been told by a dear friend of mine that I *need to never pass up an opportunity to keep my mouth shut.* Since I naturally talk so much, I miss out on opportunities to learn about and know others. To benefit the people in our lives, women with strong personalities are called to develop a *quiet* confidence in group settings. A quiet spirit allows room for others to express their ideas and come to their own conclusions. Even if we come to a conclusion quickly, we demonstrate grace and care when we listen well and others are invited into the process of discussing and developing their own conclusions.

Toni was the new superintendent at a Christian elementary school. The teachers were apathetic and were not being challenged by the fact that they were entrusted with the young lives of their students. Toni had a lot of new ideas on how to improve the school.

> When I came in, I thought that I would just whip these teachers into shape. I instituted a lot of new processes and requirements, but there began to be a lot of conflict. Some appreciated being pushed, but others could not understand why on earth I was picked to lead. After a lot of prayer, I had to confess that I was trying to take over and implement my own agenda rather than seeking the Lord to discover what he would have me do.
>
> I came to realize that the teachers needed encouragement and help to grow in their ministry. We worked together to come up with a

vision for the school. We began to spend time together and started to enjoy each other. Instead of regular business meetings, we began to devote a lot of time to prayer, hearing from one another about what God was doing in our lives. My experience at the school dramatically changed as we all focused on the Lord and his ministry rather than my agenda. So many of my ideas have been implemented, but it all has come out of humbly working on our relationships with one another.

People are blessed when we listen to them, even if we end up not following their suggestions. By listening carefully to them, we show that we value and respect them. We also demonstrate genuine humility and care when we pay attention to others and hear them out.

Submit to and support those in authority. No one has authority except by God's permission and plan. Whether civil authorities (Rom. 13:1–2), church authorities (1 Thess. 5:12), or "masters" (1 Tim. 6:1), God himself has established those who are to be in positions of authority. Rebelling against authority is a serious matter.[4]

Just as we emphasized in the previous chapter, female Christian leaders are called to submit to those in authority, regardless of whether they are gentle or harsh. Even when doing so is difficult, we can learn to say to our leaders, "I am going to trust the Lord to lead me through you." Whether it seems to make sense or is costing us what we hold dear, we are like Christ when we entrust ourselves to God and remember that he works out his will through authority.

We all, including women leaders, can easily submit to authority when we agree with the attitudes and actions of the people in power. Women with powerful personalities can be affirming to their leaders, causing them to delight in the joys of having someone who believes in them and supports them with great passion. When those times arise that women with powerful personalities are called upon to submit to decisions with which they don't agree, their same powerful personalities can cause terror in others. Leaders can fear angering strong women because they do not want to endure our wrath and disdain.

Having worked in the education field for years, Athella was a leader who was considered an expert in curriculum development.

Helping to co-found a classical Christian education school in her community afforded Athella a wonderful outlet for her gifts and an excellent education for her children. But when the school board decided against one of her well thought out and professionally presented proposals, Athella was initially hurt and angry. "How could they go with Amanda's idea?" she fumed. "Amanda doesn't even have a college education! These people don't know what they're talking about." Thankfully, however, Athella sought godly counsel about the situation, remembering that her work was for the Lord. God's grace enabled her to humble her heart and embrace both Amanda's ideas and the board's decision. Later Athella reflected on this experience as a turning point in her understanding of leadership. "You never really know if you are a true leader unless you have true followers. And you never really know if you have true followers unless they have the freedom and ability to choose to not follow. I am a better leader today because I value and respect, rather than assume, others' choices to submit to and follow me. I never really embraced the importance of leadership until I embraced the importance of submitting in love to those who lead me."

In Scripture, two powerful passages speak relevant wisdom to our lives as we seek to submit to those in authority over us—especially when we disagree. While these passages specifically name slaves and masters, our twenty-first-century equivalents would clearly include employees and employers, and the principles can apply to all sorts of authority relationships. The principles embedded in these passages speak to our hearts and motivations: "Serve wholeheartedly, as if you were serving the Lord, not men, because you know that the Lord will reward everyone for whatever good he does, whether he is slave or free" (Eph. 6:7–8). "Slaves, obey your earthly masters in everything; and do it, not only when their eye is on you and to win their favor, but with sincerity of heart and reverence for the Lord. Whatever you do, work at it with all your heart, as working for the Lord, not for men, since you know that you will receive an inheritance from the Lord as a reward. It is the Lord Christ you are serving" (Col. 3:22–24).

The blessings of submitting to and supporting authority are rarely highlighted in our Christian culture, but I (Judy) have experienced many. I am admittedly a woman with a strong personality, and over the course of my ministry I have occasionally disagreed with the decisions made by my leaders. Some of these situations have caused me great suffering—but much greater blessing. Whether disagreeing with a decision about how to handle a church discipline case or frustrated with the reappropriation of resources in the church away from my ministry, God has graciously enabled me to freely choose to bear up under the pain with gentleness and respect. Through this I am humbled by the blessing of experiencing the "Spirit of glory and of God" resting on me (1 Peter 4:14), just as Peter promises will be the joyful result of suffering in Christ.

One of the most important and meaningful aspects of serving in my leadership role is that over the years I increasingly enjoy the privilege of earning the trust and respect of my leaders. By God's grace, they know that even if I disagree with their decisions, I genuinely love and value them and I willingly submit to their authority. My pastors and elders frequently ask for my opinion. Since they trust my commitment to them, they feel just as free to take my advice as to leave it. In one meeting, my friend and elder Phil asked for my input. After listening to my ideas, Phil immediately decided on a different path. When I laughed out loud, Phil asked me, "What's so funny?" I told him, "You just gave me the best compliment I've had in a long time." "What do you mean?" "You obviously trust my love and commitment so much that you have the complete freedom to not use my ideas. But you respect my thoughts highly enough to ask my opinion."

I consider myself among the most blessed of women in the church. I am accepted for who I am, strong personality and all, and I am empowered to use my gifts under the loving protection of my elders. While few things have hurt as much as the suffering I have experienced in ministry, few things have enriched my heart and touched my soul more than the blessings of submitting to God and to those God places in authority over me.

Serve wholeheartedly and with great love. While women ought to be able to speak to issues with which they don't agree, women with powerful personalities have another weapon in their arsenal of love—the opportunity to apply their gifts and strengths to serving wholeheartedly with sincerity and reverence (1 Peter 2:17). We don't always have circumstances ordered as we would prefer, but we always have the opportunity to honor God in uncomfortable situations: "Love must be sincere. Hate what is evil; cling to what is good. Be devoted to one another in brotherly love. Honor one another above yourselves. . . . Do not be overcome by evil, but overcome evil with good" (Rom. 12:9–10, 21).

Powerful *and* Peaceful

I (Judy) had an identity crisis in early 2002 when I was named the executive director of the counseling center at my church. I called my pastor, Wilson Benton, and asked for some time to talk through my concerns. My question was this: "Wilson, I've read the books on leadership and I think I understand what it takes to lead well. The only problem is that these books are written by men for men. How do I lead as a woman?" He answered by speaking words that changed my life and forever impacted the way I use my gifts and exercise my authority as a leader. He asked me, "In what ways have you been successful as a woman?" I answered, "Well, I think I've been reasonably successful as a mother." Wilson replied, "Then that is how you will lead; you will lead as a mother. Mothers strive to be tender, compassionate, strong, and able to discipline because they have genuine love and a desire to see others grow to their full potential. Your leadership at work will be the same type of leadership you show at home with Ryan and Robyn."

Women with leadership gifts and powerful personalities have great opportunities to promote *shalom* or to destroy it. Few female leaders better instruct us with regard to their power to promote peace than the Old Testament figure of Deborah, whose service to God and leadership of God's people were used to bring forty years of peace to Israel (Judg. 5:31). Deborah, acknowledging herself as a "mother in Israel" (Judg. 5:7), was in the position to advise powerful leaders even while she worked and worshiped alongside them.

My powerful personality has often made me (Judy) feel like a square peg trying to fit in a round hole. Over the years, despite my attempts to "fit in," I have been told more times than I care to admit that I intimidate people. Few things disappoint and hurt me more than to hear these words. So, when recently two men told me that I was the strongest woman they had ever met, I felt my heart go cold, dreading their next few words. Yet both men indicated that while they had felt intimidated by strong and competent women in the past, neither felt intimidated by me. Fully aware of my ability to be selfish, demanding, and intimidating, I was humbled by their words. In their view, God's grace has enabled me to use my strength with compassion and love, not to dominate but to serve. These words are among the finest words of praise I have ever received, especially as I reflect on the conflicts I have caused in previous years. I know that this growth in me is only by God's grace. We have every confidence that God will grow you, and those you love with "powerful personalities," in similar ways.

Personal Reflection

Questions for Reflection

1. Summarize chapter 9 in two sentences. Do these truths apply more to you or to someone you know? What are three ideas you take away from this chapter about female leaders with strong personalities?
2. Read Romans 8:5–6. Divide a sheet of paper into two columns, one with the heading "Relating according to My Sinful Desires" and the other "Relating according to the Spirit's Desires." In what ways would you say you relate to others according to "the sinful nature"? In what ways would you say you relate to others in accordance with the Spirit? List these on your sheet of paper. What three changes can you make this week in the way you relate to others to help you to set your mind on what the Spirit desires concerning your relationships?
3. How would you describe your natural personality (you may want to consider going to your library to check out some books on different temperaments and personalities)? How do you tend to think and feel about people who are different from you? Do you treat people whom you perceive to have a different personality the same as those who are similar to you? Why or why not?

4. What kind of listener do you think you are? Ask three people who know you well to honestly evaluate you as a listener. How well did you listen to their answer? In what ways did others see you the same as you see yourself, and in what ways did they see you differently? Reflect on Proverbs 18:13 and write a short paragraph about what you discovered about yourself. Consider using the L-U-A-U model of communication on pages 246–47 as the basis for your self-evaluation.

5. What natural talents and spiritual gifts would you say you possess? How would you complete the following? "I utilize my talents and gifts in ways that . . ." Read Galatians 5:22–23. Which of these fruits of the Spirit are revealed most in you? Which fruit of the Spirit do you most lack?

6. Why are you called to submit to those in authority over you *even if you are convinced that you would do a better job than they do*? What two Bible verses can you memorize to encourage you as you seek to build them up, honor them, and respect the authority that God has ordained in your life?

7. Think of a female leader with a powerful personality who might be considered to be intimidating to others. How might you encourage her?

8. Have you ever been told by others that you are intimidating? Have people ever informed you that you have offended them but you had no idea that they felt that way? In what ways might you be blind to the damage that you have caused to your relationships? Who can you reach out to today for counsel, help, and accountability as you seek to grow into a more gentle and relational woman?

Praying Scripture to God

Lord, I thank you that you are the compassionate and gracious God, slow to anger, abounding in love and faithfulness, maintaining love to thousands, and forgiving wickedness, rebellion, and sin. Please, God, help me to never lord my authority or leadership skills over the people around me, but please cause me to be a humble servant. May I do nothing out of selfish ambition or vain conceit, but in humility may I consider others better than myself. By your grace may I be humble like a little child. Father, please help me to turn away from demanding perfection that frustrates the people around me. Instead may I use the resources you give me to prayerfully do the best I can at the time. Remind me of my weaknesses that I might not be quick to condemn others but be quick to treat them with grace and kindness. In response to your love for me, please help me to love my neighbor and joyfully submit to the authority that you have placed over me. In all things may I serve wholeheartedly, as if I were serving you and not people. By your grace, please cause me to serve with sincerity and reverence.

(Prayer based on Exod. 34:6–7; Matt. 20:25–27; Phil. 2:3; Matt. 18:4; John 8:1–6; Matt. 22:39; Rom. 13:1–2; 1 Thess. 5:12; 1 Tim. 6:1; Eph. 6:7; 1 Peter 2:17.)

Recommended Resources for Further Study and Consideration

Ajith Fernando, *Jesus Driven Ministry* (Wheaton: Crossway, 2002).

Susan Hunt and Peggy Hutcheson, *Leadership for Women in the Church* (Grand Rapids: Zondervan, 1991).

Tim Kimmel, *Powerful Personalities* (Colorado Springs: Focus on the Family, 1977).

Les Parrott, *Shoulda, Coulda, Woulda: Live in the Present, Find Your Future* (Grand Rapids: Zondervan, 2003).

Paul David Tripp, *War of Words: Getting to the Heart of Your Communication Struggles* (Phillipsburg, NJ: P&R Publishing, 2000).

Richard Winter, *Perfectionism* (Michigan City, IN: L'Abri Cassettes, 1996), audiocassettes 2273–2274.

PART THREE

CONFLICTS WITHIN

You will keep in perfect peace him whose mind is
steadfast, because he trusts in you. Trust in the LORD
forever, for the LORD, the LORD, is the Rock eternal.

Isaiah 26:3–4

The two major causes of most emotional problems
among evangelicals are these: the failure to understand, receive and live out God's unconditional love,
forgiveness, and grace; and the failure to give out that
unconditional love, forgiveness, and grace to other
people. We read, we hear, we believe a good theology
of grace. But that's not the way we live.

David Seamands[1]

In the quietness of your most private thoughts, are you at peace?
As you lie on your bed at night, are you calm, content, and
joyful? Or is your heart restless? Do you sometimes feel a vague
sense that all is *not* well?

Sometimes the conflicts we face within ourselves cause our greatest turmoil. To live as peacemaking women, we are called to face
and address our misplaced shame, dark depression, and ungodly
fears. It is not enough that our "outsides" appear to be at peace.

As we live out faith in Jesus Christ, one good fruit we enjoy is internal peace. As John Calvin reminds us, we must first turn to the Lord if we are to gain understanding into our hearts: "Again, it is certain that man never achieves a clear knowledge of himself unless he has first looked upon God's face, and then descends from contemplating Him to scrutinize himself."[2]

In this section we will address the three most common internal conflicts women face: shame, depression, and fear. I (Tara) remember a time as a teenager, new to the faith, when all three internal struggles crashed together in one sad moment. My mother had just attempted suicide, and I was living with a Christian family from my church. One Saturday we were doing chores and I unplugged the vacuum by pulling on the cord. I was gently and appropriately corrected—"Don't pull on the cord. Reach down and pull the grip out of the socket; otherwise, the cord could detach and fray." Immediately I was flooded with shame, fear, and depression. I thought, *I shouldn't be here! Their house is beautiful. This is a perfect family. I'm unworthy, stupid, a loser. Now that they know what an idiot I am, they're going to kick me out. Will I be homeless? I don't even know how to live in a nice house. I hate myself and I hate my life.*

In this situation, I was bound by shame—*I am no good.* The correction that I received seemed to confirm it—*I am stupid and deserve to be rejected.* I was gripped by fear—*I'm going to be kicked out.* My dark thoughts led to depression—*My life is awful and it will never change.*

As I reflected on this memory with Judy, she helped me to see that the gospel of Jesus Christ sets us free to look within ourselves and face whatever is unseemly there. The gospel tells us that we are completely loved by God; he made the way for our relationship with him to be restored through the finished work of his Son, Jesus, on the cross. We are fully accepted by God because the righteousness of Christ has become our own. No darkness in us can change the wonderful truth that our relationship with God does not depend on us but on his gift of grace.

We are emboldened to look within and pursue *shalom* because we are already living that eternal life promised to us through our faith in Jesus Christ. The gospel is the foundation upon which our internal peace rests because by it our peace with God has been fully accomplished. Without the gospel we are hopeless and lost, constantly looking for answers to satisfy our doubts and soothe our despair. But in Christ we have peace.

Of course, the gospel calls us to live for God's glory, not because he makes us happy—which he does—but simply because he is God. As J. I. Packer reminds us, "We must return to the authentic gospel—not some substitute that occasionally shares similarities. The true gospel produces deep reverence, repentance, humility, a spirit of worship and a concern for the church. It makes men God-centered in their thoughts and God-fearing in their hearts. Too often, a substitute gospel is promoted to 'help' people—to bring peace, comfort, happiness, satisfaction—not to glorify God."[3]

As we come to the conclusion of this book, we will incorporate the truths about God presented in part 1 and the application of those truths learned in part 2 as we consider how to develop that quiet inner confidence that brings about the good fruit of righteousness and *shalom*. And as always, to find rest for our souls, we turn to Christ who promises, "Come to me, all you who are weary and burdened, and I will give you rest. Take my yoke upon you and learn from me, for I am gentle and humble in heart, and you will find rest for your souls. For my yoke is easy and my burden is light" (Matt. 11:28–30).

10

SHAME

No one whose hope is in you will ever be put to
shame.

Psalm 25:3

If we are to live the kind of free and radically loving
and holy lives Christ calls us to, we must understand
the place of shame and how to fight against its crip-
pling effects.

John Piper[1]

The Midwest is home to an awful little spider called the brown
recluse. This spider is famous for its bite. Once a person is
bitten, the small red dot quickly disappears, and the victim has little
awareness that she just received one of the most venomous spider
bites known to mankind. Over time, however, a terrible infection
begins beneath the surface of the skin. By the time she is aware
that she has been bitten, significant damage has occurred. In fact,
surgery into the undamaged flesh is usually necessary to stop the
rapid spread of the spider's venom. The treatment often leaves visible reminders of the destruction left by that tiny spider.

Ungodly shame works in the human heart much like a brown recluse bite works on the body. On the surface, everything may look fine, but beneath the surface a decaying, infected wound is doing serious damage to the heart and soul. Sadly, shame is prevalent in the lives of many Christian women. It is often experienced as a vague but overwhelming sense that *no matter how hard we try, we will never be good enough.* When shame lives in our hearts, we feel as though no matter how much we may desire relationships with others, *no one will ever really want us.* Although we may teach the gospel of God's grace and love to others, easily believing it to be true for *them*, we have a hard time believing that it is actually true for *us.* Women infected by shame often withdraw from God and others in an attempt to prevent the spread of this lethal disease or to disguise the truth that they are carriers of it. When shame lives in our hearts, our internal conflicts are often the fertile soil for conflicts with God and others. Shame has great power to destroy *shalom.*

Godly and Ungodly Shame

Godly shame is a blessing. Shame comes in two main varieties, godly and ungodly. Godly shame is our soul's response to the Spirit of God when we have sinned. It is one aspect of sorrow and remorse and can be an integral part of repentance. Godly shame is a gift from God that flows out of an awareness and sorrow that we have sinned and done wrong. Godly shame sickens us with the realization of our sin and makes us rightly crave the restoration that comes through repentance and forgiveness. The Giver of godly shame uses it as the hook to reel us back into his forgiving, purifying arms. When we sin, if our hearts are soft and responsive, we will experience appropriate and godly remorse that quickly turns us back to God. We flee to our heavenly Father to receive forgiveness and freedom as we delight in our status as redeemed sinners.

I (Tara) remember a time when I was really struggling with bitterness toward a friend who had betrayed my confidence and embarrassed me publicly. I felt weighed down and miserable as I nursed the offense—I knew it was wrong to continually replay it in my mind and harbor bitterness, yet I stubbornly continued to do so. On one of our long walks, my husband, Fred, said to me, "I'm glad you're miserable and ashamed, Tara, when you are tempted to hate your sister in Christ. If you weren't, I'd go and get help from our pastor because then I would know that you are hardening your heart to the Lord. But the fact that you are ashamed and miserable is a good thing. Your shame shows that the Spirit of God is in you and your heart is open to correction." God graciously granted me the gift of godly shame in order to help bring me to repentance.

Godly shame that drives us back to the Lord for healing and hope is a blessing—it is a sensitivity to sin coupled with faith that Jesus Christ forgives completely and restores fully. Who would not rush into the arms of her dear Savior to receive grace when convinced that he alone purifies her from her shame and sets her free from its pain?

Ungodly shame is an unbearable burden. Ungodly shame does not come from God as a result of our sin but comes from many different sources: our own hearts, other people, and the philosophies and values of the world. These sources of ungodly shame all serve to produce in us a sense of "badness" that usually drives us away from God and toward our futile efforts to restore ourselves. While godly shame results from the Spirit of God working in our hearts to prompt us to deal with our sinfulness, ungodly shame results from our responses to our fallenness and the fallenness of the world in which we live. Fallenness is a larger category of experiences that includes sin but also includes so much more (see discussion of this in chapter 4).

When a woman is filled with ungodly shame, her response to her own sin or fallenness is to say, "Something is wrong with me and I need to work harder to make this right." Ungodly shame is a self-indictment that overrides the truth of the gospel that Jesus Christ loves me and in him I am accepted. Another way to think about godly shame and ungodly shame is to note that while godly shame may have a component of legitimate and appropriate guilt, "I *did* wrong," ungodly shame condemningly says, "I *am* wrong." Sadly, ungodly shame directs people away from God and others, effectively trapping them in a lifestyle of shame-based living. Ungodly shame is an unbearable burden.

Janelle struggles with ungodly shame. In her childhood home, her parents disciplined her by saying, "You are such a bad little girl. For shame! For shame!" Instead of lovingly shepherding her heart and disciplining her behavior ("You *did* a bad thing"), they told her *she* was bad. Janelle grew up in an environment of conditional "love" where she received love when she did things well and was a "good girl" but was personally rejected when she was "bad" and struggled with sin. As an adult, Janelle has a hard time trusting in God's love toward her because she never feels that she is being "good enough." Janelle is burdened by ungodly shame as a result of her parents' sin and fallenness colliding with her own sin and fallenness.

A lack of shame can be a curse. Guilt is different from shame. True guilt is an objective fact that says the holiness of God has been transgressed by our thoughts, words, or deeds.[2] When we are guilty, we *ought* to experience godly shame. We don't *feel* guilt, since it is the fact rather than the feeling, but we *feel* godly shame. When true guilt and godly shame exist together, we are filled with a godly sorrow that leads to repentance and leaves no regret (2 Cor. 7:10). But, sadly, guilt may or may not be accompanied by the experience of godly shame.

True guilt that is *not* accompanied by the experience of shame is a horrible thing. As Jeremiah reminds us, we can be genuinely guilty of wrongdoing but not experience the emotion of godly shame at all: "Are they ashamed of their loathsome conduct? No, they have no shame at all; they do not even know how to blush. So they will fall among the fallen; they will be brought down when they are punished, says the LORD" (Jer. 8:12). Such a lack of shame is terrifying evidence of a heart hardened by sin's deceitfulness (Heb. 3:13).

Interestingly enough, while godly and ungodly shame come from different sources and are the result of different forces in our lives, both the effect of them in our lives and the cure for them are largely the same. From this point on, we will discuss shame broadly, making the distinction between these two types of shame only when necessary for clarity's sake.

The Faces of Shame

We see expressions of shame in many of the people we know and meet. We also see the insidious marks of shame in our own hearts. Several examples from Scripture illustrate what shame often looks like and help us to understand and recognize shame. The first chapters of Genesis provide examples of the "faces" of shame in the lives of Adam, Cain, and Lamech. Today shame is as much a driving force in our lives as it was in theirs. Once we are able to recognize the presence of shame and understand how it affects our relationships and our hearts, we are better prepared to address it in a biblical manner.

Diversion. The first place that shame is described in the Bible is in Genesis 3. A fascinating drama unfolds when Adam and Eve are confronted with recognition of their sin: "Then the eyes of both of them were opened, and they realized they were naked; so they sewed fig leaves together and made coverings for themselves" (v. 7). Our first parents were stunned by their own sin but diverted their feelings of shame toward something that previously had not been a source of shame at all. They indicted their nakedness rather than their act of rebellion. That state of nakedness, which had previously been God-approved and associated with no feelings of shame (Gen. 2:25), now became the focus of Adam and Eve's shame and self-contempt.

We often transfer our feelings of shame from the source of our shame to something altogether different. For example, even though Lisa did nothing wrong when she was sexually abused as a young child, she struggles with overwhelming shame. Instead of preaching truth to her unbiblical shame, she diverts her shame to her own body by covering it with excess pounds. Weight gain is a common way women try to divert their shame. Of course, thirty extra pounds cannot release us from our shame.

In another example of diverted shame, Melissa refuses to allow herself to enjoy sex in her marriage. Premarital promiscuity, once a source of deep shame, is all but forgotten in her mind as Melissa redirects her shame at her own sexual responses. Rather than confess the guilt of sexual immorality and find forgiveness and restoration, Melissa instead condemns her sexual feelings for her husband as dirty and disgusting. She has diverted her condemning shame to something that should be beautiful and God-honoring—her sexual intimacy with her husband—rather than allowing it to drive her toward the One who cleanses and makes her whole.

Joan, having had an abortion at sixteen, refuses to care for her own body. She channels her shame over the abortion into bouts of anorexia and bulimia, never finding freedom from the guilt that haunts her. Joan's shame no longer points to her real problem but has been diverted to her "obese" 110-pound, five-foot-six-inch body.

Hiding. In Genesis 3:8, Adam and Eve "heard the sound of the Lord God as he was walking in the garden in the cool of the day, and they hid from the Lord God among the trees of the garden." Ungodly shame often results in covering up and hiding from others. Godly shame, on the other hand, results in the opposite response. Godly shame compels us to expose our sin and run to God and others for forgiveness and restoration of relationship. To cover up and hide is to deny ourselves what we need in order to be healed. Adam hid from God because he was afraid. Fear, a common face of shame, becomes an excuse for hiding and not dealing with feelings of shame. We see an example of this in Genesis 3: "But the Lord God called to the man, 'Where are you?' He answered, 'I heard you in the garden, and I was afraid because I was naked; so I hid'" (vv. 9–10).

Laurie's father abandoned the family when she and her siblings were young. Her mother blamed the children and Laurie in particular for his desertion. She constantly told Laurie: "You are the reason my life is so bad! I wish you had never been born. I could've gone to college if it weren't for you!" Laurie grew up looking like a normal, happy little girl. But inside she was hiding. She learned to "play the game" of performing and acting like everything was okay, but she refused to allow others to know the "real" her because she feared rejection. Shame-based beliefs guided her thoughts and relationships, and she told herself, "I can't let them see the real me. If they do, they'll know how bad I am, and they won't want to be my friend." And so Laurie hid.

One of the things we (Judy and Tara) dislike the most about the grip of shame on others is that it robs us of the chance to know and experience the beauty embedded in them. Shame tempts women to hide from us and apologize for "taking our time" because "why would Judy or Tara want to hear about me?" Whenever a woman gives in to shame and holds herself back from others, she deprives them of the true blessing of knowing and loving her. People who are burdened by shame do not recognize that they are worth knowing and loving—if for no other reason than because they are made in the image of God.

Blaming. Adam and Eve, responding as so many of us do, acted on their shame in one particular way that never brings restoration from shame—blaming. Blaming others for our shame is an expression of contempt for them and for ourselves. When we blame, we accuse others of wrongdoing, and conflict is the inevitable result. As long as the focus stays on the wrong committed by others, our own shame remains unaddressed. Where shame is unacknowledged, it fails to receive the care it needs. The venom of shame is then allowed to cause unnecessary damage and greater destruction to peace.

Adam soon blames both Eve and God for his lack of obedience. "The man said, 'The woman you put here with me—*she* gave me some fruit from the tree, and I ate it'" (Gen. 3:12, emphasis added). When questioned by God, Eve blames the serpent for deceiving her (Gen. 3:13). No one ever feels godly remorse and sorrow for their sins when they are committed to blaming others.

Adam's son Cain provides another fascinating example of shame that turns to blame. Our experience of shame often seems to be a condition that spreads through families, generation to generation. Cain reflects a common face of shame in his response to God over his rejected offering: "The LORD looked with favor on Abel and his offering, but on Cain and his offering he did not look with favor. So Cain was very angry, and his face was downcast" (Gen. 4:4–5). Instead of facing up to his own legitimate guilt and taking responsibility for his own actions, Cain turns his focus away from himself and blames the closest person to him—Abel.

Anita suffered from a strong sense of feeling unlovable and unwanted. Flowing from these feelings of shame, she was largely unwilling to have sex with her husband. Rather than recognizing her ungodly shame and addressing it biblically, Anita blamed her husband for all of their intimacy problems: "If he were a better husband, then our sex life would be better too." Over time I (Judy) was able to make the following observation: "You genuinely seem to love your husband, but you feel strongly that you are worthless.

It almost seems that you believe your love for your husband would demand that you *not* give him a worthless gift such as yourself. In fact, your lack of intimate love for him might be because you actually *do* love him—too much to inflict 'trash' on him. However, this way you are 'loving' your husband (holding yourself back from him) certainly does not match up with what we have been considering in God's Word. Still, it makes sense when I think about how you feel about yourself."

Anita recognized immediately that her blaming her husband was simply one expression of her shame. She knew that she was hurting both her husband and herself. Her shame-permeated view of herself robbed them both of the sweetness of love they could otherwise know. Anita was called to speak biblical truth to her shame-based lies by asking: "Am I really 'trash'? Or am I a redeemed and beloved daughter of God?" By God's grace, Anita turned to the Lord and believed in his promises of love for her. In so doing, she was able to turn away from the shame that drove her away from loving God and her husband.

Attacking. Cain, as we know, goes on to murder his brother, Abel, rather than accept God's invitation to address his disobedience with godly change. "Now Cain said to his brother Abel, 'Let's go out to the field.' And while they were in the field, Cain attacked his brother Abel and killed him" (Gen. 4:8). The cure for shame was available to Cain, yet he chose the burden of carrying shame rather than being relieved of it. Shame often looks like hatred and always gives us two choices: take it to God or take it on ourselves. As an infection deep in the soul, shame has lethal consequences. Left unexposed and not dealt with, shame can evolve from contempt into hatred and from hatred into attacking.

Shame that matures over time is often expressed somewhere on the spectrum between attacking self and attacking others. Lynn's life demonstrates the destruction that the venom of shame inflicts on relationships. Instead of taking her shame to God and receiving the blessings of acceptance and grace, Lynn is an angry, critical woman. Unhealed shame often intensifies a fear of rejection. To protect herself from this fear, Lynn criticizes and verbally attacks the people around her so they can't get close enough to hurt her with their rejection. While Lynn longs for intimate friendship and true love from her family members, her actions and words drive people away. She couches her verbal attacks as "just being honest" and "speaking the truth."

When Lynn's husband failed to wash the gnats out of the light fixture after changing a bulb, Lynn's vicious attack surprised even her. It wasn't until later as she reflected on what was happening in her heart that Lynn realized that her actions were actually a result of her shame-filled thoughts: "I attack my husband by stating that he doesn't do enough around the house. The truth is that I feel like I'm the one who doesn't do enough. The gnats in the light fixture affirmed to me that I really am a bad wife. I bet he is going to leave me." Even though her husband had never expressed such thoughts and had never even felt that leaving was an option, Lynn's shame and fear of rejection came out as an attack—both toward him and herself.

The venom of shame spreads far and wide, leaving others desperately seeking ways to placate in order to avoid further attacks. Lynn's only hope is that she might one day find her identity fully in Christ and rest in his gracious acceptance and love of her. Until then, Lynn will remain gripped by her shame, unable to share that same gracious and merciful kindness with the people around her.

Complaining. When confronted yet again by God after the murder, Cain denied knowledge and responsibility. God asked him, "Where is your brother Abel?" "I don't know," he replied. "Am I my brother's keeper?" (Gen. 4:9). But when God placed Cain under a curse for his wicked act, Cain launched into a complaint against God. Instead of humbly repenting, Cain complained that his punishment—his loss of experiencing God's presence, belonging, and safety—was more than he could bear. Shame often reveals itself in self-pitying complaint.

For several years, I (Judy) carried the burden of ungodly shame. As most shame eventually does, my shame evolved—into bitterness, mistrust, and dislike for Christians. When Christians rejected me, I complained to God and to people. However, inside I was filled with self-pity.

One particular expression of my bitterness happened shortly after I became a Christian when I still possessed a lot of rough edges. An elder in our church refused to allow his children to play with mine, even though we lived nearby in the same neighborhood. I felt tainted, yet I carried the shame rather than trusting God with it. One day God graciously gave me a glimpse of my own heart. I recognized that in this situation and many others, I shared Cain's complaint. I knew that the day would come when I would stand before the throne of my Savior and complain to him that my punishment was too severe. I would say to God, "If only you had given me true friends to love me, my life would have been better" or "If only people hadn't rejected me, then I would not have been bitter." I was completely undone by the thought of what Jesus might say to me in reply: *"Was my grace not sufficient for you?"*

In a moment I realized that I did not want to stand before Jesus and tell him that his grace was not enough for me to live a full, blessed life regardless of my circumstance. I did not want to complain that I needed more than his perfect grace and that better friends, more understanding, deeper intimacy, and greater love were really the objects of my worship and devotion. In prayer I laid down that burden of shame that I had carried for so long. Refusing to continue down the path of complaining, I asked God to help me to forgive and love those who had hurt me.

Shamelessness and sin. Shame-filled women can change into shameless women who respond to their burden of shame by attempting to desensitize their feelings of embarrassment, remorse, and sorrow over their guilt. They normalize guilt with the rationalization that "everyone is doing it." They choose to believe that what is wrong is really right because "we are born that way." They attempt to diminish the power of shame in their lives with whatever "feels good."

When a heart becomes insensitive to guilt, it often becomes insensitive to godly shame as well. We see an example of this in Cain's descendant, Lamech: "Lamech married two women, one named Adah and the other Zillah. . . . Lamech said to his wives, 'Adah and Zillah, listen to me; wives of Lamech, hear my words. I have killed a man for wounding me, a young man for injuring me'" (Gen. 4:19, 23).

Lamech, when injured by a young man (this word for young man is often translated as "boy"), retaliates with escalating violence. A wound is repaid with murder. Yet even more astonishing is Lamech's proud, shameless speech to his wives, boasting of his deeds. Where is Lamech's remorse for killing a boy who merely injured him? Where is Lamech's sense of guilt for his deeds? There is no room for Lamech to deal with his guilt, nor is there room for anyone close to Lamech to point out his fault. Insensitivity to guilt brings insensitivity to shame. Shame that has gone cold has the face of shamelessness.

We have counseled women who have experienced terrible sexual abuse. In a quest to make themselves feel acceptable and earn a place of belonging, many of these women engage in promiscuity as a way of managing the shame they feel. Over time, they become hardened to their own action and even flaunt their behaviors. Having worked with a number of prostitutes, I (Judy) know that these precious women often feel totally unacceptable to God and others. Rather than live in the truth of the gospel, they increasingly live in ways that create greater distance between God and themselves. Apart from saving faith, they destroy any hope for *shalom* as they diminish their relationships with others and their acceptance of themselves.

Sexually impure behavior is a common way of attempting to deal with feelings of ungodly shame. Women often use sexual relationships to try to silence the voice that whispers over and over in their ears, "You are worthless." Some women, seeking profound acceptance, even attempt to address their feelings of shame through same-sex attraction. They are attracted to anyone and anything that can drown out the voice in their head and soothe the ache of loneliness in their heart. Tragically, the outcome of such shameless behavior is not only deeper loneliness but the additional burden of godly shame.

Self-righteousness. Shame often grows into self-righteousness and legalism. Rather than expose our shame and run to God, our conviction that *we are not wrong in any way* soon makes way for the conviction that *we are right in every way*. We try to stand in a position of superiority to hide our horrible shame over our inadequacies. We criticize and judge others in an attempt to feel better about ourselves.

Lamech's words demonstrate no shame, but we hear a self-righteousness in his clear threat that any who would oppose Lamech will be punished severely. "If Cain is avenged seven times, then Lamech seventy-seven times" (Gen. 4:24). Lamech, the one who declares himself right in his dealings with the boy, also feels justified in establishing the punishment that would be meted out if any were to challenge his actions.

I (Tara) am embarrassed to admit that in looking back on my first few years as a Christian, I see plainly how my ungodly shame manifested itself as legalism and self-righteousness. As a teenager I was saved by God's *grace*, but my initial response was to live as a legalistic Pharisee. Instead of humbly sharing the gospel with my family, I adopted an air of superiority as I threw away all of my "sinful" rock-and-roll audiotapes. I judged my relatives for the television shows and movies they watched. Completely failing to minister encouragement and hope to them, I sniffed piously at their lifestyles. Even more seriously, I saw true areas of sin in their lives—areas in need of rescue and love—and instead of seeking to help them, bearing their burdens, or pointing them to Christ (Gal. 6:1–2), I turned away from them. I look back on those years with true regret. I see how my own pride and shame combined to make me a "Christian jerk." Thankfully, God has led me to seek the forgiveness of all of my family members for my judgmental heart and self-righteous behavior, and they have forgiven me.

The Cure for Shame

What can we do to be free of the burden of shame that is at the root of so much of our conflict? Dick Keyes in *Beyond Identity* makes the excellent point that guilt and shame are two very different problems, rooted in two different theological realities, each with its own cure.[3] Two thought-provoking questions help us to address our guilt and shame:

- What is the cure for guilt?
- What is the cure for shame?

Nearly every believer is able to rapidly answer the first question. *The cure for guilt is forgiveness.* However, few are able to articulate the cure for shame without a great deal of reflection. Yet Scripture speaks volumes about how to cure shame. To be women of *shalom*, we must understand how the concepts of adoption, intimacy, love, and delight impact our experience of shame. These gifts of grace help us to trust that we are accepted just the way we are. The acceptance we have in Christ because we are adopted into his family is the surgeon's scalpel that begins to carve away the festering poison of shame. The intimacy, love, and delight we experience because of our adoption all provide the healing balm that soothes the painful effects of shame.

Adoption. When we know without a doubt that God has accepted us, we come to understand the amazing truth that we are brought into membership in God's family forever (1 John 3:1). The doctrine that speaks most powerfully to our guilt is *justification*, and the doctrine that speaks most directly to our ungodly shame is *adoption*. While the cure for our guilt rests only in the forgiveness of God, the cure for our shame is found in God's loving acceptance through adopting us into his family. Adoption washes away our shame in the same way that justification wipes away our guilt. Adoption says, "I love you, you belong to me, and nothing will take you out of my hand. Nothing about you will cause me to reject you. Anything wrong with you will not cost us our relationship. I am God, and I know you completely. And I love you" (see John 10:29; Rom. 8:15–17; Gal. 4:4–7).

I (Tara) *love* adoption stories. I am drawn to them like no other stories. I love to hear about the prayerful pleas for a child; the long anticipation and waiting; the actual journey to meet the child; the lifetime promise of love offered before the parents even lay eyes on the little one; the tearful moment when the child is placed in the arms of the parents and the cradle of the family of God; and the grace and love reflected in the life of a wanted and cherished child. I am mesmerized by the thought that parents would *choose*, *seek out*, and *love* a child that they had never even met. I guess it reflects both my longing for relationship with my own parents and my longing for my perfect heavenly parent, Father God.

A key aspect of adoption is that it is a lifetime commitment. Adoption is steadfast. Shame flees when people don't give up on us, but it compounds when they do. I (Tara) once had a close friend—I considered her to be my best friend at the time—give up on me with absolutely no warning. One day she just decided that my sins were too great, I was too unloving and ungracious, and she didn't want to be my friend anymore. In one of the worst conversations in my entire life, we sat in my car and she said that although we had been best friends, she never wanted to see me or talk to me again. I have tried numerous times over the years to ask her forgiveness and appeal for us to be reconciled, but she has never acknowledged my letters or calls. For years that rejection intensified my sense of shame because it was the exact opposite of steadfast and abiding love.

To think that God would choose, seek out, and love us *forever*? Never give up on us? This is adoption at its best. And shame disappears in the face of the marvel of adopting love.

Intimacy. Intimacy is a biblical concept that permeates Scripture from beginning to end. It is the relational experience of knowing others as they really are and being known for who we really are. The desire for intimacy is strongly related to how God has made us in his own image. Although sufficient in himself, God desires that we know and love him—hence the first commandment ("You shall have no other gods before me") and the greatest commandment ("Love the Lord your God with all your heart . . ."). As people made in his image, we share the same desire to be intimately known and fully loved. Our creation in God's image assumes intimacy as a normal part of relationships. Yet shame, that lethal disease, eats away at our hearts—especially the place where intimacy is desired and embraced. Shame destroys the desire and ability to be known by others. Shame kills the desire and ability to know and love others.

If genuine love flows out of true intimacy, and if love for God and others is our greatest calling, intimacy is a vital part of our human experience. We will not be vulnerable with people unless we know that we are safe with them because they love us intimately.

Trusting, loving relationships are based on genuine knowledge of others. We follow Jesus because we know who he is. He has revealed himself to us, and we can know him—not fully, but truly and increasingly as we spend time in his Word, in communion with him, in fellowship with his Spirit-filled people, and in worship. He calls us by our own names, knowing who we really are. He knows us fully, even "the secrets of the heart" (Ps. 44:21).

Intimacy is reflected in Jesus's explanation of what it means to be a true shepherd of God's people: "He calls his own sheep by name and leads them out. When he has brought out all his own, he goes on ahead of them, and his sheep follow him because they know his voice. But they will never follow a stranger; in fact, they will run away from him because they do not recognize a stranger's voice. . . . I am the good shepherd; I know my sheep and my sheep know me—just as the Father knows me and I know the Father—and I lay down my life for the sheep" (John 10:3–5, 14–15).

Note the helpful fact that in this passage, intimacy is a crucial aspect of loving leadership and ministry. So often our counseling with believers touches on the topic of how difficult it is to know Christian leaders. The hurts that are experienced by our pastors and elders often make them withdraw from people. The hurts that are experienced by all believers lead us to withdraw from relationships as well. When Christians are deprived of intimate, loving relationships with one another, shame often flourishes because we fear letting others see our weaknesses. Mistrust, bitterness, unforgiveness, and fear stand in the way of deep connection in the body of Christ.

Janet was praying with a friend, Patty, who was counseling her through a difficult conflict. During the prayer, Patty cried out for "*Abba*, Daddy" to hear her prayers for Janet. Janet cringed on the inside as she listened to her friend speak to God in such an intimate way. She knew that her relationship with God lacked that "Daddy" quality of innocent trust and intimacy. Janet began to cry because she longed to feel the loving arms of her *Abba* around her. She knew that she was accepted by God but felt that her acceptance was based on a technicality, and she subconsciously felt that he would begrudgingly allow her into heaven because he didn't have a way out of the obligation and was trapped by his own goodness and faithfulness. The thought that God desired her and intimately loved her had never crossed Janet's mind.

As is often the case, Janet's relationship with her earthly father impacted how she related to God. Janet's earthly father had not shown any interest in knowing her. He had abandoned Janet as a child, and when he did have any contact with her, he only expressed approval at certain performance-based accomplishments. Influenced by her earthly father, Janet felt any expressions of approval from God as demands for greater effort to succeed and be perfect.

To understand intimacy with God is to know that our shame is fully known and exposed before a holy God. God sees every bit of our hearts and knows us even better than we know ourselves (Ps. 139:13–16). He even knows the number of hairs on our heads. And guess what? *He loves us.* With his eyes wide open, in full knowledge of our fallenness and sin, the God of the universe tenderly loves us and accepts us. True intimacy is rooted in knowledge and depth of insight—the fundamentals of love—and it banishes shame.

Love. Paul gives the Philippians much to consider about the importance and wonder of having intimate human relationships when he writes, "And this is my prayer: that your love may abound more and more in knowledge and depth of insight, so that you may be able to discern what is best and may be pure and blameless until the day of Christ, filled with the fruit of righteousness that comes through Jesus Christ—to the glory and praise of God" (Phil. 1:9–11). Paul uses powerful words—abounding love—to describe a powerful concept. Love doesn't trickle in when love abounds and intimacy is present. Love surges forward—more and more. And shame flees in the face of love.

Jesus further defines the depth of true love and what our love for others looks like with a new commandment. (As if the second greatest commandment to "love your neighbor as yourself" in Matthew 22:39 is not enough to make us take notice, the new commandment sobers us even more.) We are called to *love others as Jesus has loved us*: "A new command I give you: Love one another. As I have loved you, so you must love one another" (John 13:34). While we are not always impressed by how people love themselves and therefore not overly eager to be loved that same way, the love of Jesus for us never fails to impress and move our hearts because this is the greatest love possible (John 15:13).

Tina was a beautiful young woman who worked as a server in a restaurant. She came to talk with me (Judy) about her deep shame. When she thought she had said something inappropriate in a conversation, Tina would literally bang her head against a wall while crying out "Stupid! Stupid! Stupid!" As I came to know Tina, I was amazed at how intelligent and thoughtful she was. Yet most people never would have known it by how she presented herself. Tina was a high school graduate with an unimpressive grade point average; she spoke with a lisp and in a way that sounded babyish. Her friends and family frequently called her a "ditz."

As we talked, however, I discovered that Tina loved history and spent hours every day watching the History Channel or reading history books. She was an avid historian who knew names, dates, and complexities of modern history. But in her family growing up, she was always the "baby" who was never taken seriously. Convinced that she was neither intelligent nor of much value and importance, Tina's shame drove her to conceal her real interests with a cloak of poor performance and baby talk. As we began to carve away at her shame, I reflected back to her how intelligent and loveable I found her to be. I remember when she asked, "Do you really think I am smart? Do you really *love* me, Judy?"

Tina eventually came to recognize herself as a creation of God gifted with talents and abilities. She turned away from false shame and embraced biblical truth as she learned to steward her gifts for God's glory and the benefit of others. She recognized her desire to learn and soon enrolled in a local college. The last time I saw her, Tina's lisp had disappeared, and she was enjoying great success in her college courses.

Acceptance and delight. We can love many people, but *delightful acceptance* with intimate knowledge is a foretaste of the exquisite grace that awaits us when we are reunited with Jesus Christ face-to-face. Delight is a special form of acceptance that profoundly heals shame.

In the early 1990s, my (Judy's) pastor told me that he did not think I should enter the field of counseling because he thought I would do more harm than good. His reason for his belief was the way I related to my husband. I tried to control Jim so that he would think and act the way I thought he should. In other words, I tried to make Jim into my own image. I was hurt by my pastor's words, yet I knew they were true. After many weeks of suffering, I had a life-changing realization: *God has accepted Jim.* If God has accepted Jim just as he is, who am I to reject him? Am I above God? As I reflected on Romans 15:7, I knew I was called to accept Jim "just as Christ accepted you, in order to bring praise to God."

In coming to the startling realization that God had already accepted Jim just as he is, I was able to choose to accept him as well. My marriage was radically transformed. Shame began to melt away, and both of us began to grow as individuals. We came to know and understand each other for the people we really are, the people God created us to be. Within a few years, however, something new began to happen. Acceptance, bathed in intimate love, grew into delight for one another. To this day, the man I married is a huge source of delight for me. I sing his praises to everyone I meet.

What do you delight in? The fuzzy little kitten that begins to purr when you hold it to your chest? The toddler who takes his first step and squeals with joy, clapping for his own efforts? The drawing a friend creates and gives to you so that you know how special you are to her? Delight is a wholehearted, emotional response of enjoyment, appreciation, and love. Delight is a powerful antidote to shame.

I (Tara) recall with crystal clarity the first time I ever saw a father absolutely *delighting* in his family. It happened in college when I was visiting a family from church. As the mother, father, and children walked me around their home, the father stopped time and time again to *marvel* at his family's photographs. "Wasn't Katie a beautiful baby?" "Have you ever seen such a smile as Tori's?" "Look at this one, Tara, isn't my wife amazing? This was just after we lost our beloved son, and yet there June is, believing on the Lord even in her grief." At the dinner table, George was quick to show his pleasure in his family. "Tori is growing so much in her faith. She is showing so much wisdom." "Katie encouraged me the other day with her kindness and love." "God has given me such a gift in my wife. I can't believe I get to be her husband and raise our girls together. God is so good to me."

As I listened to my friend's delight, I tucked the thought away into a quiet piece of my heart, "I pray that one day I might have a husband who delights in me and in our children like George delights in his family." Why does this memory stick with me after so many years? Because delight dispels shame. Shame cannot breathe or live in the flood of loving, rejoicing delight. Of course, the ultimate foundation for our delight is found in Jesus Christ. He is the lover of our souls who delights in us and eternally dispels our shame.

Even if we do not yet experience delight in earthly relationships, we can rest secure in God's delight in us.

From Shame to *Shalom*

Even as I (Tara) have spent the day working on this chapter, I have struggled with shame. My husband is caring for our little baby so that I can concentrate on writing. Shame tells me, "If you weren't such a lousy wife, you would take better care of your husband." I look around my home and see my attempts at cobbling our used furniture and old lamps into a warm and inviting home. Shame whispers, "If you were a better homemaker, you would know how to decorate and create a beautiful environment. You can't even take care of a home. There's dog hair everywhere." We are working on having our daughter, Sophia, take naps in her crib instead of in our arms. But as she cries in protest, my shame indicts me, "You don't have any idea what you're doing with your baby. What makes you think *you* can be a mother?"

Can you imagine? Even as I am here meditating hour after hour on the many truths of Scripture as to how the gospel speaks directly to my shame, *I still struggle.* Some of you reading this will not be able to relate to what I'm saying. I thank God for that! I am always refreshed and blessed to share fellowship with people who do not struggle with the foreboding, horrible, vague sense that they are not good enough. Their confidence and trust in the Lord is like a refreshing breeze or a sweet melody. To not live in shame is a glimpse of heaven.

But others of you know exactly what I am talking about. You know what it is like for your shame to condemn you. You too struggle with horrible thoughts of your own unworthiness, dirtiness, and inadequacies. Dear sisters in Christ, there is hope! Let us *run* to our saving, forgiving, adopting, and accepting God. The Prince of Peace knows our hearts, our pasts, our futures, and our every deed—and he *delights* in us. *God delights in you!* He, in his awesome act of love, offered himself as a sacrifice that we might live eternally as righteous children of God.

To know that Jesus knows us, loves us, accepts us, and has declared us righteous is the first step toward seeing shame forever washed away. Being known, loved, and accepted by others dispels that shame even more. When we, as fallen and sinful creatures, can view ourselves with the eyes of Christ, *shalom* abounds richly. In the light of the love of Christ, shame gives way to *shalom*. In grateful and humble response we cry: "Thanks be to God for his indescribable gift!" (2 Cor. 9:15).

Personal Reflection

Questions for Reflection

1. Do you ever struggle with a vague sense that you are not good enough no matter how hard you try? What comes more easily to you—believing that God delights in you or that he is disappointed in you?
2. Write out one sentence summarizing the difference between godly and ungodly shame. How can you identify either of these types of shame in your life? How might the presence of shame impact your relationships with others? With your spouse or children? What response might God be calling you to?
3. Grace, adoption, intimacy, delight, and love are all key to combating shame. Who delights in you? Who gives you grace and accepts you just as you are? Read Galatians 4:6–7 and 1 John 3:1. Write a few sentences reflecting on how these passages speak to your shame.
4. When you talk about yourself, what kinds of words do you use? Make a list of the words used in Philippians 4:8 about what we are to think about. Take each word and write it into the following question: "What is _____ about me?" Write out short answers to these questions.
5. As you review the list of the faces of shame, which "face" are you most prone to manifest in your own life? Why is this so?
6. What are the top five things that you are most ashamed of in your life? Is your shame tied to true guilt for transgression of God's law? If so, have you confessed your sins to God? Are you forgiven? On what basis are you forgiven?

7. Often we know what the Bible says but have a hard time *feeling* that it is true. Do you know the truth that God loves and accepts you but have a hard time *feeling* loved and accepted? Read Mark 9:23–24 and reflect on the meaning of this passage. Write out a short prayer reflecting the words found in verse 24.

8. How do you think Scripture memory can help you develop a grace-based view of yourself instead of a shame-based view? Choose two verses to memorize to help you to best understand how God views you. You may want to consider memorizing Zephaniah 3:17 or Isaiah 62:4.

9. Meditate on Psalm 51. How did David deal with the guilt and shame of his sin? In what ways does God restore the joy of our salvation (Ps. 51:12)?

Praying Scripture to God

Father, I approach your throne of grace with confidence, for I find mercy and grace to help me in my time of need. I thank you, Lord, that you have adopted me, you love me intimately, and you delight in me. O God, I thirst for you and long for you. I thank you that you do not withhold your mercy from me, Lord. You protect and save me. I rejoice in you and give thanks to you, O Lord Most High. I thank you that because of your great love, when I confess and renounce my sins, I find your mercy. Dear Lord, please enable me to trust in you, and please develop in me by the power of your Holy Spirit the mind of Christ.

(Prayer based on Heb. 4:16; Ps. 63:1; Ps. 40:11, 13; Ps. 7:17; Prov. 28:13; Ps. 112:7; Phil. 2:5.)

Recommended Resources for Further Study and Consideration

Dan B. Allender and Tremper Longman III, *Cry of the Soul* (Colorado Springs: NavPress, 1994).

Jerry Bridges, *The Discipline of Grace* (Colorado Springs: NavPress, 1994).

Jerry Bridges, *Transforming Grace: Living Confidently in God's Unfailing Love* (Colorado Springs: NavPress, 1991).

Michael Card, *A Violent Grace* (Sisters, OR: Multnomah Publishers, 2000).

Cynthia Spell Humbert, *Deceived by Shame, Desired by God* (Colorado Springs: NavPress, 2001).

Dick Keyes, *Beyond Identity: Finding Your Way in the Image and Character of God* (Cumbria, UK: Paternoster Press, 1998).

Robert A. Peterson, *Adopted by God* (Phillipsburg, NJ: P&R Publishing, 2001).

Terry Schlossberg and Elizabeth Achtemeier, *Not My Own: Abortion and the Marks of the Church* (Grand Rapids: Eerdmans, 1995).

Lewis B. Smedes, *Shame and Grace* (San Francisco: HarperSanFrancisco, 1993).

Sandra D. Wilson, *Released from Shame* (Downers Grove, IL: InterVarsity Press, 1990).

11

DEPRESSION

My thoughts trouble me and I am distraught. . . .
My heart is in anguish within me;
    the terrors of death assail me.
Fear and trembling have beset me;
    horror has overwhelmed me.

Psalm 55:2, 4–5

Are you too bad to receive grace? Grace woos and
comforts us when we think we are too far gone to be
rescued. How could you be too bad to receive what is
for the bad?

David Powlison[1]

The "Great Flood" of 1993 saw St. Louis flooded as it had never been flooded before. The Missouri and Mississippi Rivers were swollen with exorbitant amounts of rainwater. It seemed the rain would never stop. As the rivers rose, onlookers anxiously watched. And then it began to happen: right before our eyes, first one levy split, then another crumbled, and finally levies everywhere just melted under the pressure of the fast-moving waters. The river left its course and poured into towns and cities. Livelihoods were lost, homes were destroyed, and the cost of damages rose into the billions. When the waters finally receded, the unspeakable mess of worm-filled mud meant months spent cleaning. Much was lost, and a dark irony became a part of everyday life: water was everywhere, yet bottled water sales were at an all-time high. Given time and the commitment of the entire community, the spirit of the people revived. Improved levies, stronger floodwalls, and lives were rebuilt.

Depression often begins in the same way the Great Flood of 1993 began: a rainstorm, and then another, and finally another. When our normal resources to manage the storms of life prove inadequate, the building pressure of our circumstances bursts out of control. Despite our attempts to build protective sandbag walls, we are swept away. Devastation and destruction occur as anger, hurt, sadness, and bitterness pour out of our hearts and into the lives of those around us. We feel overwhelmed as we see our difficulties wash away what we have worked so hard to build. We feel helpless to rebuild our lives to what they once were or what we believe they should be. When the damage is done, we are left horror-stricken and hopeless at the mess left behind.

In my (Tara's) darkest season of depression, my journal shows the overwhelming flood of emotions I experienced:

It felt like the room was spinning—voices from everywhere—mocking me and hating me, so I left the party. Did my husband come to check on me even once? No. Does anyone even care about me? No. Why am I even here? I hate my life and myself. I hate everyone and everything. I wish I were dead. Please help me, God. I'm drowning. I can't breathe. Maybe I should just jump off this balcony and end it all. I am so sick of feeling this way but I don't think it's ever going to end. I don't think I can take it anymore.

Depression like I experienced is considered by psychiatrists to be the most common form of mental illness. Pharmaceutical companies make billions of dollars every year selling prescription medication designed to treat depression. Depression has been referred to as "public enemy number one" and is a common part of our experience. We see it in ourselves, in those around us, and in Scripture. Some of the heroes of our faith struggled with the despair that comes from deep discouragement and depression. The *shalom*-killer of depression must be understood and addressed, especially as it impacts our ability to be at peace with God, others, and ourselves.

What Is Depression?

A number of simplistic descriptions of depression exist: depression is anger turned inward; depression is a chemical deficiency in the brain; depression is a result of bad thinking and bad choices; depression is a genetic tendency; depression is not believing God's promises. Some of the confusion over depression arises because it is a complex concept that has many sources. Depression is not a single emotion; it is a blend—a *flood*—of many emotions running together. Among other things it is fear, anger, sorrow, grief, bitterness, hatred, self-contempt, and disappointment. Depression may be the result of many things, including the failure of our personal resources to cope with life challenges or the outcome of unconfessed sin. In this chapter we will not address depression in the clinical sense but as a pervasive experience of sadness, discouragement, and despair.

A real difference of opinion exists in our evangelical world about depression. Some people think that most people are depressed, and others don't believe that depression is real at all. Many Christians believe that depression ought never to be experienced by true believers and is a sign of faithlessness and sin. Other Christians fail to adequately address any sin and behavioral issues associated with depression, simply using medication to mask the symptoms.

In the Great Flood, St. Louis experienced devastation due to distant rainstorms in northern states and an aging sewer system that was not designed to handle the high levels of water. In addition, the water table had risen over the previous years and was only a few feet below ground. Invisible forces can have powerful ramifications. So it is with depression. Invisible factors impact us in ways that we can see but do not always understand. Depression strikes a woman at every level of her being: emotional, relational, spiritual, and physical. It is an all-encompassing experience that finds its culmination in visible storms and invisible destruction. Consider some of the ways that depression manifests itself in our lives.

Loss of hope. When we are depressed, we lose hope (Eccles. 4:1–3). And when we lose hope, we can easily become depressed (Prov. 13:12). This is a vicious cycle that can lead us to foreboding and terrible thoughts that deny the truths of Scripture and bring us to despair. When we take our eyes off of the Lord and put them on our circumstances and ourselves, we often lose hope and become depressed.

This happened in my (Tara's) life. Having been an overachiever my entire life, I strived to excel at everything I did. I found comfort in my orderly and purposeful life. When I lost my job suddenly, I entered into a dark season of extreme depression. As I took my eyes off of the Lord and put them on my circumstances, I saw only devastation and chaos. My reputation, financial security, and daily purpose seemed instantly wiped away. I felt no peace with God, my husband and friends, or myself. I wrote in my journal: "During that terrible time, I didn't know who I was. It was as if my very identity had been ripped from me. I hated those responsible for my suffering. I hated myself for being such a failure. Most of all, I felt overwhelmed and alone. My life was ruined and I had no hope!"

Despair. The apostle Paul vividly describes his own despair. With great transparency he speaks to the believers at Corinth so that they will know what he personally experienced and share in the comfort of seeing a purpose in suffering. "We do not want you to be uninformed, brothers, about the hardships we suffered in the province of Asia. We were under great pressure, far beyond our ability to endure, so that we despaired even of life. Indeed, in our hearts we felt the sentence of death. But this happened that we might not rely on ourselves but on God, who raises the dead" (2 Cor. 1:8–9).

Imagine the great apostle who spoke with Jesus directly, the missionary who saw multitudes of lives transformed by the power of God and who "was caught up to paradise" (2 Cor. 12:4), feeling overwhelmed by his hardships to the point of despairing of life itself. Like Paul, we all will experience profoundly painful disappointment. And such disappointments will sometimes lead to despair and depression.

Shelly was a new missionary. All her life she had dreamed of the joy of serving on the mission field, so it was a horrible shock to her when she began to experience conflict with her team leader. She did not mind the other hardships of missionary life, but she felt powerless and terrified by the domineering and capricious way her leader ran their team. Their clashes grew to such a point that he actually ordered Shelly off of the field. She was sent home in disgrace. In her sorrow and anger, she made appeal after appeal to her sending agency. But nothing changed. She was branded a troublemaker within the organization. People at her home church began to gossip about her. She felt as if her life purpose, her ministry calling, her very *self* were all being condemned and rejected. Soon her despair led to depression that forced Shelly into a year of intensive biblical counseling and treatment.

Escape. In our depression, we are often physically exhausted, emotionally sad or numb, spiritually dry, and relationally strained. Depression is often accompanied by dark thoughts and unproductive choices that reflect a strong desire to escape painful circumstances. We say things like, "Nothing is right in my life! Everything is terrible!" "I sleep all the time now. I never want to get out of bed." "All I want to do is be by myself, eating and watching television." "I want to live in a cabin in the mountains, reading books and staying away from everyone."

Elijah's story in 1 Kings 19 illustrates both depression and the desire to escape from a troubling situation. On the heels of a great spiritual victory in which Elijah witnessed the power of God in destroying the prophets of Baal, Elijah becomes frightened when Jezebel threatens to kill him. "Elijah was afraid and ran for his life. When he came to Beersheba in Judah, he left his servant there, while he himself went a day's journey into the desert. He came to a broom tree, sat down under it and prayed that he might die. 'I have had enough, LORD,' he said. 'Take my life; I am no better than my ancestors'" (1 Kings 19:3–4).

As many people do when overwhelmed by a flood of emotion, Elijah runs. Escape often seems the only reasonable reaction when we become engulfed by distressing difficulties. Elijah runs a long way, over a hundred miles, all the way from Jezreel in Israel to Beersheba in southern Judah. At the end of his flight, he escapes even further by leaving his companion and going away by himself to pray that he might die. Just like Elijah, we intuitively long for peace when we are depressed. But false peace bought through temporary escapes is not true *shalom* at all. Attempts to escape from God, others, and ourselves may bring moments of relief, but they ultimately inhibit true *shalom*.

Donna was devastated when she was diagnosed with a fast-growing bone cancer. Instead of telling others and reaching out to loving friends to help her bear this frightening burden, Donna began to abuse her prescription painkillers in an effort to escape the dark cloud of depression that had overtaken her. The problem was, every time she awoke, the cancer was still there. Escape granted her no comfort from her depression.

Grief. Depression is often a part of the grieving process. Nearly all of us will at one time or another endure a process of grieving. Even Jesus wept at the tomb of his friend (John 11:35). Grief can be brought on by many types of losses: the death of loved ones, the loss of a job or financial security, health setbacks, and relationship struggles. Several years ago, my (Judy's) closest friend terminated our friendship. For more than a year I grieved the loss and experienced the common stages of grieving. I experienced a sense of shock when I received her letter indicating that our relationship was over. The shock soon became anger and eventually melted into a frantic period of trying to do all that I could to get my friend to reengage with me. When my efforts failed, I struggled with depression. I had difficulty sleeping and functioning. Eventually I grieved the loss of the relationship, reached a place of acceptance, and moved on, but I look back on that season of depression as one of my most trying times in life.

Overwhelming troubles. Scripture teaches that righteous people will not avoid troubles: "A righteous man may have many troubles" (Ps. 34:19). Being righteous does not mean that somehow we have attained some level of wisdom and goodness that prevents us from experiencing calamity. Trials and troubles in the lives of God's people are a *reality*. Many of the psalms of David transparently reflect struggles with anger, fear, loneliness, bitterness, confusion, hopelessness, and despair. God allows his people, even people with a "heart after God," to experience the overwhelming storms of life.

The apostle Paul frequently spoke about the reality of his troubles: "We are hard pressed on every side, but not crushed; perplexed, but not in despair; persecuted, but not abandoned; struck down, but not destroyed" (2 Cor. 4:8–9). "When we came into Macedonia, this body of ours had no rest, but we were harassed at every turn—conflicts on the outside, fears within" (2 Cor. 7:5). "Do your best to come to me quickly, for Demas, because he loved this world, has deserted me. . . . Alexander the metalworker did me a great deal of harm. . . . At my first defense, no one came to my support, but everyone deserted me" (2 Tim. 4:9–10, 14, 16).

Overwhelming troubles can lead us to depression. Marie has not gotten out of bed for more than a few hours at a time for *decades*. When her infant son died of SIDS and her husband divorced her, leaving her with thousands of dollars in credit card debt, Marie's troubles felt overwhelming. Instead of trusting the Lord and reaching out to the church for help, Marie tunneled down into her dark, depressive thoughts. She moved in with her parents, hid away from everyone and everything, and has spent years living in her dark basement room watching television.

Overcoming Depression

Depression often occurs when we feel like God is forsaking us and we are overwhelmed by the great pressures that life brings. Depression makes us feel as if life has lost all purpose, joy, and meaning. It is a sentence of death in the soul. Misunderstood and mishandled, depression is a thief of peace. In order to be peacemaking women, we learn to rely in faith on the God who does indeed raise us up from death—even the death of our souls drowned by depression. He promises: "I will lead the blind by ways they have not known, along unfamiliar paths I will guide them; I will turn the darkness into light before them and make the rough places smooth. These are the things I will do; I will not forsake them" (Isa. 42:16). Let us consider some of the ways that God's grace enables us to overcome depression.

Address all aspects of the depression biblically. The journey through depression requires us to biblically address every aspect of our lives: physical, emotional, spiritual, and relational. We are called to "unpack" the specifics of our depression using biblical terms so that we can wisely discern biblical responses. Elijah's experience in 1 Kings 19 helps us to understand these truths. *Spiritually*, Elijah was invited to encounter God's presence. Nothing refreshes our spirits more than experiencing God personally as the one who knows us and cares for us. *Physically*, Elijah was given food and rest. When we are physically exhausted, nothing refreshes our bodies more than sleep and good food. *Relationally*, Elijah was provided with Elisha to be his attendant and eventual successor. When we are alone, nothing refreshes more than a faithful friend who attends to us and shares the burden of our work. *Emotionally*, Elijah was comforted by the truth that he was a part of a small army of faithful believers. Nothing renews our commitment to serving God more than to know that we are a part of something larger than ourselves.

Our depression will probably not lift if we fail to address all aspects of it. Helen was offended when her pastor dared to imply that some aspect of her depression might have a component of sin. She refused his biblical counsel. Barb was sure that her depression would lift if she could just get on the right medicine. Sue didn't think that her depression had anything to do with the fact that she was morbidly obese, had no physical activity in her life, and spent hours every day eating junk food and reading romance novels. By God's grace, these precious women were all called to address the physical, spiritual, emotional, and relational aspects of their depression in order to find deliverance.

Call on the name of the Lord. Psalm 34 instructs us to respond in certain ways in order to experience the sweet hope that, "The LORD redeems his servants; no one will be condemned who takes refuge in him" (v. 34:22). By faith, believers are to extol the Lord (v. 1), boast in the Lord (v. 2), glorify the Lord (v. 3), look to him (v. 5), call out to him (v. 6), delight in him (v. 7), taste and see that the Lord is good and take refuge in him (v. 8), fear the Lord (v. 9), seek the Lord (v. 10), listen to the Lord (v. 11), guard our mouths from speaking evil (v. 13), turn from evil, do good, and seek and pursue peace (v. 14). Faith is actively turning to God, calling on his name, and depending on him.

Psalm 34 reminds the Christian that she will have many troubles, and yet it is primarily a psalm of hope—hope in the God who answers and delivers (v. 4), who hears and saves (v. 6), who protects (v. 20), and who redeems (v. 22). Depression too is turned to good by God through his active working of his purposes in our lives. God is glorified when we trust in him and open our hearts to receive his many good gifts. God is pleased when we turn to him and cry out for his help and protection. When we open our mouths and our hearts to call on the name of the Lord, he delights in delivering us from all our troubles (Ps. 34:6).

When I (Judy) was molested as a child, I remember that on the other side of the door, people's voices could be heard. Just feet away from where I was, others talked and laughed. But I never called out. I was convinced that calling out would have caused me to be discovered, rejected, and punished. Until recently, I never learned to call out for help when I was in trouble. I never learned to really call on the name of the Lord until I was in the midst of writing this book. My spiritual advisor and friend, Carl Gans, helped me to cross this line of voicelessness, to learn to call out to God, and to find myself safely in his hand.

I had spent several months fighting deep discouragement. With gentle questions, Carl drew out the true purposes of my heart (Prov. 20:5) and lovingly reminded me of the biblical truths that breathe hope into the many aspects of my struggles. Carl told me over and over, "God hears you. He loves you. He holds you; you don't hold him" (see Ps. 73:23). And one day, the darkness lifted. I finally realized, deep in my heart, for the first time, that if I were to let go of God completely, he would still be the one who holds me by his right hand. As the psalmist writes, "When I said, 'My foot is slipping,' your love, O LORD, supported me. When anxiety was great within me, your consolation brought joy to my soul" (Ps. 94:18–19). And the writer of Hebrews reminds us: "God has said, 'Never will I leave you; never will I forsake you.' So we say with confidence, 'The Lord is my helper; I will not be afraid. What can man do to me?'" (Heb. 13:5–6).

Even in our depression, God enables us to call on the name of the Lord. By finding our strength in God (1 Sam. 23:16), we call to the One who hears us, loves us, and holds us forever.

Take the steps you can take. When you are depressed, you probably won't *feel* like doing much. And yet any step toward the

Lord produces positive momentum that can help move you forward. God uses our struggles to develop faith and trust. Peter stood convinced that his troubles and testing were for the purpose of growing his faith, that precious gift from God that is "of greater worth than gold" (1 Peter 1:7). Jeremiah, in a moving poem of depression and despair, confesses that his troubles and trials ultimately led him back to reliance on God, to "wait for him" (Lam. 3:24). James highlights the truth that our troubles have a special link with our faith in God. He boldly instructs his readers to consider the trials and troubles of life to be a source of joy. Why? Because they test our faith, bringing it to maturity (James 1:2–4).

What steps can you take to address your depression? Cathryn had struggled with depression for years, but she began her journey toward peace when she took one step of faith and turned off the television for one hour each day and spent that time reading the Bible. The next month she reached out to one person with a card. Over time, she began to take short walks in the mall and gradually began to take walks around her neighborhood. Instead of hiding from her troubles, Cathryn prayed and consecrated them to the Lord. Scripture memory helped her to meditate on the attributes of God, his goodness, and his sovereignty. Over ten years later, Cathryn has a particularly effective ministry to the people in her church struggling with depression.

One of my (Judy's) first counseling clients was David, a man in his mid-thirties whose wife brought him to counseling to deal with his depression. He had been out of work for a couple of years and spent a good deal of time sleeping every day. He had been treated with medication for his depression for nearly ten years. I was an inexperienced counselor, but I had also struggled with severe depression several times in my adult life. I intuitively knew what David would spend the next year teaching me. He taught me that depression occurs when our resources break down on many different fronts because our difficulties and troubles are too much to bear with the resources we have available. But depression also brings many opportunities that would not otherwise come. While the answers for curing depression are not simplistic, there is hope. We do not find freedom without great struggle and without being changed along the way.

In my first counseling session with David, when I suggested that he could actually do something about his depression, the response I received was shocking. David jumped to his feet, shook his fist in my face, and shouted obscenities. He stormed out of the office, and I was left looking at his equally shocked wife. We set another appointment, but I never expected to see him again. Yet David returned and we began a process that took over a year. David explored his past experiences and his present thoughts and actions, exposing his hurts, frustrations, and desires to the truth in God's Word. David learned that he was not an unfortunate accident but a man dearly loved by God. He discovered that he alone was responsible for his feelings and choices, and he eventually released others in his life through forgiveness. David also discovered that he had special gifts that could be used to bless others. He struggled but eventually was restored to his wife and children, found a new job, and began to engage deeply with the Lord. Not only did he change, so did I. When I encounter depressed people today, I am filled with hope for them. If David could find freedom from a decade of depression, so can the rest of us. *God raises the dead.*

Grieve with hope. Grief can be without hope or a grief with hope: "Brothers, we do not want you to be ignorant about those who fall asleep, or to grieve like the rest of men, who have no hope" (1 Thess. 4:13). We grieve when we experience loss. Prolonged grief without hope can lead to bitterness and depression.

Hope is the miracle drug that cures depression—a powerful medicine that is often "time released" rather than instantaneous. As we see again from 1 Kings 19, God allows Elijah to reach the end of himself. He did not demand that Elijah snap out of his depression; instead, God guided Elijah through it. Working through the flood of depression, coming to hope in the Lord, requires us to see God as he is—the "everlasting God, the Creator of the ends of the earth" (Isa. 40:28). Hoping in the Lord requires us to see ourselves as we really are—people who grow tired and weary, vulnerable to stumbling and falling. Hoping in the Lord is a taste of *shalom* because we know what lies ahead for us—renewed strength and "soaring" joy.

> Do you not know?
> Have you not heard?

The LORD is the everlasting God,
  the Creator of the ends of the earth.
He will not grow tired or weary,
  and his understanding no one can fathom.
He gives strength to the weary
  and increases the power of the weak.
Even youths grow tired and weary,
  and young men stumble and fall;
but those who hope in the LORD
  will renew their strength.
They will soar on wings like eagles;
  they will run and not grow weary,
  they will walk and not be faint.

Isaiah 40:28–31

When we counsel grieving people, their ability to persevere is enhanced if their expectations are properly set. We help them understand the "DABDAH" model of grief so that the effects of this draining process can be managed better instead of worsening their despair and depression.[2] "DABDAH" stands for Denial, Anger, Bargaining, Depression, Acceptance, and Hope and is a simple reminder of the stages people go through when working through grief. Each stage has its own difficulties, but depression is often the longest of these stages. Complex grief, such as the loss of a loved one, usually needs to be worked through many times. The human heart seems able to be refilled over and over again with fresh grief over past losses. Grieving is the draining of those swelling reservoirs and is an appropriate response to loss.

Christians are able to grieve with hope because they are not ignorant about the truth. Those who do not know the gospel of Jesus Christ and the truth of God through his Word are those who do not have the hope of eternity with God. Without the truth, we cannot grieve with the hope that lightens our sorrow. Mere acceptance, rather than true hope, is often the final result. In Christ, however, we have hope.

View depression as an opportunity. Elijah's story reminds us of a key aspect of overcoming depression. Just as Elijah's experience spanned many weeks, our own efforts to move out of depression can take a long time. Paul recognized the need to be "patient in affliction" (Rom. 12:12) because even when hope dawns and depression draws to an end, a time of rebuilding or "cleaning up" is just beginning. When the floodwaters of 1993 receded, the survivors were left sorting through the damage. The shells of countless homes were still intact, but their drywall and electrical wiring had to be ripped out and replaced. Belongings once held dear had to be tossed in the trash.

Like a flood, depression brings the opportunity to let go of worthless things such as pride, self-confidence, and the appearance of strength. It brings the opportunity to rebuild using better and more enduring materials. Depression, in other words, is an opportunity to upgrade life. Depression also gives us the opportunity to learn to live with things that are damaged and irreparable. But it comes at a high cost. Letting go of our worldly treasures and learning to live in a fallen world is difficult, but we are called to do so: "Do not store up for yourselves treasures on earth, where moth and rust destroy, and where thieves break in and steal. But store up for yourselves treasures in heaven, where moth and rust do not destroy, and where thieves do not break in and steal. For where your treasure is, there your heart will be also" (Matt. 6:19–21).

The treasures of this world are heavy weights. They impose a sense of responsibility and burden. The treasures of heaven warm our hearts and give us delight and hope. Many financially blessed people say they wish they could return to the simpler life they enjoyed before their belongings came to own them.

People who have been flooded with negative emotions and brought to the point of despair rarely enjoy *shalom*-filled lives. Depression slows them down and robs them of energy. Yet we often need a season of depression before we embrace the great opportunities brought about by heartfelt reflection. Reflection that takes us back to the Word of God causes us to grow in spiritual maturity. Depression often slows us down long enough to make reflection possible—even as it drives us to ask for help from others. Allowing others to minister to us deepens our chances for rich Christian community. Depression is an opportunity to become vulnerable before God and others. It is an opportunity to evaluate our relationships and our longings. It is an opportunity to ask ourselves the hard questions: Who am I? Who is God? What is my purpose in life? Depression is not always our enemy, but it can actually serve us as an opportunity and as a friend.

Respond like the soldier, athlete, and farmer. In 2 Timothy 2, Paul gives us biblical illustrations about how God's people are to respond to the difficulties and troubles that they will surely face, including depression.

Paul writes that we are to endure hardship like a good soldier, one who is focused on pleasing his commanding officer and refuses to be distracted by the many other demands that surround him. What are the qualities of a good soldier? First, he is part of a unit. He doesn't exist on his own but works with a group of well-trained, committed comrades who share his common purposes. Overcoming depression is not a one-man act. It involves community and relationship with others, depending on others and trusting even your life to their protection and help. The qualities of a good soldier—courage, obedience, loyalty, and endurance—are strengthened and polished by others as we share in the pleasure of working as a unit. When depression comes, a good soldier knows to look to his commanding officer for new directions. He never gives up. He is committed to "fight the good fight of the faith" (1 Tim. 6:12).

Paul instructs us to endure hardship like an athlete who competes according to the rules of the game. Athletes train with dedication, staying prepared at all times for the challenges that lie ahead. Rather than write their own book of rules, they stay within the parameters set forth for them. Overcoming depression is not a lazy process but one that calls for diligence and excellence in all we do and all we are. An athlete needs a coach to help spot weaknesses and eliminate them. She who competes on a team must learn to respect and value the contributions of others. She needs the encouragement of others. When depression comes, the athlete perseveres and does not give up. She forgets what is behind, strains toward what is ahead, and presses on toward the goal to win the prize (Phil. 3:13–14).

Paul tells us that we are to endure hardship like a hardworking farmer who does all that he can to provide for himself. There is a right way of addressing our depression: we are called to responsibly work at the tasks we are designed to accomplish while also looking in faith to the God who sends the rain and makes the plants to grow. A farmer is patient, knowing that his labors will not produce immediate results. He keeps careful watch and regularly takes care of weeds and pests. At harvest his task is exhausting but rewarding. The good farmer calls in his crew to help him harvest the good gifts God has given, storing them to satisfy the needs of those close to him. When depression arrives in response to natural, uncontrollable disasters—blight, fires, floods, and pestilence—the farmer prepares to go through a lean time while also preparing to plant again. His sadness does not destroy his commitment to fulfill the purposes for which he was made. He turns his gaze to God's great and precious promises that encourage him to "add to your faith goodness; and to goodness, knowledge; and to knowledge, self-control; and to self-control, perseverance" (2 Peter 1:5–6).

Rest in God's presence. Consider again Elijah's experience as recorded in 1 Kings 19. In exhaustion, after expressing his deep discouragement that the value of his work was "no better than his ancestors," Elijah falls asleep. An angel ministers to Elijah's physical needs until he is strong enough for the journey that lies ahead. Forty days later, Elijah reaches his destination: a dark, empty cave. When God confronts Elijah, Elijah expresses his feelings of isolation and fear as well as anger at those he believes are responsible for his situation. "And the word of the LORD came to him: 'What are you doing here, Elijah?' He replied, 'I have been very zealous for the LORD God Almighty. The Israelites have rejected your covenant, broken down your altars, and put your prophets to death with the sword. I am the only one left, and now they are trying to kill me too'" (1 Kings 19:9–10).

God does not reason with Elijah. Not at first. Instead, God allows Elijah to encounter God's own presence—his surprising, unexpected, and gentle presence. But Elijah's complaint does not change. Elijah remains angry and self-pitying. God listens and then calls Elijah to return to his responsibilities. God ends his instructions by correcting Elijah's wrong thinking—the very thinking upon which Elijah's feelings of anger and self-pity rest. Specifically, God tells Elijah that he is not the lone prophet as he had wrongly thought, because God himself has set aside seven thousand additional faithful followers (1 Kings 19:18). Elijah finds hope in the truth and rest in the presence of God.

"Now faith is being sure of what we hope for and certain of what we do not see" (Heb. 11:1). God blesses us with the gift of faith, and he calls us to use that gift by responding to him in ways that fill us with blessed hope. Depression has a difficult time thriving when we are watered and fed by hope through the Word of God. We pray with the psalmist, "My soul is weary with sorrow; strengthen me according to your word" (Ps. 119:28). Consider Julia's testimony of resting in God's presence even though depressed: "I spent an entire year in a dry wasteland of feeling separated and far from God. Nothing soothed my soul. I 'did my duty' of reading Scriptures and praying. I even cried out to my sisters in Christ, 'What do I do?' Everyone told me to 'buck up!' I received nothing from them. I used to weep through every sermon. In the end, all I could do was preach truth to myself: God is faithful. God will test, try, and discipline me—but he will not leave me. Even when life is dark and lonely, he is with me. That is enough." By resting in God's presence and clinging to what is good (Rom. 12:9), Julia worked through her dark time to eventually find herself restored to the peace that transcends all understanding (Phil. 4:7).

From Depression to *Shalom*

When I (Tara) was struggling with depression after the birth of my first child, I once asked my husband, Fred, "When you wake up in the morning, do you feel like there is a pool of gray muck above your head that is ten feet deep; and you have to claw your way to the top of it just to get a breath; and then you have to force your way into your day, choosing by faith to take joy in things that really *do* make you happy, but you just don't *feel* happy because even though *nothing* is actually wrong it feels as though *everything* is wrong?" He said, no, he did not feel that way. I think it was after that conversation that we both knew it was time to get help for my depression.

Our first step was to pray and seek biblical counsel from our pastor. We did this because depression often has issues of sin and unbelief tied to it. But we also talked to my brother-in-law, who is a licensed clinical social worker, and my medical doctor, because we knew that both my maternal and paternal family lines have had a history of chemical imbalances associated with depression. I knew that I did not want to simply go on antidepressants as a "cure-all," and yet I did not want to avoid them if, in fact, they might be one way that God would minister his grace to me. "If your ankle were broken," Fred told me, "we would seek medical help. If there is a chemical component to this depression, we should prayerfully consider seeking appropriate medical help to treat it."

Between my private study of the resources recommended at the end of this chapter, pastoral counseling, and the clinical advice I received, I learned more about the symptoms of depression (sleeping too much or not at all, overwhelming fear, eating too much or not at all, panic attacks, constantly reliving troubling memories, hiding away). I also learned how to "unpack" the gray muck in order to address the fallenness and sin issues one by one. Instead of being overwhelmed by an amorphous blob of sorrows and struggles, I learned to list them out and apply Scripture to them. I didn't end up going on antidepressants, mainly because I was still nursing our baby, but I would prayerfully consider them in the future if I were in a serious and prolonged depression.

By God's grace, my depression did lift. If you are struggling with depression, we have every hope and confidence that you can receive similar help in your time of need. For Jesus truly gives us all we need to experience peace: "I have told you these things, so that in me you may have peace. In this world you will have trouble. But take heart! I have overcome the world" (John 16:33). Jesus has overcome the world and deprived it of its power to ultimately harm us. Jesus is our hope and our peace. We will have many troubles, but even during our times of greatest depression, God's grace empowers us to hope in the Lord and to rest in his care. As we long for our eternal home in heaven—where there will be no more sadness—we have peace as we call on the name of the Lord. We pray with the psalmist:

> I love the LORD, for he heard my voice;
> he heard my cry for mercy.
> Because he turned his ear to me,
> I will call on him as long as I live.

The cords of death entangled me,
    the anguish of the grave came upon me;
    I was overcome by trouble and sorrow.
Then I called on the name of the LORD:
    "O LORD, save me!"

The LORD is gracious and righteous;
    our God is full of compassion.
The LORD protects the simplehearted;
    when I was in great need, he saved me.

Be at rest once more, O my soul,
    for the LORD has been good to you.

For you, O LORD, have delivered my soul from death,
    my eyes from tears,
    my feet from stumbling,
that I may walk before the LORD
    in the land of the living.

Psalm 116:1–9

Personal Reflection

Questions for Reflection

1. Read 1 Corinthians 6:9–11, paying particular attention to verse 11. What does it mean if we forget that we have been cleansed from our past sins? How does remembering this amazing truth—the gospel—speak practically to our hearts when we are depressed?

2. Sometimes we are depressed because we do not get what we want in the way we want it. We become disappointed, and continued disappointment and frustration can lead to depression. Read Proverbs 13:12. Is there any area of your life where you have experienced continual disappointment? Write a short letter to God, expressing how you feel about this area of disappointment and how you feel about God when you think of this situation.

3. Make a list of the burdens that you carry. Which of these burdens add to feelings of discouragement or depression? Could you take any specific actions this week to improve these situations? Who can you reach out to for help to entrust your concerns to the Lord and address them biblically?

4. What resources are available to help you when you feel depressed? How might you help others who struggle with depression? If someone were to tell you that they were suicidal, what would be the first thing you would do? If someone you knew were abusing alcohol or drugs to deal with their feelings of hopelessness, how might you respond? Reflect on your answers with another person whom you believe has the resources to help people. What thoughts or suggestions did this person have for you regarding your answers to this question?

5. Depression does not live in an atmosphere of rejoicing. Read Philippians 4:4–7. Write about three ways that God has blessed you in the past. If any of these blessings include actions by other people, consider writing them a letter thanking them for how they have encouraged you.

6. Meditate on Psalm 119:67; Hebrews 5:8; and James 1:2–4. Write out three *benefits* of hardship and suffering. Read Romans 5:2–5. What are we to hope in? Write out a prayer to the Lord incorporating the ideas of these four Scriptures.

7. Sometimes we get depressed when people reject us. Read Psalm 27:10 and Hebrews 13:5. What does it mean to you to know that even though people may reject you, God never will?

8. Has your depression grown stronger and bleaker? Do you feel hopeless? Have you ever considered suicide? Are you currently considering suicide? Such thoughts and feelings are common, even in the church. You are not alone! If you are experiencing prolonged depression and would describe your pain as unbearable, using alcohol or drugs to escape your feeling of hopelessness, feeling that you do not have a support network of friends and family to help you, or planning out ways to end your life, *then you should get help today.* Please consider calling a pastor, counselor, or doctor immediately.

Praying Scripture to God

I thank you, God, that you are compassionate to me and that you protect me. Thank you, Lord, for forgiving my transgressions and showing me mercy. Dear God, I know that my life is not my own. Please strengthen me with power through my inner being so that Christ may dwell in my heart through faith. Please teach me to walk continually in your truth and not run away from my troubles. God of all hope, please fill me with all joy and peace even though I grieve and experience many sorrows. I trust in you. Please, God, help me to address all aspects of my depression and honor you in my body, mind, and speech. Father, I thank you that you enable me to fight the fight of faith as I call on your name, flee from sin, and pursue righteousness, godliness, faith, and love. I thank you that you are my hope and you renew me when I am weary and faint.

(Prayer based on Ps. 116:5–6; Prov. 28:13; Mic. 7:18–19; Jer. 10:23; Eph. 3:16–17; Ps. 26:3; Rom. 15:13; 1 Cor. 6:19–20; Ps. 34:6; 1 Tim. 6:11–12; Isa. 40:28–31.)

Recommended Resources for Further Study and Consideration

William Bridge, *A Lifting Up for the Downcast* (Carlisle, PA: Banner of Truth Trust, 1649, 1995).

Jeremiah Burroughs, *The Rare Jewel of Christian Contentment* (Carlisle, PA: Banner of Truth Trust, 1648, 2000).

D. Martyn Lloyd-Jones, *Spiritual Depression: Its Causes and Its Cures* (Grand Rapids: Eerdmans, 1965).

Timothy Rogers, *Trouble of Mind and the Disease of Melancholy* (Morgan, PA: Soli Deo Gloria Publications, 2002).

Edward T. Welch, *Blame It on the Brain? Distinguishing Chemical Imbalances, Brain Disorders and Disobedience* (Phillipsburg, NJ: P&R Publishing, 1998).

Edward T. Welch, *Depression—A Stubborn Darkness* (Winston-Salem, NC: Punch, 2004).

Edward T. Welch, *Depression: The Way Up When You Are Down* (Phillipsburg, NJ: P&R Publishing, 2000).

1 2

FEAR

In my anguish I cried to the LORD,
   and he answered by setting me free.
The LORD is with me; I will not be afraid.
   What can man do to me?

Psalm 118:5–6

There is nothing like suspense and anxiety for barricading a human's mind against [God].

C. S. Lewis[1]

You might remember a movie called *Holy Man*.[2] While this movie is unlikely to become one of the great classics, I (Judy) found it fascinating. Throughout the movie, the holy man interacted with people according to his ability to discern what was true about them beneath the surface, not as they were accustomed to being treated. The movie makes the point that people frequently are not on the inside what they appear to be on the outside. We aren't always who we seem to be, and we are often quite the opposite of what we appear to be. The same is often true of fear.

I (Tara) recall a season when Fred and I were experiencing marital tension and frequent conflicts. One day I journaled,

Our day started off with a fight. Fred said something in the middle of a yawn that I couldn't understand. When I asked him to repeat it he said, "It's not worth repeating." I got hurt and suddenly we were in the middle of a fight. Again. Fred says it's my fault—I'm too sensitive. But then he grudgingly says, "Well, okay, I could be more gentle." Give me a break. I'm afraid! I'm afraid that Fred will never get a better job and we won't have enough money to pay our bills or stay in our home.

Isn't that a telling progression? Initially you may read that example and think, "They need better communication skills." However, the reality is that my heart had given in to fear. Underlying my frustration over our poor communication was a fear that my family would not be financially secure. My problem wasn't just that I needed to learn how to communicate better. My problem was ultimately fear. Instead of trusting in the Lord, I was relying on my husband and myself. When I looked at our out-of-balance budget each month, I was terrified. In my fear, I was forgetting the Lord. As Ed Welch writes, "In the biblical sense, what we fear shows our allegiances. It shows where we put our trust. The problem is when fear forgets God."[3]

In this chapter we will look carefully at the peace-shattering, troubling emotion of fear. What is fear? What does it look like? What can we do about it? To be women of *shalom*, we are called to grapple with fear so that we may live in obedience to Jesus's words, "Do not let your hearts be troubled" (John 14:1). One thing that makes fear difficult to grapple with is that it rarely looks like fear.

Faces of Fear

Fears that are felt deeply have great power over the human heart. Fear has the power to drive out *shalom*—robbing us of peace with God, others, and ourselves. We need to identify our deep fears and bring them to the surface so that they can be evaluated in light of the truth of Scripture. Once we have evaluated them, we choose to live either according to our fears or according to the truth. Most of us live according to fear because we have not taken the time to reflect and evaluate our lives and our hearts. Perhaps no condition of the heart is easier to misdiagnose than fear. In a culture where fear is frowned upon and people are made to feel like "losers" if they struggle with it, fear has gone underground. It is difficult to spot in others and also in ourselves.

Worry. We are prone to worry. Worry is that constant obsessing about the worst possible outcome to a situation. Worry is misplaced faith. When we worry, we call God a liar and deny him as our heavenly Father. Worry is the soul's usurpation of God's sovereignty and is the distinguishing mark of the pagan world.[4] When we worry, we usually engage in thoughts, words, and actions that are rooted in unbelief.

Tammy is bound by worry that comes from unbelief. "I worry that my husband has been injured because he is late coming home. I worry that we won't have the money to pay the bill on the minivan repairs. I worry that we will be mugged on the train coming home or that the 'D' on my son's report card means that he will grow up without a bright future. I wake up worrying about my daughter's illness and I go to bed worrying about terrorists—not that I sleep much." Do you see how Tammy's fears and worries are rooted in unbelief? Instead of trusting in God and believing his Word, Tammy is acting as though she is the lord of her life and the sustainer of the universe. She claims to trust God, but really she lives as though she believes that *she* has to control her circumstances and keep everyone in her life safe and happy. Her fearful heart is a heart of unbelief and worry.

One reason we worry is that it gives us something to do when we feel powerless. Worrying is a mental action that fully absorbs us—it gives the illusion that we can change what is beyond our control. Deep in our hearts, we have the sense that worrying makes us better prepared, smarter, and more powerful to act. Worry, however, is futile and useless. It chokes the Word of God out of our lives: "The one who received the seed that fell among the thorns is the man who hears the word, but the *worries* of this life and the deceitfulness of wealth choke it, making it unfruitful" (Matt. 13:22, emphasis added).

Both the New and Old Testaments confront us with the fact that worry has no real power to change things: "Who of you by worrying can add a single hour to his life?" (Matt. 6:27). "Since no man knows the future, who can tell him what is to come? No man has power over the wind to contain it; so no one has power over the day of his death" (Eccles. 8:7–8).

Another biblical word for worry is "fret." Psalm 37:8 exhorts us to not worry or fret because "it leads only to evil." How does worrying lead to evil? It distracts us from the important things in life. It takes our focus off of the most important thing of all—our relationship with Christ. When speaking to Martha about her complaint that Mary was not assisting in the housework, Jesus's response was enlightening: "'Martha, Martha,' the Lord answered, 'you are worried and upset about many things, but only one thing is needed. Mary has chosen what is better, and it will not be taken away from her'" (Luke 10:41–42). Fear and worry cause us to lose perspective—to lose sight of that which is truly important.

Anxiety. Anxiety is that pervasive sense of hypervigilance and discomfort that something bad might happen. Anxiety is the bread and butter of psychotherapy. Sometimes specific situations can cause anxiety. At other times anxiety may be a generalized feeling that pervades all of life. At all times, "an anxious heart weighs a man down" (Prov. 12:25).

Anxiety causes many physical problems, including hypertension, headaches, stomach discomfort, and fatigue. Anxiety pollutes other emotions, and the "panic attack" is an increasingly common experience for people who suffer from anxiety. Anxiety is a combination of worry and doubt that brings a spiritual restlessness that robs a believer of the precious peace found in Christ.

Anne is an anxious woman. She rarely lets anyone else drive because she has to be in control; otherwise she grips the armrest in panic. She doesn't sleep at all until her children—even her college-aged adult children—are home for the night. And when she does sleep, she is restless and fitful, thinking that she might be hearing someone calling for help or an intruder breaking in. She is compulsive in crowds, vigilant against someone trying to cause her harm. Anne's fears bind her in anxiety.

Anger. We live in a culture that often applauds anger. Action films idolize and admire control, power, and anger. Yet the Bible states that anger is cruel (Prov. 27:4) and that anger "resides in the lap of fools" (Eccles. 7:9). Anger is often a cover for fear. In response to feeling out of control and powerless, frightened people often lash out in anger, experiencing a momentary sense of control. Anger is often a manifestation of worry and fear.

Janice and Eric appeared to be an angry woman and a fearful man when they came to me (Judy) for counseling. Janice raged at Eric, blaming and accusing him of causing their relationship breakdown. Meanwhile, Eric sat dejected, looking at his hands in his lap. He rarely looked up and would not speak. Janice said of her husband, "He is such a fearful man. And I am angry. I can't get him to stop being afraid and start being a real husband." By God's grace, I discerned that Eric was in fact angry at how his wife treated him and chose to control his emotions by shutting them down. I also came to understand how frightened his wife was because she felt the weight of responsibility for repairing their damaged relationship.

When I suggested to the couple that they had their diagnosis backwards, that it was the husband who was angry and the wife who was frightened, they began to look at themselves and each other differently. They began to change as they responded to their real heart conditions. Eric addressed Janice's fear with assurance of his love and commitment. Had he maintained that she was angry rather than afraid, he would have continued to "tune her out." Janice responded to Eric's anger by seeking his forgiveness for her disrespect. Had she maintained that he was afraid, she would have continued in her efforts to make him change. Slowly this couple saw their marriage transformed by understanding, love, and gentleness.

Fear and anger are often two sides of the same coin. How quickly fear turns into anger! How many times have anxious mothers and fathers, waiting for their overdue teenager to arrive home, become enraged the moment the headlights appear in the driveway? I (Tara) realize just how often I come across as angry and impatient when in fact I am terrified. For example, in my twenties I was frequently promoted to positions which were actually beyond my abilities. I didn't realize it when I accepted the work, of course, but the truth was that I did not know how to do the jobs well. Never one to give up easily, I would work and work, pouring myself into my commitments, trying desperately to do a good job. Yet people

304   Conflicts Within

often found me difficult to work with. Why? Many thought I was
angry and impatient, but the mature, wise, and loving people with
whom I worked knew the truth: I was afraid. Fear is often masked
as anger.

Doubt. During the writing of this book, my (Judy's) father passed
away. I loved my father, even though he was a wounded man who
hurt others profoundly. He was a fearful man, nagged by many
doubts. He doubted that people loved him. He doubted that he
mattered to others and that others had his best interests at heart.
What does a person who doubts deeply do? He often causes his
fears to come true. One way to dispel fear and doubt is to make
what we fear a reality.

Often when we are troubled by doubt we become testers. We
test others in order to prove our doubts false and end up realizing our greatest fears. When we doubt that we are loved, we
test others by pushing them away. When we doubt that we are
significant or important, we live as if our actions and words are
meaningless. When we fail to trust others, we become untrust-
worthy ourselves.

My father wrote this poem and gave it to me one Christmas
Day a few years ago. It clearly illustrates how strongly doubt—as
fear—is experienced and how powerfully it motivates us in the way
we choose to live:

Doubt

I watched the evening sunset
So orange in grand array,
Bringing me closer to darkness,
Ending a most doubt-filled day.
It causes me to think back,
To measure my good deeds
If any; and did I contribute
To someone's simple needs?
I wonder as I watch the sun,
Fade slowly out of sight,
While I hope and pray
To see dawn's early light.
Determined to try even harder
To make tomorrow really count,
So that when facing yet another day
I'll have shed my fear of doubt.

Fear that shows itself as doubt makes people constantly evaluate themselves to determine how they must try harder in order to be found worthy or acceptable. A person who doubts is "like a wave of the sea, blown and tossed by the wind. . . . a double-minded man, unstable in all he does" (James 1:6, 8). We can sink under the weight of our doubts, as Peter did when he was walking on the water towards Jesus. Yet knowing that Peter's fear was unfounded, Jesus asked Peter, "Why did you doubt?" (Matt. 14:31).

Control. Most people dislike being told that they are controlling individuals. Most people dislike working for or living with a controlling person. In this "age of tolerance," controlling people are viewed as immature and irritating, forever manipulating people and activities in an attempt to guarantee the outcome they desire. For example, I (Tara) remember with chilling regret a statement I made when I was only nine years old. I intimidated another child in an attempt to control her behavior by stating: "You'd better do what I say because I have a lot of friends, and if you don't, you'll be sorry! They won't want to be your friends if you're not nice to me."

What a bully I was! What a frightened child I was. I was so afraid of rejection and the thought of having no friends that I actually intimidated and sought to control another child. Controlling people are fearful people. Control is an attempt to reduce fear by taking the ambiguity out of life. Life, however, is full of mystery and has multiple surprises embedded in it. The sense that we can control our own futures and avoid our worst fears is an illusion—an illusion to which many of us devote much time and energy.

Linda had separated from Alex because he was "controlling," frequently making threats to force his family to comply with his wishes. The final straw came when Alex threatened his teenage children that they would be taken from their Christian school and placed in public school if their grade point averages fell below a 3.5. Devastated, Linda took her two children and left the home. After many hours of conflict coaching, Alex began to see that he threatened others with punishment in an attempt to control because he was afraid of the possible "outcomes" to the situation. Alex feared that children who did not perform well in school would have no future, no financial blessings, and no status. He feared financial ruin for himself and felt great stress over the high cost of tuition. Angry that his fears were not shared, Alex felt that he alone had to carry the burden of making sure everything turned out okay. To justify the risk of the financial strain and to guarantee that his children would have positive futures, Alex drove his children to excel with threats of removing them from their beloved school. When his family complied with his threats, he felt comforted that he had brought control into an out-of-control situation. His fears were temporarily alleviated. When others did not agree with Alex or comply with his demands, his threats escalated because Alex believed that he had to control the future, even if it took threatening his family and breaking his relationships.

All who grasp at the illusion of control eventually find themselves empty-handed. A lonely Thanksgiving and Christmas, separated from his family, confronted Alex with the fact that control was just a shallow façade for fear in his life.

Defensiveness. I (Judy) dislike nothing more than defensiveness in the counseling room—not because defensive people are irritating (although they can be) but because defensiveness is so sad. Defensiveness guarantees that people will not get what they long for. Why are people defensive? Often it is because they feel misunderstood, which usually results in feeling unaccepted, unappreciated, and devalued. Defensive people are afraid. They fear loss of relationship and love, but their very actions turn others off and push them away. Defensiveness guarantees isolation, which is the opposite of the very understanding and acceptance hoped for.

Perhaps no character in Scripture is more defensive than the "proverbial fool." In Proverbs, the fool is one who does not invest her energy in listening and understanding others but airs her own opinions (Prov. 18:2). She embarrasses herself by answering others without having listened to them first (Prov. 18:13). The fool is quick to quarrel (Prov. 20:3) and rejects the wisdom offered to her by others (Prov. 23:9). A fool is difficult to change (Prov. 27:22); fools trust in themselves (Prov. 28:26) and give free rein to their anger (Prov. 29:11). The fool brings ruin on herself but blames God (Prov. 19:3). People who cling to their defensiveness, controlled by their fear, will not listen to and consider the words of others. Defensive people foolishly spurn wisdom and the God of wisdom.

I (Tara) spent years responding to my fears with defensiveness. Instead of admitting that I was afraid, I tried to micromanage situations and did not take counsel well. For example, I remember an important team-based project when I was in graduate school. I was terrified of failure, but I did not have the skills or wisdom to do the job well. I was exhausted, scared, and just wanted to get the job done and go home. When I felt that our team was floundering, I dominated the meetings, tried to force the project to completion, and bristled at criticisms and suggestions. In my fear I was defensive, and my team members reacted accordingly. I was not well liked or respected. At the root of it all was fear.

The fear of man. The "fear of man" is probably the most common manifestation of fear.[5] Most women—even Christian women—spend an inordinate amount of time trying to impress people. We are afraid of being judged unworthy or rejected. We try to impress even people we neither respect nor care about.

I (Tara) remember the exact moment as a junior-high age girl when I first realized that I could attract the attention of boys. My family was on a vacation, and I smiled at a boy from the car window. He smiled back, and I was hooked. Intoxicated with my newfound power, suddenly every gas stop had a purpose—for me to try to attract attention. When I got home I wouldn't leave the house without full makeup and a color-coordinated outfit. I was enraptured with the idea of gaining men's approval, and I began to live in bondage to the fear of man.

Scripture is clear that the fear of man is a curse and a snare. "This is what the LORD says: 'Cursed is the one who trusts in man, who depends on flesh for his strength and whose heart turns away from the LORD. . . . But blessed is the man who trusts in the LORD, whose confidence is in him. He will be like a tree planted by the water that sends out its roots by the stream. It does not fear when heat comes; its leaves are always green. It has no worries in a year of drought and never fails to bear fruit'" (Jer. 17:5, 7–8).

If you fear God, you will not fear your life circumstances. You will not worry. But if you are trapped in the fear of man, you will be bound by anxiety, fear, and worry. To help identify the fear of man in your own life, answer the following questions:

- If I could play a videotape of my daydreams and fantasies, what would I see?
- When I make a mistake or fail at a task, what are my thoughts? Am I sad because I fail to please the Lord or because I look stupid in front of other people?
- Am I afraid to try, really try, because if I fail, it would crush me? Do I need an "out" in case I don't succeed?
- Are my days far too busy and overcommitted because I don't dare risk offending people by saying "no" to their requests and demands?
- Do I have true friends and genuine, intimate relationships? Or do I dare not show any other person my true self for fear of being rejected?
- How often do I exaggerate (lie)? Do I cover up and tell white lies to mask reality because it isn't good enough?

That last question goes quickly to my (Tara's) heart. I distinctly remember a time in the second grade when the teacher invited a violinist to come to class for a demonstration. She asked if anyone in the class played the violin and I replied, "I *used to* play but I don't remember how—it was *years ago*." I chuckle as I recall this memory, for I was only seven years old at the time. I can only imagine the laughter in the teachers' lounge after my showy performance trying to impress people.

What about you? Do you fear people and live for their approval? Do you fail to invite people into your home because you think it isn't clean enough or nice enough? Or do you value love and hospitable ministry more than performance and looking good in front of others? "Fear of man will prove to be a snare, but whoever trusts in the LORD is kept safe" (Prov. 29:25).

The Cures for Fear

If your life is full of fear, then where is your heart? Our fears reveal what we treasure—we fear losing something important, experiencing pain, or failing to get something pleasurable. Simply said, we have two choices in life: to seek God's kingdom or to seek our own kingdom. We cannot have peace when we have divided loyalties. When we are caught up in the pursuit of our own purposes and pleasures, we will often stumble in the darkness, gripped by fear because we do not have the resources required to provide for ourselves in this life or the next.

To be rid of our fears, we are called to pray for the grace to follow Jesus's teaching and store up our treasures in heaven, not on earth: "Provide purses for yourselves that will not wear out, a treasure in heaven that will not be exhausted, where no thief comes near and no moth destroys. For where your treasure is, there your heart will be also" (Luke 12:33–34). Jesus never worried even though he did not have an easy life. He was often exhausted. He carried the vast pressures of a growing ministry. Yet he was not gripped by fear. Instead, he sought his Father's kingdom first. What does it look like to turn away from fear by seeking God's kingdom?

Identification. The first step in overcoming our fears is to find biblical ways to identify and describe them so that we can apply God's Word to the real issues. Keri felt bound by fear, but the books she read used words like "codependency," "self-esteem," and "post-traumatic stress disorder." She just didn't know how to find Scriptures that applied to her fears. In counseling with her pastor, Keri learned how to prayerfully list out her concerns using scriptural terms to describe what she feared: betrayal, rejection, financial devastation, ongoing suffering, unresolved conflict, failure. Then he led her in prayerfully looking at God's commands and promises related to her fears. By reminding Keri of the gospel and guiding her in worship, study, meditation, and prayer, Keri's pastor helped her to overcome her fears by experiencing many evidences of God's grace.

Faith and trust in God. By faith we are called to reconcile our circumstances with the fact that God is in control. We are to trust God. That's why Peter says that wives are to win over their husbands with a quiet and gentle spirit, not giving way to fear (1 Peter 3:1–6). When we give in to fear, we nag, micromanage, and push people around. When our hearts are fixed on our fears, we feel vulnerable, in doubt, and afraid. David proclaimed, "When I am afraid, I will trust in you. In God, whose word I praise, in God I trust; I will not be afraid" (Ps. 56:3–4). To be at peace with God, we are called to understand who he really is and how he addresses our fear. Unless we turn to God in faith, fear will destroy any hope for peace with God, others, and ourselves. Fear is a huge stumbling block to *shalom*, but peace comes through faith in Jesus Christ.

"Now faith is being sure of what we hope for and certain of what we do not see" (Heb. 11:1). Instead of living in our fears, we are called to turn in faith to the Lord and believe on his goodness both in this life and in eternity to come. Alissa is a young woman who is learning to turn away from her fears and to the Lord. After she was mugged and beaten coming home from school one day, Alissa became terrified that the man would follow her again and hurt her. She began to fear all strangers and didn't want to leave her home. But with help from her family and church, Alissa is beginning to walk in faith each day and turn away from her fears. In many ways Alissa's fear is legitimate—it happened to her once! Yet the beauty of faith in Christ is that we can commit both our painful past and our unknown future to our loving Savior.

No one knows the future except God. Alissa does not have the power in herself to bring about the future outcomes she desires. There is One who does. God says, "I make known the end from the beginning, from ancient times, what is still to come. I say: My purpose will stand, and I will do all that I please. . . . What I have said, that will I bring about; what I have planned, that will I do" (Isa. 46:10–11). While our actions do have power to impact our life circumstances, we are given this power only by God. God remains the Sovereign Lord whose purposes prevail even though human beings act out their own plans (Prov. 19:21). To trust God and his sovereign power over our lives is to turn from fear, knowing that the outcome of our lives is safely in his hand.

Fear. Firefighters have a strange but effective way of fighting out-of-control wildfires. *They fight fire with fire.* Firefighters burn a patch of ground in the path of an oncoming firestorm in order to destroy any fuel that could be consumed by the raging fire. Its power is diminished, and the weakened fire can be extinguished. So it is with fear. Our out-of-control fears are extinguished by a stronger fear, the fear of the Lord. "He will be the sure foundation for your times, a rich store of salvation and wisdom and knowledge; the fear of the LORD is the key to this treasure" (Isa. 33:6).

Fearing the Lord means that we turn to God with a reverential trust. Fearing the Lord involves a worshipful faith and reliance on God. "In the fear of the LORD there is strong confidence" (Prov. 14:26 NASB). As you grow in the fear of the Lord, you will grow to fear nothing else (see Matt. 10:28–31; Deut. 31:6). We are to fear God and to love and serve people for the glory of God—instead of looking to people to meet our felt needs or approve of us.

When my (Judy's) son, Ryan, was six years old, he experimented in "fashion design." For some reason he was enamored with a chef's cap (which I had purchased from a garage sale), a plastic necklace with a big pink jewel, and a little brass can that slipped snugly over his ear. I tried to say, "Let's wear something different to church," but Ryan was not interested. He felt good about his outfit, and his sweet face glowed with delight—delight he was sure was shared by his parents. As I spoke to Ryan, I could not detect any desire in him to ruin my life. He was just being a six-year-old, and he liked the way he looked. I had to ask myself, "Is he trying to make me look bad? Or is this exposing in my own heart the truth that I fear people and want their approval more than I want to bless and encourage my son?" My husband and I decided to let him wear his "special outfit" to church. Upon seeing him, people gasped. One man shook his head and said, "I can't say anything." People tried to shame us, but for us it was a moment of freedom. Our son's joy was more important than what others thought.

Many women are gripped by the fear of man. Our sense of okay-ness is based on things like: Do our kids look and act perfectly? Are our bodies and outfits beautiful? Is our home stylishly decorated? Is our spiritual life in order? If any of the answers are no, our fears say that somehow *we* are not okay. But the fear of the Lord says that we are to seek God's kingdom and his glory first, instead of looking to "mere man" for our approval and purpose in life. We can never get our act so together that everyone approves of us at every moment. To live for everyone's approval is to be trapped by fear. But to live for God's glory, knowing that we are already fully loved in Christ and secure in him? This is to live in the safety and security of the fear of the Lord.

I (Tara) received an encouraging email from a woman who attended a conference at which I spoke. In it she wrote:

Do you remember me? After we prayed together you recommended
the book *When People Are Big and God Is Small* by Ed Welch. It has
been a tremendous help to me! I realize how deeply the fear of man
was rooted in my heart. I can remember the exact day I said in my
heart at age 11 that I was going to be popular no matter what it
took. I established my idol of pleasing people to maintain a sense of
acceptance and self-worth. God has been doing major heart surgery
on me! He has challenged me with the question "To what extent do
you trust me?" I have realized that I can be content with his grace
and forgiveness even if I never receive it from other people. I know
that God will be with me, and I feel I am better prepared to face
whatever may come. I have hope for my future. Thank you.

We have two options: will you trust in man, or will you trust in
the Lord? Scripture is clear that we are to trust in the Lord: "It is
better to take refuge in the LORD than to trust in man" (Ps. 118:8).
"Do not put your trust in princes, in mortal men, who cannot save.
When their spirit departs, they return to the ground; on that very
day their plans come to nothing" (Ps. 146:3–4). The fear of the
Lord banishes all other fears.

Truth. Psalm 77 beautifully illustrates how truth is a cure for
fear. The psalmist poignantly displays his fear and doubt through
many probing, heartfelt questions: "Will the Lord reject forever?
Will he never show his favor again? Has his unfailing love vanished
forever? Has his promise failed for all time? Has God forgotten to be
merciful? Has he in anger withheld his compassion?" (vv. 7–9).

In working through these doubt-filled questions, the psalmist
moves toward the cure for fear—remembering what is true and
real, meditating on the trustworthy words of God, and reflecting
on God's holy character. "Your ways, O God, are holy. What god
is so great as our God? You are the God who performs miracles;
you display your power among the peoples. With your mighty arm
you redeemed your people, the descendants of Jacob and Joseph"
(vv. 13–15).

Tabitha, a young college student, is learning to speak truth to
her fears. In the past, when one thing would go wrong, Tabitha's
thoughts rapidly accelerated in a progression of horrible fear. For
example, when her car broke down, Tabitha's fears told her, "You
don't have a car. That means that you won't be able to go to work,

so you won't be able to earn enough money to pay your tuition. So you won't be able to graduate, you'll never get a decent job, and you'll end up working in a diner your whole life or living on the street." How does truth comfort her fears? Truth tells her, "Your car has broken down before. Your parents are quick to help, and if they can't afford the repairs, you can always reach out to your deacons at church. If you really can't get your car repaired, there are definitely jobs close enough to campus to walk or ride your bike. Of course the school isn't going to kick an honor student out halfway through her senior year. And even if all of these bad things were to happen, God is still sovereign over your life. He is with you. You are going to be okay." Like Tabitha, we can learn to overcome our fears by speaking truth to them instead of indulging them.

Rest. Nothing brings greater peace to the Christian than the sure knowledge that God is near, cares deeply, and is a safe refuge where we can find rest. Psalm 23 is a psalm of rest, reflecting the peace that comes from living in the awareness of God's presence, an awareness born out of a lifetime of experiencing his presence many times and in many ways. "Even though I walk through the valley of the shadow of death, I will fear no evil, for you are with me; your rod and your staff, they comfort me" (v. 4).

W. Phillip Keller wrote his book *A Shepherd Looks at Psalm 23* based on his experience as an actual shepherd. He wrote, "I know of nothing which so stimulates my faith in my heavenly Father as to look back and reflect on his faithfulness to me in every crisis and every chilling circumstance of life. Over and over he has proved his care and concern for my welfare. . . . Storms may break about me, predators may attack, the rivers of reverses may threaten to inundate me. But because he is in the situation with me, I shall not fear."[6] Even after losing his wife to cancer, Keller knew God's presence profoundly—especially at the darkest times of life. Keller rested in the Lord and did not give way to fear.

Love. Perfect love is a cure for fear. "There is no fear in love. But perfect love drives out fear, because fear has to do with punishment. The one who fears is not made perfect in love" (1 John 4:18). Yet what is John talking about when he describes perfect love? In discussing this passage, many Christians fail to understand the richness of the term *perfect love*. We often think of perfect love as speaking to a "quality"—perfect as opposed to flawed. Yet in John's usage of perfect love, he seems to be talking instead of a "quantity" of love—complete rather than incomplete. This verse must be read in context. In chapters 2 and 3, John writes about the love of God's people for each other as a response to God's love for all of us. In chapters 4 and 5, John emphasizes the love we have for God in response to his love for us. A right understanding of 1 John recognizes that perfect love is a complete version of the love God intends—God's love for us, our love for God, our love for our brothers and sisters in Christ, and their love for us. All of these loves combine to provide the perfect love that drives out fear.

Perfect love is a multifaceted network of loving relationships. In the words of Jay Adams, "The enemy of fear is love; the way to put off fear, then, is to put on love."[7] In the same way that perfect love can drive out fear, perfect fear can drive out love. When we give our hearts over to the fears that besiege us, those same fears can diminish our ability to love God and others as we have been created to do.

Consider the following questions and responses concerning love:

- What if others love me, but I do not know that God loves me? I would fear for my eternity.
- What if I know that God loves me, but I do not love him in return? I would doubt the existence of God because he doesn't change my heart.
- What if I know and return God's love, but I do not know that others love me? I would anxiously live in fear of the sorrows of life in a world where I was alone.
- What if I fail to genuinely love others, even though they may love me? I would worry that love has not penetrated my heart and doubt that love is real after all.

When we know God loves us, we lose our fear of the future and we find freedom. When we love God, we find hope. When we love our brother, we find peace. When our brother loves us, we find joy. Our experience of God grows as our experience of love grows. Where there is fear, there is not love. Let us love each other deeply from the heart—so much so that fear cannot take root and grow. "The only thing that counts is faith expressing itself through love" (Gal. 5:6).

Rejoice! Nowhere in Scripture is fear (in the form of anxiety) more clearly addressed than in Philippians 4:

> Rejoice in the Lord always. I will say it again: Rejoice! Let your gentleness be evident to all. The Lord is near. Do not be anxious about anything, but in everything, by prayer and petition, with thanksgiving, present your requests to God. And the peace of God, which transcends all understanding, will guard your hearts and your minds in Christ Jesus.
>
> Finally, brothers, whatever is true, whatever is noble, whatever is right, whatever is pure, whatever is lovely, whatever is admirable—if anything is excellent or praiseworthy—think about such things. Whatever you have learned or received or heard from me, or seen in me—put it into practice. And the God of peace will be with you.
>
> Philippians 4:4–9

Paul exhorts the reader to not be fearful and anxious and gives clear direction on how our fears and anxiety ought to be dispelled. We cannot read these verses without realizing that self-control and self-discipline are both means of addressing and dealing with fear. While many fearful people attempt to control others or their situation in order to deal with their uncomfortable feelings, it is in the arena of *self-control* that fear is best managed.

What does Paul call the fearful and anxious believer to do? First, we are to rejoice. Joy is a healing balm for anxiety, and joy abounds when we are reminded that God is near. God is not distant, unable to hear our pleas for help. God is close by and ready to respond to our prayers. Therefore, knowing God is near, we can thankfully bring our many requests to God. As we pray, giving God our concerns—not snatching them back and carrying them with us—God blesses us with peace. Peace is nurtured as we discipline our thinking. To pray for God's help but then to dwell on the possible bad outcomes of the situation, is to miss the peace of God that transcends all understanding. Self-control is exercised as we choose to think truthfully. To dwell on what *might* be is to dwell on what is not true. Even if it might become true at some point, what is not *yet* true is not true.

From Fear to *Shalom*

Few people who know me (Judy) would describe me as a fearful person. Yet fear has been a prevailing problem for me. I never realized how fearful I was until several years ago when I traveled with a friend. Getting ready for bed, doing the things I usually did when I traveled, I heard my friend's voice call across the room, "What do you think you're doing?" I froze. Why would she ask me that? I was doing what any reasonable person would do when staying in a hotel in a strange city. "I'm building my intruder alert system . . . why do you ask?" Having dragged furniture and trash cans in front of the door to create a delicately balanced alarm system designed to notify me if a stranger tried to enter the room, all of a sudden I had the uncomfortable sensation that I was not doing what others would do in the same situation. After a long discussion, with the pieces of furniture returned to their places, I realized that I had a lot more fear in me than I ever knew.

As you consider how fear may be manifesting its debilitating effects in your life, we urge you to turn toward the Lord in renewed faith, hope, and love. Instead of fearing future suffering, punishment, or rejection, Christ enables you to meditate on the joy, reward, and eternal acceptance that are yours in him. As the Holy Spirit fills your heart with faith, you will begin to trust in yourself less and less and find security and *peace* more and more in Christ alone. You will pray with the psalmist: "The LORD is the stronghold of my life—of whom shall I be afraid? When evil men advance against me . . . when my enemies and my foes attack me . . . even then will I be confident. One thing I ask of the LORD . . . that I may dwell in the house of the LORD all the days of my life, to gaze upon the beauty of the LORD" (Ps. 27:1–4).

Imagine what your life would be like without fear, anxiety, and worry. Instead of knots in your stomach when you send your children off to summer camp for the first time, your heart and body are at peace as you entrust them to the loving care of the Lord and rejoice in him. When joining a new women's Bible study, your pulse will no longer race as you wonder, "Do I fit in? What are they thinking about me? What if I say something stupid?" Instead, your heart is filled with anticipatory joy as you consider the riches you will mine from God's Word and how you might encourage and edify the other women and be blessed by them. When financial difficulties come, you sleep well because you know that God is with you and he cares for you. You rejoice in God, and your fears are dispelled. As Elyse Fitzpatrick reminds us, "The Lord Jesus Christ has faced every fear and has done so on your behalf. It's because of his triumph over fear that you can grow toward true freedom."[8]

God cares for you! He knows your troubles. He weeps with you. We need not be afraid because God's eternal, adopting love banishes fear from our lives and leads us in the way of *shalom*.

Personal Reflection

Questions for Reflection

1. One way to begin to deal with the vague, unnamed fears and worries we carry is to name them. Complete the following: *I am afraid and I worry about*:

   ☐ Money
   ☐ My work
   ☐ My marriage / finding a husband
   ☐ My children / having children
   ☐ My unsaved relatives

   ☐ My weight and looks
   ☐ My church
   ☐ My ministry
   ☐ How people view me
   ☐ Whether someone is mad at me

   ☐ Conflicted relationships
   ☐ Disease
   ☐ What will happen if people find out about _____
   ☐ What people say about me behind my back
   ☐ A big project or commitment _____

   ☐ Whether I might be going crazy
   ☐ Everything! My life is a mess!
   ☐ That I'm really as bad as I feel
   ☐ Other: _____

   Read Psalm 31 prayerfully, bringing your fears and worries to the Lord.

2. Read Isaiah 41:10 and Psalm 46:1–3. Why are we to not fear? How do you feel at the thought that God upholds you? Read Isaiah 66:13. Write down two ways that God comforts and helps you when you are afraid.

3. Think about a situation that you could find yourself in that causes you to feel fearful. Describe this situation in a paragraph. Then ask yourself, "What if my worst fears came true?" In a second paragraph, write down three things that fall into your "worst-case scenario." Where is God in *your* story? Write down your answer in a third paragraph.

4. Read Psalm 91. What does the Lord promise to us when we dwell in his shelter, rest in his shadow, and find refuge in him? Write down the promise from Psalm 91 that is most significant to you.

5. Fear is a common temptation that reveals itself in many forms. Read 1 Peter 1:13. What three actions are commanded in this verse? In what ways might you take one or more of these actions to counter your fears? How might these actions impact your fears?

6. How are you tempted to respond when you are afraid? What does fear look like in your life? Write a paragraph that describes how you act and feel when you are burdened by fear. Read 1 Thessalonians 5:16–18 aloud. How do these verses speak to your fears?

7. Meditate on Philippians 4:6–7 and Luke 12:22–34. What promises of Jesus apply to your fears and worries?

Praying Scripture to God

Dear God, I am weighed down by my anxieties. Please help me to cast off my troubles, and please deliver me from my worries. Father, what I feared has come upon me, and I have no peace or rest but only turmoil. Please comfort and guard me; please keep me in perfect and constant peace, for my mind is fixed on you. I thank you, God, that you sow the seed of your Word deep into my heart. Please keep the desires and concerns of my heart from choking out your grace. I thank you, God, that when I call to you, you are faithful to answer me. You are with me. I am secure in you, Lord, for you love me as your own beloved child. When I am afraid, I will trust in you, God, for I am certain of your goodness and sovereignty. Please help me to fear you, Lord, more than anything or anyone else, for you are my strong confidence. Lord, I fear no evil, for you are with me. I thank you that you are my peace.

(Prayer based on Prov. 12:25; Matt. 6:34; Job 3:25–26; Isa. 26:3; Mark 4:13–20; Isa. 58:9; Deut. 33:12; Ps. 56:3; Heb. 11:1; Prov. 14:26; Ps. 23:4; Phil. 4:9.)

Recommended Resources for Further Study and Consideration

Elyse Fitzpatrick, *Overcoming Fear, Worry, and Anxiety* (Eugene, OR: Harvest House, 2001).

Nancy Leigh DeMoss, *Lies Women Believe and the Truth That Sets Them Free* (Chicago: Moody Press, 2001).

Rose Marie Miller, *From Fear to Freedom: Living as Sons and Daughters of God* (Wheaton: Harold Shaw Publishers, 1994).

David Powlison, *Worry: Pursuing a Better Path to Peace* (Phillipsburg, NJ: P&R Publishing, 2004).

Edward T. Welch, *When People Are Big and God Is Small: Overcoming Peer Pressure, Codependency, and the Fear of Man* (Phillipsburg, NJ: P&R Publishing, 1997).

CONCLUSION

Now may the Lord of peace himself give you peace at all times and in every way. The Lord be with all of you.

2 Thessalonians 3:16

Learn to say "Come, Lord Jesus" (Rev. 22:20). This reminds you that your hope is in a person and such a hope is certain. His response is, "Yes, I am coming soon" (Rev. 22:20).

Edward T. Welch[1]

In the introduction we promised to tell you about the conflicts we faced when coauthoring this book. We must admit that it is hard to relive just how painful and unpleasant the last year was for both of us. You see, we actually love one another dearly—not only as coauthors but as sisters in Christ and as friends. So we are embarrassed to reveal our sinful words, actions, and hearts to you. But we do so now because *conflict is inevitable in every relationship*. Our heartfelt prayer is that our story will encourage and motivate you to faithful obedience as you seek to be a peacemaking woman in your own relationships.

Our Stories

As we reflect on the past year, we are both struck by just how quickly our love and relationship deteriorated when we began to work on this manuscript. At the very time we were writing a book on peacemaking, we were experiencing one of the worst relational conflicts either one of us has ever had. The irony was not lost on us even in our pain. Our conflicts darkened every word we wrote, our relationship was all but destroyed, and this book project was almost scrapped (even after most of the manuscript had been written), all because of our conflict. And yet God was faithful, even to prideful and fearful sinners like us.

Judy's story. I experienced a spiritual and emotional crisis about a year ago, six months into writing this book. A series of stressful experiences overwhelmed me to the point that I felt as though I were standing in a crowd screaming for help but no one heard me. At the very time, I was overseeing the purchase of a new building for the counseling center, my mother had major surgery, and my husband was hospitalized for over a week after a terrible accident. My father-in-law grew critically ill and passed away, and a short time later my own father died. To top it all off, two key leaders in our ministry relocated to other states, leaving a leadership vacuum in the ministry with only myself to fill it. And as if that wasn't enough, I found myself forced to deal with a complaint brought against me by a former mediation client who, after three months of reporting satisfaction with the mediation process, experienced a new conflict with the other party but chose to focus her rage against me. All the while I was a doctoral student in seminary, a counselor and mediator, director of a counseling center, a wife and mother, *and* trying to write this book. I began to experience panic attacks. I thought I was having a heart attack, but two trips to the emergency room gave me a different diagnosis—anxiety. My traumas were eating me alive, and I felt forsaken by my friends and even God.

I was broken. I grew numb, cold, distant, and robotic. Unable to invest any energy into my relationships, I grew angry as I saw them wither and no one came after me. I withdrew further, resolving to never extend my heart to another person. I could no longer feel the presence of God in my life. I had grown fearful and untrusting, even informing Tara that I was unwilling to have a relationship with her other than through email. But then, after a season of rest, fasting, and prayer, a transformation began. In all my suffering, I began to know God in a deeper, truer, and closer way than I had ever known him in my life. The gospel of grace through Jesus Christ took on a meaning and importance that I had never before experienced. My friend Paul Vazquez lovingly helped me evaluate my thoughts, attitudes, and motives about God, this book, my broken relationship with Tara, my fears, and my idols.

I came to see vividly that I had lost so much grace—love, friendship, and compassion—that I otherwise would have had if my conflict with Tara had been addressed sooner. Never has Jonah 2:8 been more clear to me: "Those who cling to worthless idols forfeit the grace that could be theirs." As God graciously showed me my heart, I began to see my idols. Specifically, I wanted to be loved, but loved according to my terms. I expected to be understood, but understood not because I was doing the work of being vulnerable but because I was being pursued by others who "proved" to me through their pursuit that they cared about me and could be trusted. I wanted others to acknowledge that I was right in what I said, did, and thought. I wasn't willing to be honest about the sin raging in my heart. I wanted to be respected. I wanted to never need anyone ever again. Not only had I stopped loving Tara but my hardness of heart had permeated many other areas of my life. As I saw my desperate sin, I was finally ready for help. Even more than that, I was finally ready for help *with my heart wide open*. I wanted to reconcile with Tara not out of duty but out of love. A tender and earnest love began to grow in me as I reflected on God's love for both of us and how that love had rescued us from death.

Tara's story. In many respects, the task of writing this book and the breakdown in my relationship with Judy felt like a strange, disorienting, *very* bad dream. I knew that I loved Judy, but everything I did and said seemed to communicate the opposite to her. I knew that Judy was one of the most loving, godly, and wise women I had ever met, but somehow I seemed to have lost her. I wanted to reach out to her and help carry her burdens, but instead it seemed like *I* was one of her worst burdens. I remember watching the days, weeks, and even months pass by as our relationship struggled and progress on the book lagged. I longed to work on writing and improving the book, but I was trapped and unable to move. I craved reconciliation with Judy, but she said "not now." I wanted to wake up and shake off the nightmare! But as our conflicts continued, I began to sin grievously against God and against Judy.

Over time, although I would *never* have wanted to admit it to anyone, I began to take on a "victim" and "martyr" complex. I grew self-righteous and defensive. Instead of mercy, I began to harbor bitterness and resentment toward Judy. I began to allow selfish, petty, and critical thoughts to reside in my mind. Instead of giving charity, I judged her. Instead of helping her, I hurt her. At the very time she needed care, compassion, encouragement, and tangible help and love, I failed her.

I was sitting in my little world, withholding my heart from her and even resenting her. I too was clinging to my idols. The tension between us got so bad that I couldn't even receive emails and calls from Judy without experiencing a huge amount of adrenaline and stress. But through it all, my husband counseled me to *love Judy* and *do good to her*. He rebuked my sinful heart. He lovingly brought the gospel to bear on how I was interacting with her. He wisely screened my emails to her in order to help me to have a gentle tone and gracious attitude. He steadfastly encouraged me to continue to appeal to Judy for help to work through our conflicts. And he prayed for both of us. Then one day Judy emailed me that she was ready to meet for a mediation.

Our Reconciliation

One can easily lose hope when a relationship is as broken as ours was. We see this all the time in our counseling and mediating. Decades of hurts and offenses have piled up to the point where it is easy to feel as though there is no possible way that friendship and love could ever be restored. For all practical purposes, the relationship is dead. Apart from God's miraculous, redeeming, resurrecting grace, no hope remains. But in Christ, the God of wonders intervenes and brings new life. This is what happened to us: "At one time we too were foolish, disobedient, deceived and enslaved by all kinds of passions and pleasures. We lived in malice and envy, being hated and hating one another. But when the kindness and love of God our Savior appeared, he saved us, not because of righteous things we had done, but because of his mercy" (Titus 3:3–5).

God's mercy was shown to us in many ways but especially in the help we received from two gifted peacemakers and biblical counselors, Ted Kober, president of Ambassadors of Reconciliation, and Pastor Jason Barrie of Rocky Mountain Community Church (PCA). For three days these men helped us to address our conflicts and do the hard work of peacemaking. The first day was difficult. The incredible pain, hurt, and anger we both felt were nearly insurmountable. Yet we persevered because we knew that reconciliation was close to God's heart and God was calling us to this task. The chapters of our book took on new life. We fought to remember the truth about who God is, we struggled to persevere through our suffering, and we anxiously allowed our hearts to be evaluated and our idols revealed. Shame, fear, and depression were prominent in our stories. With horror we came to realize how the consequences of our conflict with one another had far-reaching effects in our own lives and the lives of others.

For three days we followed the conciliation process we both knew so well, taught regularly, and used in our professional ministries. We told our stories to one another and worked hard to help the other person understand our perspective and our pain. We tried to communicate humbly and carefully, and we *still* misunderstood each other. So Ted and Jason persevered and helped us try again. We worked harder to listen, seeking to truly understand one another. Our conciliators exhorted us to persevere and put our faith in the Lord, to truly trust him even when things seemed hopeless. We listened. We cried. We gently engaged and confronted one another. We confessed our sins to one another, and then *we forgave one another.*

It's true. It *is* possible to forgive even horrible hurts and offenses—not because the other person's confession is "good enough" to merit our forgiveness and not even because we have absolute assurance that they will never do the same thing again. *We forgive because in Christ, we have been forgiven a debt we could never pay. Therefore, we do not hold onto the debts and offenses of others.* Out of gratitude for God's forgiveness for us, we forgave one another. Our hearts changed as they were flooded with grace—much of the grace that we would have experienced during the previous months had we not been clinging to the worthless things of the world. The coauthors who had once loved but had grown to hate became precious and dear to each other—even more than previously. We found the freedom to step away from many of the idols that kept us in bondage and to step toward right worship of God and loving service of one another.

With the shackles of bitterness broken, our original love for one another took new depth and new height. We could not help but express to each other how much we loved one another. For the few hours before we parted, we successfully worked through an agreement on how to complete the book. We finished the mediation exhausted but refreshed. A huge burden had been lifted, and we embarked together on the journey of rebuilding our trust and love. Just as we talked about in chapter 4, even after we forgave one another, we knew that true reconciliation would take *time* and *effort* to build and grow strong. When conflicts come (as they inevitably do in any relationship), we talk them out, pray together, and when necessary *get help*. Through it all, God's love and grace cover us and help us to persevere as each other's friend, protector, encourager, and *helper*.

This is what it means to be peacemaking women! Our lives are not conflict-free. But because of Jesus Christ, we can experience *shalom*-filled relationships: the exhilarating, frightening, painful, and joyful unfolding of steadfast love, gentle understanding, and abiding acceptance.

Our Final Charge to You

Our book is now complete and we offer it to you not as coauthors but as friends—dear friends who are learning to love one another well.

I (Judy) leave the last eighteen months a different person. As I write this, I say honestly that I have never been more committed to serving the Lord through my relationships while at the same time I now hold relationships with a lighter and looser grip. A week after Tara and I reconciled, I stood with my family on vacation looking over a railing at the Roman Forum. While gazing upon those ancient and ghastly ruins, I suddenly began to have words for the many things I had learned. I realized that all that we strive for, all that we build and imagine, everything we do, will come to ruin. No book we write, no speech we give, and no vision we pursue will make it into eternity. Only people make it into eternity. Our relationships with one another will endure throughout all time, even as all that we have accomplished will fade away. Every human being will live in eternity—some in blissful joy because they have placed their trust in Jesus Christ and some in unending agony because they have rejected his saving grace. The glory of man dissolves away. The glory of God endures forever and is most profoundly revealed in us and in our relationships.

I (Tara) continue to marvel at God's sovereignty over this entire project. Although my sin grieves God, he is not surprised or dismayed. He knows the first from the last, the beginning from the end. He is not bound by time. He *is* the Alpha and the Omega. So, as I reflect on the strange truth that two women could be so painfully conflicted while writing a book on peacemaking, I am drawn to worship God even more deeply than ever before. Why? Because it is true that there is *no good in us*, none at all, save for Jesus Christ and his righteousness apportioned to us. Yes, the biblical truths contained in this book are true. And yes, these peacemaking principles have helped many and will continue to help many even as they have been a blessing to Judy and me. God's truth is absolutely and completely life changing, but *not because of us*! It is because of God and God alone. Only God softens hearts and leads sinners to repentance. Only God turns our hearts away from idols and to himself. Only God comforts us with his eternal, perfect love. And he often uses broken, sinful people in the process. I marvel that God would give me such gifts as the friends I have, especially Judy Dabler. Life is hard! And it is a gift of God's grace that we get to journey through this life with people who love and forgive us.

We both pray that as you read these final words, you will turn to the Lord and know "the hope to which he has called you, the riches of his glorious inheritance in the saints, and his incomparably great power for us who believe" (Eph. 1:18–19). Sharing our lives with you in this book has been our honor and our joy. Our prayer is that sweet *shalom* will flood your soul and your joy will be complete as you experience the transforming work of God in your heart and mind. May the peace of God be with you, and may you love well, just as Christ commands: "As the Father has loved me, so have I loved you. Now remain in my love. If you obey my commands, you will remain in my love, just as I have obeyed my Father's commands and remain in his love. I have told you this so that my joy may be in you and that your joy may be complete. My command is this: Love each other as I have loved you" (John 15:9–12).

Until we meet in eternity, may the Lord bless you on your journey as peacemaking women.

NOTES

Introduction

1. David Powlison, *Seeing with New Eyes* (Phillipsburg, NJ: P&R Publishing, 2003), 81.

2. The names and identifying information of many of the people mentioned in this book have been changed to protect confidentiality.

3. Bob and Gretchen Passantino, *Psychology and the Church: Laying a Foundation for Discernment*, CRI (Christian Research Institute) Statement DP-220-1, Rancho Santa Margarita, CA.

4. The Barna Research Group reports, "33% of all born again individuals who have been married have gone through a divorce, which is statistically identical to the 34% incidence among non-born again adults." Barna Research Group, "Family," 2001, available online at http://www.barna.org/FlexPage.aspx?Page=Topic&TopicID=20.

5. D. Martyn Lloyd-Jones, *Spiritual Depression: Its Causes and Its Cure* (Grand Rapids: Eerdmans, 1965), Foreword.

6. Eugene H. Peterson, *A Long Obedience in the Same Direction: Discipleship in an Instant Society* (Downers Grove, IL: InterVarsity Press, 1980), 52.

7. Phillip Yancey, *What's So Amazing About Grace?* (Grand Rapids: Zondervan, 1997), 93.

Part One: Conflicts with God

1. J. I. Packer, *Knowing God* (Downers Grove, IL: InterVarsity Press, 1973), 14–15.

2. John M. Frame, *The Doctrine of the Knowledge of God* (Phillipsburg, NJ: P&R Publishing, 1987), 81.

3. Powlison, *Seeing with New Eyes*, 177.

4. Carolyn Custis James, *When Life and Beliefs Collide: How Knowing God Makes a Difference* (Grand Rapids: Zondervan, 2001), 25.

Chapter 1: Thinking about God

1. A. W. Tozer, *The Knowledge of the Holy* (San Francisco: Harper, 1998), 7.

2. For much of this chapter I (Judy) am indebted to my systematic theology professor from Covenant Theological Seminary, Dr. Robert Peterson. Under his care and especially through his course entitled "God, Man and Christ," I came to know God in a deeper way than I ever imagined possible. See Robert A. Peterson, *God, Man and Christ: Including The Doctrines of God, Man, Sin, Christ, and Christ's Saving Work* (Covenant Theological Seminary, 1995).

3. Lloyd-Jones, *Spiritual Depression*, 155.

4. We will not attempt to make a thorough defense of God or presentation of a systematic theology. Instead we will present only a few key attributes of God and encourage you to consider the resources listed in our bibliography for further study.

5. C. S. Lewis, *The Lion, the Witch and the Wardrobe* (New York: Collier Books, 1950), 76.

6. We refer to the Fall as the historical time recorded in Genesis 3 when the disobedience of Adam and Eve brought brokenness to their relationship with God and their descendants.

7. John Piper, *Desiring God: Meditations of a Christian Hedonist* (Portland: Multnomah, 1986), 47.

8. John Murray calls adoption "The apex of grace and privilege." *Redemption Accomplished and Applied* (Grand Rapids: Eerdmans, 1955), 134. See also J. I. Packer, *Knowing God*, 206.

9. Packer, *Knowing God*, 208.

10. D. H. S. Nicholson and A. H. E. Lee, eds., *The Oxford Book of English Mystical Verse* (Oxford: The Clarendon Press, 1917), www.bartleby.com/236/.

11. Martin Luther, *Defense of All the Articles*, quoted in Grace Brame, *Receptive Prayer* (Chalice Press, 1985), 119.

12. To impute is to charge to a person's account. Christ's righteousness is credited to all believers (Rom. 4; 1 Cor. 1:30; 2 Cor. 5:21; Phil. 3:9).

13. C. S. Lewis, *Letters to Children*, ed. Lyle W. Dorsett and Marjorie Lamp Meade (New York: Touchstone Books, 1996), 52–53.

14. Lloyd-Jones, *Spiritual Depression*, 89.

Chapter 2: Idolatry

1. Charles Spurgeon, *The Treasury of David*, Vol. 1 (Grand Rapids: Zondervan, 1950), 137.

2. John Calvin, *Institutes of the Christian Religion* (Philadelphia: Westminster, 1960), 108.

3. J. R. R. Tolkien, *The Lord of the Rings* (New York: Houghton Mifflin, 1954), 619, 671, 922.

4. Paul David Tripp, *Instruments of Change: How God Can Use You to Help People Grow* (Philadelphia: Christian Counseling and Educational Foundation, 2000).

5. Ibid., 4.

6. John Piper, *Future Grace* (Sisters, OR: Multnomah, 1995), 20.

7. John Piper, "Repentance, Forgiveness, and the Gift of the Spirit," sermon, November 25, 1990, http://www.desiringgod.org/library/sermons/90/112590.html.

8. Edward T. Welch, *Addictions—A Banquet in the Grave: Finding Hope in the Power of the Gospel* (Phillipsburg, NJ: P&R Publishing, 2001), 32.

9. Martin Luther, *The Bondage of the Will*, quoted in Welch, *Addictions—A Banquet in the Grave*, 33.

10. Alfred Poirier, *Faith's Fight Against Sin*, published by Rocky Mountain Community Church (PCA), Billings, MT (www.rmccmontana.org).

Chapter 3: Suffering

1. Attribution to Elisabeth Elliot and publication permission granted on April 28, 2004, by Mr. Lars Gren, husband of Elisabeth Elliot.

2. W. Robert Godfrey, "Nothing but a Constant Death," in *Modern Reformation* 11, no. 2 (2002): 44.

3. Powlison, *Seeing with New Eyes*, 206.

4. John Piper, "Counseling with Suffering People," *Journal of Biblical Counseling* 21, no. 2 (2003): 25.

5. C. S. Lewis, *Mere Christianity* (San Francisco: HarperSanFrancisco, 1952), 137.

6. Peterson, *A Long Obedience*, 134.

7. Charles Spurgeon quoted in John Piper, "Men of Whom the World Is Not Worthy: Charles Spurgeon—Preaching through Adversity" (sermon given at Bethlehem Conference for Pastors, Minneapolis, MN: 1995).

Part Two: Conflicts with Others

1. Ken Sande, *The Peacemaker: A Biblical Guide to Resolving Personal Conflict* (Grand Rapids: Baker, 2003), 12.

Chapter 4: Biblical Peacemaking

1. Francis Schaeffer, *The Church Before the Watching World* in *The Complete Works of Francis A. Schaeffer: A Christian Worldview* (Wheaton: Crossway, 1982), 151.

2. Concepts in this chapter adapted from *The Peacemaker* by Ken Sande. Used by permission. For more information visit the website of Peacemaker Ministries at http://www.HisPeace.org.

3. For an excellent, biblical teaching on honestly looking at our faults, we highly recommend Pastor Alfred Poirier's Culture of Peace booklet entitled *Words that Cut: Receiving Criticism in Light of the Gospel* (Billings, MT: Peacemaker Ministries, 2003). This article is also available at www. HisPeace.org.

4. The third G, "Gently Restore," might occur in the same conversation as the second G, "Get the Log Out." However, wisdom sometimes reveals that the two should occur at separate times. If we are too quick to seek to restore or confront the other person, we may seem to be confessing only so that we can confront them. Deciding on an appropriate time to confront takes wisdom. We encourage you to pray and seek godly counsel in this regard.

5. Permission for attribution granted in private correspondence with Matthew D. Smith, study assistant to Rev. Dr. John Stott, April 8, 2004.

6. Please do not interpret this example as meaning that we approve of people being too thin-skinned. Proverbs 19:11 exhorts us to be quick to overlook the faults of others.

7. Alfred J. Poirier, "Pastor as Peacemaker: Twelve Lectures for an M.Div. Course in Biblical Conflict Resolution" (applied research project, Westminster Theological Seminary, 2004), 132, 144.

8. An example of true forgiveness is overlooking. When we overlook a person's sin, we make a decision unilaterally to forgive her without even speaking with her about it. This is an action that is very different from

denial (which pretends that there is no conflict and therefore nothing to forgive).

9. Susan Hunt, *Spiritual Mothering* (Wheaton: Crossway, 1992), 161.

Chapter 5: *Shalom*-Filled Relationships

1. Alfred Poirier, "Life Together" (sermon, Rocky Mountain Community Church, Billings, MT, November 24, 2002).

2. Edgar Metzler quoted in Ajith Fernando, *Reclaiming Friendship: Relating to Each Other in a Frenzied World* (Scottsdale, PA: Herald Press, 1991), 11.

3. For a winsome look at personality differences, we recommend Bob Phillips, *The Delicate Art of Dancing with Porcupines: Learning to Appreciate the Finer Points of Others* (Ventura, CA: Regal Books, 1989).

4. C. S. Lewis, *The Four Loves* (London: Geoffrey Bles, 1960), quoted in Ajith Fernando, *Reclaiming Friendship*, 30.

5. Harper Lee, *To Kill a Mockingbird* (New York: HarperCollins, 1960), 33.

6. The term "breathe grace" and much of the content in this section comes from a sermon that Ken Sande gave at my (Tara's) church in the summer of 2003 and is discussed on page 170 in the revised and updated version of *The Peacemaker*. Ken Sande, "Our Triune God Breathes Grace" (sermon, Rocky Mountain Community Church, Billings, MT, July 27, 2003).

7. If you struggle to breathe grace with your speech, we highly recommend that you apply the truths in Paul Tripp's book, *War of Words: Getting to the Heart of Your Communication Struggles* (Phillipsburg, NJ: P&R Publishing, 2000).

Chapter 6: Romantic Love

1. William Shakespeare, *The Complete Works of William Shakespeare* (Garden City, NY: Nelson Doubleday Inc.), 1108.

2. Powlison, *Seeing with New Eyes*, 226.

3. Dr. Henry Cloud and Dr. John Townsend, *Boundaries* (Grand Rapids: Zondervan, 1992). They write, "Things can hurt and not harm us. In fact they can even be good for us. And things that feel good can be very harmful to us" (p. 94).

4. Charles Williams, *Descent into Hell* (Grand Rapids: Grand Rapids Book Manufacturers, Inc., 1937).

5. Of course, if a husband is physically abusive to his wife or children, then it is neither loving nor wise to remain in harm's way. In that sad

circumstance, church leaders have a responsibility before God to protect their sheep—both the victims and the abuser—by intervening. For counsel in this regard, we highly recommend the resource by David Powlison, Paul David Tripp, and Edward T. Welch, *Domestic Abuse: How to Help* (Phillipsburg, NJ: P&R Publishing Company, 2002).

6. If your marriage is extremely conflicted and you are overwhelmed with unhappiness, it can be easy to be tempted to divorce. You might think that the only possible options are to divorce or to stay in an unhappy marriage. There is another option: a redeemed marriage. Again, we fully realize that we cannot do justice to this crucial topic. We urge you to study the recommended resources at the end of the chapter and seek help if you or someone you love needs help in this area.

7. Warren, *Purpose-Driven Life*, 72.

8. Of course, actions have consequences and abuse should be punished so that no further harm will come to others and so that the abuser can receive the help to change. But even when we are terribly abused, God calls us to not respond in bitterness, resentment, or prolonged rage.

Chapter 7: Families

1. Susan Hunt, *Heirs of the Covenant* (Wheaton: Crossway, 1998), 107.

2. We recommend *The Young Peacemaker* curriculum by Corlette Sande. It includes twelve activity booklets and twelve lessons that are packed with biblical and practical advice. Corlette Sande, *The Young Peacemaker* (Wapwallopen, PA: Shepherd Press, 1997).

3. Dan Doriani, *The Life of a God-Made Man* (Wheaton: Crossway, 2001), 95.

4. Sande, *The Peacemaker*, 234.

5. Powlison, *Seeing with New Eyes*, 214.

6. Tara Barthel, "Healing the Conflicts between Mothers and Daughters," audiotape of workshop by Tara Barthel presented at Big Sky, Montana, October 2001 (Billings, MT: Peacemaker Ministries, 2001).

Chapter 8: The Church

1. Ted Kober, *Confession and Forgiveness: Professing Faith as Ambassadors of Reconciliation* (St. Louis: Concordia Publishing House, 2002), 32.

2. I am blessed to report that in the years since that sad church split, many members of this wonderful church have repented of the way they handled the conflict. Many have come back together and share unity and fellowship again.

3. For further study on this topic, we recommend: Susan Hunt and Peggy Hutcheson, *Leadership for Women in the Church* (Grand Rapids: Zondervan, 1991).

4. For an excellent book on mentoring, we recommend Susan Hunt, *Spiritual Mothering* (Wheaton: Crossway, 1992).

5. J. R. R. Tolkien, *The Return of the King* (Boston: Houghton Mifflin, 1994).

6. Of course, if our church leader or any other authority over us is in sin or requiring us to sin, then we are called to humbly and graciously appeal to them as we seek to gently restore them. However, if the authorities continue in sin, we are to gently refuse to submit. Submission to headship is not a license for abusive leaders to require cult-like absolute obedience and allegiance. But in our experience, conflicts with church leaders are *rarely* about sin issues; they are most often about preferences, hurt feelings stemming from poor communication or misunderstanding, and relational conflicts.

7. Stephen E. Ambrose, *Undaunted Courage* (New York: Simon & Schuster, 1997), 230–35.

8. Thomas M'Crie, *The Unity of the Church* (Dallas: Presbyterian Heritage Publications, 1989), 64.

Chapter 9: Female Leaders with Powerful Personalities

1. Tim Kimmel, *Powerful Personalities* (Colorado Springs: Focus on the Family, 1977), 4.

2. C. S. Lewis, *Mere Christianity* (San Francisco: HarperSanFrancisco, 1952), 125.

3. Susan Hunt, *Your Home a Place of Grace* (Wheaton: Crossway, 2000), 87.

4. Due to space constraints, we will not even attempt to address in this chapter the important issue of the role of biblical manhood and womanhood, especially when it comes to authority relationships. We urge you to study on these important topics further and pray for the grace to wisely and graciously live in accordance with God's Word.

Part Three: Conflicts Within

1. David Seamands, quoted from the "Christian Perspectives" Sunday school class at Arlington Heights Evangelical Free Church, 1998. Permission for use granted by David Seamands on July 16, 2004.

2. John Calvin, *Institutes of the Christian Religion* (Philadelphia: Westminster Press, 1960), 37.

3. J. I. Packer, *An Introduction to John Owen's "The Death of Death in the Death of Christ"* (Carlisle, PA: Banner of Truth Trust, 1989), 1–2.

Chapter 10: Shame

1. John Piper, *Future Grace* (Sisters, OR: Multnomah, 1995), 131.

2. False guilt, the idea that we have sinned when in fact Scripture does not support the notion that the action is sinful, will not be addressed in this chapter.

3. I (Judy) am indebted to Dick Keyes for his useful and powerful explanation of this material in his book, *Beyond Identity: Finding Your Way in the Image and Character of God* (Cumbria, UK: Paternoster Press, 1998), 41–60.

Chapter 11: Depression

1. Powlison, *Seeing with New Eyes*, 49.

2. Elisabeth Kübler-Ross, *On Death and Dying* (New York: Macmillan, 1991).

Chapter 12: Fear

1. C. S. Lewis, *The Screwtape Letters* (New York: Macmillan, 1959), 28.

2. *Holy Man*, VHS recording, directed by Stephen Herek, Burbank, CA: Touchstone Pictures in association with Caravan Pictures, a Roger Birnbaum production, a Stephen Herek film, written by Tom Schulman, distributed by Buena Vista Home Entertainment, 1998.

3. Edward T. Welch, *When People Are Big and God Is Small: Overcoming Peer Pressure, Codependency, and the Fear of Man* (Phillipsburg, NJ: P&R Publishing, 1997), 47, 60.

4. Many ideas for my (Tara's) contributions on worry have been adapted from a sermon by Alfred Poirier, "Seek First His Kingdom" (sermon, Rocky Mountain Community Church, Billings, MT, November 30, 2003).

5. This entire section on "fear of man" has been greatly influenced by Dr. Ed Welch's excellent book, *When People Are Big and God Is Small.* We strongly commend this book to you for further study.

6. W. Phillip Keller, *A Shepherd Looks at Psalm 23* (Grand Rapids: Zondervan, 1970), 88–89.

7. Jay E. Adams, *The Christian Counselor's Manual: The Practice of Nouthetic Counseling* (Grand Rapids: Zondervan, 1973), 414.

8. Elyse Fitzpatrick, *Overcoming Fear, Worry, and Anxiety* (Eugene, OR: Harvest House, 2001), 210.

Conclusion

1. Edward T. Welch, *Depression: A Stubborn Darkness—Light for the Path* (Winston-Salem, NC: Punch Press, 2004), 260.

INDEX

Proverbs

Tara Klena Barthel (J.D. and M.B.A., University of Illinois Urbana-Champaign) formerly served as the director of the Institute for Christian Conciliation, a division of Peacemaker Ministries. As such, she oversaw the delivery of all mediation and arbitration services as well as advanced conciliator training. Currently she serves her family as a homemaker while regularly mediating and speaking on biblical peacemaking. Tara is the vice-president of the board of directors for the Montana Christian Legal Society, an adjunct instructor and Certified Christian Conciliator with Peacemaker Ministries, and a consultant to businesses and Christian ministries on issues attendant to conflict. Tara, her husband, Fred, and their daughter, Sophia Grace, are members of Rocky Mountain Community Church (PCA) in Billings, Montana. For information on Tara's speaking and conciliating services, visit www.tarabarthel.com.

Judy Dabler, president of Live at Peace Ministries (www.liveatpeace.org), serves nationally and internationally as a mediator, counselor, educator, and consultant. Currently pursuing her PhD in educational studies, she holds a Master of Arts in Theological Studies and a Master of Arts in Counseling from Covenant Theological Seminary as well as a Bachelor of Science in Business Administration from the University of Missouri-Columbia. Judy is an adjunct professor at Trinity Evangelical Divinity School and an instructor and conciliator for Peacemaker Ministries. She is a licensed professional counselor in Missouri and a Certified Christian Conciliator™ with the Institute for Christian Conciliation™, a division of Peacemaker Ministries.

More Great

Peacemaking Resources!